SEXUAL DEVIANCE

SEXUAL DEVIANCE

A READER

edited by
CHRISTOPHER HENSLEY
RICHARD TEWKSBURY

LYNNE
RIENNER
PUBLISHERS

BOULDER
LONDON

Published in the United States of America in 2003 by
Lynne Rienner Publishers, Inc.
1800 30th Street, Boulder, Colorado 80301
www.rienner.com

and in the United Kingdom by
Lynne Rienner Publishers, Inc.
3 Henrietta Street, Covent Garden, London WC2E 8LU

Library of Congress Cataloging-in-Publication Data
Sexual deviance : a reader / edited by Christopher Hensley and Richard Tewksbury.
   Includes bibliographical references and index.
    ISBN 1-58826-100-X (alk. paper)—ISBN 1-58826-125-5 (pb. : alk. paper)
    1. Sexual deviation. 2. Deviant behavior. 3. Sex crimes. 4. Sex customs.
   5. Social values. I. Hensley, Christopher, 1972– II. Tewksbury, Richard A.
  HQ71.S3977   2002
  306.77—dc21

                           2002073970

British Cataloguing in Publication Data
A Cataloguing in Publication record for this book
is available from the British Library.

Printed and bound in the United States of America

The paper used in this publication meets the requirements
of the American National Standard for Permanence of
Paper for Printed Library Materials Z39.48-1984.

5 4 3 2 1

Contents

Acknowledgments

We would like to thank the Institute for Correctional Research and Training staff, Mary Koscheski, Amanda Jarrells, Judy Carpenter, Brittney Meguire, and Jeremy Wright, for their assistance in the preparation of the manuscript for this book. We are also grateful to the anonymous reviewers who provided us with critiques regarding the content and organization of the book. Finally, we wish to extend our appreciation to Bridget Julian, acquisitions editor at Lynne Rienner Publishers, for her commitment to this project.

Introduction:
The Social Construction
of Sexual Deviance

Christopher Hensley and Richard Tewksbury

Social deviance is perhaps one of the most discussed and debated issues among sociologists and criminologists today. Definitions of deviant behavior vary depending on time, place, and individual. In simple terms, deviance incorporates behaviors that stray from accepted standards and social expectations. Behaviors considered deviant range from improper table manners to cheating on tests to cold-blooded murder.

What society considers "deviant" changes to accommodate the social and political agendas of those in power. Those who veer from accepted standards as well as those who set those standards of acceptance are both of interest when examining the social construction of deviance.

For example, the war on drugs has historically been a war on powerless groups, particularly minorities. Around the start of the twentieth century, many states passed cocaine laws that were—by contemporary standards—essentially racist in nature. Cocaine was mainly used by African Americans during that time. Many whites believed that the drug caused blacks to be more violent and to function with superhuman abilities. It was not until this fear manifested itself in the minds of the dominant, white culture that using cocaine became a deviant and illegal act.

More recently, cocaine has shifted from being a "black/poor drug" to being a drug of the rich, powerful, and white society. Prosecution efforts now often center on crack, a cheaper form of cocaine used primarily among poor, minority populations. Despite the lack of distinct chemical differences between crack and cocaine, the legal standards and penalties for crack use are far more stringent and severe than those for cocaine. As this example illustrates, deviant acts are defined based on the social structure in which they exist.

Understanding the social construction of deviance helps us gain a firmer grasp on the role that individuals, or groups, in power have over cultural standards and values. Laws, standards, and values are defined to best suit the dominant group. Once a law against a certain behavior loses its benefit to a particularly powerful group, the act is likely to lose its deviant quality as well.

It is not enough to simply consider the deviant act in and of itself. In order to understand the severity of the labels attached to different forms of deviance, we must look at who committed the act as well as who the act was committed against. Is the forcible rape of a female next-door neighbor as deviant as the forcible rape of woman known to be a prostitute? Is the young man who steals to be accepted into a gang more deviant than a poor woman who steals to feed her starving children? The degree of deviance varies depending on the situation, the motives of the offender, and the reaction that the behavior arouses from those who observe or hear about the deviance. Almost any behavior, characteristic, or belief can be accepted in some social circles while condemned in others. Every person or group will have different notions of conduct that is defined as right or wrong, acceptable or unacceptable.

Sexual behaviors and desires are especially vulnerable to this type of inconsistency. Certain individuals may participate in a sexual activity in one situation, but may avoid that same activity in another setting. What is acceptable sexual behavior for one person may not be socially defined as acceptable for another. For example, the very act of sex can be considered deviant when it is between two unmarried teenagers, but is expected and accepted conduct between two consenting married adults. Between these extremes lie an array of sexual activities on the continuum of sexual deviance.

If definitions are socially constructed, and can vary with time, place, persons, and specifics of activities, why do we even need to address the issue of sexual deviance? The answer here is the same as it is for most sociological perspectives. Understanding sexual deviance is important for understanding the broader picture of social life, social organization, and how societies identify and respond to the needs of their members. If we want to truly understand how the social world functions and how individuals experience their lives, we need to understand the full range of actions that comprise life, and this includes our socially constructed sexual behaviors. Sexual activities also give rise to a variety of social needs, including legal needs, educational needs, health care needs, and emotional/psychological needs. As a result, both governments and social activists respond by developing policies to regulate actions and responses, and services to meet these emerging needs. In other words, our sexual behaviors—including our socially defined "deviant" sexual behaviors—are intricately connected to a wide range of other aspects of our social lives. However, these connections are not always immediately evident. It is our hope that the chapters that follow illuminate these connections and help to show how sexual behavior is both socially constructed and integral to the social experience.

It is also important to keep in mind that definitions of social actions, including sexual behaviors, are not simply a matter of being deviant or not deviant. Deviant actions come in varying degrees and forms. In this book, we have chosen to conceptualize sexual deviance as of three primary forms: normal, pathological, and sociological. All three forms are socially defined and constructed, although in different ways.

Furthermore, our intent here is to present both the range of sexual deviance in our society and to highlight the significance of the socially constructed nature of social (especially sexual) behavior. Some of the sexual behaviors discussed in the book may disturb some readers and excite others, and some individuals may read about behaviors in which they currently engage. Our intent is not to either encourage or discourage any particular form of sexual activity. Rather, it is our hope that readers will recognize that sexual behavior (both our own and that of others) is diverse and can be viewed in widely differing ways. Only when we recognize these facts can we move beyond simplistic perceptions of and reactions to forms of sexual behavior that seem to us to be odd, strange, uncomfortable, or wrong.

Defining Sexual Deviance

A sexual act is commonly perceived as deviant according to one or a combination of the following conditions: (1) the degree of consent, (2) the nature of the sex object, (3) the nature of the sex act, or (4) the setting in which the sex act occurs. However, sociologists often address two additional dimensions in determining which activities are deviant (Wheeler, 1960): the degree of outrage felt by others concerning a certain behavior and how common the activity is practiced in general society (Gagnon and Simon, 1967).

When most people hear the phrase "sexual deviance," they assume that it involves some form of pathology or psychological disorder. In reality, however, sexual deviance can have little to do with either. Sexual deviance merely refers to socially disapproved characteristics and behaviors that incite negative reactions, punishments, ostracism, or ridicule.

What society considers "normal sex" depends on both the person and the circumstances. At least four types of standards exist that commonly determine "normalcy" in terms of sexual behavior: statistical, cultural, religious, and subjective (Holmes, 1991). When more than half of the people in a particular population commit or perform a particular act, this behavior can be validated by the statistical standard. According to the statistical standard, if more than 50 percent of individuals have sex before marriage, premarital sex would be considered "normal." Using this standard alone can be risky because it validates conduct based solely on how the majority of people behave. If more than half of all Americans cheated on their spouse, would adultery no longer be considered deviant? This standard also ignores the social implications of defining the act as either "deviant" or "normal."

Cultural standards are those developed by society to govern and regulate individual action. These standards determine what sexual behavior is tolerable and intolerable. The majority of U.S. citizens would consider pedophilia, incest, rape, and exhibitionism as aberrant sexual behavior. This does not necessarily mean that all people condemn these acts, but that the rules, norms, and values of society render them deviant. Furthermore, the degree and severity of these acts vary depending on time, place, and culture. Although rape may always be considered deviant, what constitutes rape is, unfortunately, not always clear. In fact, it was not until 1993 that marital rape became a crime in all fifty states (Bergen, 1996). This should not be surprising given our cultural standards of "appropriate" gender roles in the family. Values and standards, then, are clearly reflected in the ways in which definitions of deviant acts vary.

Religion also plays a vital role in the development of the value systems that characterize a culture. Religious standards guide individual behavior, usually through the enforcement of strict and absolute guidelines. Acts considered sinful, including acts sexual in nature, are often guaranteed certain punishment and condemnation in the absence of true redemption or sorrowfulness. This standard is pivotal in the lives of religious persons and their sexual conduct. Religion and culture are often at odds with each other in terms of what is defined as "deviant." For the most part, individuals who divorce and remarry are readily accepted by society, according to our cultural standards. On the other hand, the standards of some religions condemn divorce under the belief that one is married "until death do us part." Conflicting standards such as these can further blur the line.

Finally, the subjective standard acts as another determinant and definitional element of sexual behavior. This is perhaps the most common, and most important, standard by which people measure deviance—with the assumption that true "deviants" are always able to rationalize their behavior based on social, religious, and statistical measures. Using the example of marital rape again, men who rape their wives might justify their actions based on the "obligations" or "duties" of the wife inherent in a marriage contract. Those who adhere to subjective standards feel that what they are doing is really not bad or abnormal (that is, deviant). In their minds, the actions are both justifiable and acceptable, despite the reprimands and stipulations dictated by society. An individual who engages in an extreme form of deviance such as child molestation, however, may in fact acknowledge his behavior as deviant. People from these groups, who knowingly commit deviant acts without an attempt to justify their behavior are often deemed sociopathic or mentally ill, as opposed to "deviant."

As standards of sexuality evolve and change, certain activities lose their deviant qualities and become more acceptable. Masturbation, for example, has become more commonly accepted by society. Prostitution, on the other hand, is a deviant act that continues to provoke societal condemnation. Often, there is a significant amount of overlap between sexual deviants and nondeviants.

According to Gagnon and Simon (1967), there are different categories of deviance. Each has distinct characteristics that separate them from one another. However, they all have the potential of violating the subjective standard. Any form of deviance, therefore, is likely to invoke a reaction from a personal standpoint. The three main types of deviance are normal, pathological, and sociological.

Normal deviance, the most common type, occurs with low visibility and involves a significant number of participants. From a statistical standard, this type of deviance is "normal." It is often referred to as "secret deviance" by some researchers. Although an act, such as oral sex, is considered deviant by many individuals, a majority of adults have engaged (in one way or another) in such activities. Premarital sex is also an example of normal deviance. Normal deviance may not always be viewed as negative. For example, religious abstinence could possibly be viewed as a form of normal sexual deviance.

Pathological deviance is the second category of sexual deviance.

These behaviors are regarded by many as harmful, are usually against the law, and are practiced by relatively few individuals. Examples of pathological deviance include sexual contact with children, incest, some forms of voyeurism and exhibitionism, and rape. Pathological deviance is similar to normal deviance in that it does not have significant or sizable supportive group structures to maintain the participants of the activities.

The third category of sexual deviance is referred to as sociological deviance. Both sociological and pathological deviance violate cultural and religious standards, but sociological deviance involves behavior that creates a structure to produce or sustain such activities. The structures serve to recruit participants, socialize them, gather people together to perform the act, and/or provide social support for the actor. For example, some homosexual men engage in and depend on contact with other homosexual men to develop a homosexual identity. Pornography, prostitution, and swinging are other examples of sociological deviance.

Scope of the Book

These three categories of sexual deviance—normal, pathological, and sociological—serve to structure the subsequent discussions and research in this book. While this framework organizes the chapters that follow, this should not be interpreted to mean that these categories are mutually exclusive. In fact, there is likely to be debate and disagreement about how best to interpret particular sexual acts and varieties of participating individuals. Each part begins with a short introduction that presents the major themes of sexual deviance as illustrated by the chapters that follow.

We have attempted to provide an overview of many behaviors that people currently understand as sexually deviant; in addition, we include some behaviors that most might not consider deviant in the same way. As might be expected, however, we have not dealt with every deviant behavior, and there are some—for example, transgendered sexual behaviors—that we have not covered due to a lack of research. Readers may also notice that Part 4, Sociological Sexual Deviance, is longer than the other two parts. Because sociologists tend to interest themselves in group behaviors, the category of sociological sexual deviance is more frequently studied than is normal or pathological sexual deviance.

References

Bergen, R. K. (1996). *Wife Rape: Understanding the Responses of Survivors and Service Providers.* Thousand Oaks, CA: Sage.

Gagnon, J. and W. Simon, (eds.), (1967). *Sexual Deviance.* New York: Harper and Row.

Holmes, R. (1991). *Sex Crimes.* Newbury Park, CA: Sage.

Wheeler, S. (1960). "Sex Offenses." *Law and Contemporary Problems* (Published by the Duke University School of Law) 25:2.

PART I

COMPLEXITIES OF CATEGORIZATION

The following two introductory chapters address controversial sexual deviant acts that are generally considered sociological deviant sexual acts. However, they also provide in-depth definitions and insights concerning all three categories of sexually deviant behavior. In the first chapter, DeAnn Gauthier and Craig J. Forsyth examine men who explicitly seek out opportunities to contract HIV in what they call "bug chasing." These HIV-negative men search for HIV-positive men with the desire/intention of becoming infected with HIV. The authors present four explanations of why men seek to become infected with the deadly virus. First, the fear throughout the gay community of becoming infected with HIV affects the relationships of those engaging in sexual activities. Many bug chasers feel that it is inevitable that they will become infected. Another reason for bug chasing is the thrill of the risk. To many bug chasers, the risk of becoming infected with HIV is erotic as well as dangerous. Safer sex significantly lowers the likelihood of infection and in turn lowers the bug chasers' sexual stimulation. Third, many bug chasers seek HIV in response to loneliness. While they remain in the ranks of HIV-negative men, many of their friends and significant others have died of AIDS. This leaves some of those that are "left behind" feeling deserted and alone. Finally, many bug chasers engage in this type of sexual activity as a political statement in reaction to homophobic attitudes. As demonstrated by this multitide of motivations, categorizing even a single act as unquestionably normal, pathological, or sociological in its deviance can be problematic.

In Chapter 2, Forsyth provides information on various forms of voyeurism through the observation of two groups of voyeurs. The author discovered that while many voyeurs began their peeping alone, it sometimes develops into a group activity. While voyeurism has traditionally been categorized as pathologically deviant, the data reported by Forsyth—that these groups generate social structures to recruit and socialize others, and gather people together to perform the acts and provide social support for the actors—suggests that certain voyeuristic behaviors should be considered a form of sociological rather than pathological sexual deviance. This chapter also illuminates the difficulty inherent in assessing and classifying deviant behavior definitively. Together, these selections provide a cogent introduction to the complexities revealed in the chapters that follow.

I

Bareback Sex, Bug Chasers, and the Gift of Death

DeAnn Gauthier and Craig J. Forsyth

Unprotected sex has occurred throughout the AIDS epidemic, as evidenced by the thousands of new infections that occur each year. Since the mid-1980s, AIDS educators have focused primarily on gay men in their campaign to reduce the frequency of barebacking [sexual intercourse without the use of a condom] as a route of transmission for the deadly virus that causes AIDS. This strategy seemed to effect real behavioral changes, leading to a marked decline in the proportion of new AIDS cases due solely to male homosexual transmission (Siegel, Mesagno, Chen, and Christ, 1989). On the other hand, there continued to be simultaneous evidence that subgroups within the male homosexual community were not effecting behavioral changes (Ames, Atchinson, and Rose, 1995). Whether such activity is actually increasing in frequency, or whether discourse about such activity is only increasing, recent media attention to the subject has been alarmist in tone (McCoy, 1997; Peyser, 1997; Rotello, 1997; Signorile, 1997b). In this exploratory study, we argue that the panicked controversy surrounding the recent discussions of bareback sex is a reflection of a larger cultural division over the complex meanings of sexual behavior in the formation and maintenance of personal identities.

Barebacking is considered to be a form of sexual deviance only in certain contexts. If the partners are married heterosexuals, little to no social disapproval occurs. Should the partners be unmarried but romantically involved heterosexuals, social censure increases, but is still rela-

Reprinted from *Deviant Behavior,* Vol. 20, No. 1 (1999), pp. 85–100. © 1999 Taylor & Francis, Inc. Edited and reprinted by permission of the publisher.

tively mild in the United States of the 1990s. When the behavioral exchange occurs between unmarried heterosexual partners who are not romantically involved, the social censure increases further. But when barebacking involves homosexual male partners, it receives serious social censure, particularly since the identification of this route of transmission for the virus that causes AIDS. What is considered serious deviance, then, often depends on the context in which a behavior occurs more than on the actual content of the acts that comprise that behavior. As West (1987) noted, "Many deviant behaviors are merely exaggerated versions of familiar components of ordinary sexuality" (75).

Research has identified three categories of sexual deviance: normal, pathological, and sociological (Forsyth, 1996; Gagnon and Simon, 1967; Little, 1983, 1995). Normal sexual deviance occurs often, and among a large number of participants, thus making it statistically "normal," despite its designation as deviance. This includes such activities as oral sex and masturbation. Although many individuals consider oral sex to be deviant, a majority of adults have engaged in the act (Benokraitis, 1996).

The second category of sexual deviance is labeled pathological. Generally, these behaviors are considered to be harmful and are against the law, and few individuals participate. Examples include sexual contact with children, incest, exhibitionism, some forms of voyeurism, and rape (Forsyth, 1996; Gagnon and Simon, 1967; Little, 1983, 1995). This category is similar to the first in one respect: The deviant behaviors exist without the evolution of supportive group structures to maintain participants in the activity.

The third type of sexual deviance is sociological. It consists of precisely those sorts of behavior that generate distinctive forms of social structures that serve to recruit participants, train them, gather people together to perform the act, and/or provide social support for the actor. Examples are pornography, homosexuality, prostitution, swinging, and nudism in nudist camps. Although some individuals develop a homosexual identity without having had contact with other homosexual individuals, most homosexual men engage in, and in many ways depend on, contact with other homosexual men (Forsyth, 1996; Gagnon and Simon, 1967; Little, 1983, 1995). "The social structures engendered by this category of deviance are implicit when one speaks of the homosexual community with its bars, steam baths, publications, organizations, and argot" (Little 1983: 29). Such social structures also make use of emerging technology. With regard to sexual deviance, the application of new technology can be seen (among others) in the use of telephones for phone sex industry, CB radios for the prostitution industry, telescopes for voyeurism, and home video players for the prostitution movie industry (Durkin and Bryant, 1995; Forsyth, 1996; Luxenburg and Klein, 1984). Most recently, the personal computer and the Internet have provided a linking mechanism for individuals interested in identifying like-minded partners for sexual experimentation. Such may be the case with the particular form of barebacking known as bug chasing. Many forms of deviance do not spread (Douglas, Rasmussen, and Flanagan, 1977), but those that do, do so because there is a sociological structure to generate or maintain them (Forsyth and Benoit, 1989; Forsyth and Fournet, 1987; Toolan, Elkins, and D'Encarnacao, 1974; Weinberg, 1981a, 1981b). Thus,

> On any given night one can log on to the Internet and find lively discussions going on in chat rooms called Bareback M4M or I Like It Raw. . . . A sizeable portion of the poz [HIV positive] population (as well as a segment of the negative population) is openly forgoing the use of generally accepted safe-sex practices when engaging in intimate contact with each other (Bergling 1997: 71).

Method

Web sites, chat rooms, mailing lists, and personal ads devoted to the subject of barebacking have become part of the Internet landscape in the past few years. The primary data for this project were obtained chiefly from these Internet sources, ultimately constituting an availability sample of men who bareback and others who have information regarding the practice. Secondary data include the scant existing literature on barebacking, especially as expressed in the form of bug chasing, in the popular and academic presses.

Findings

The population of gay male barebackers includes an unknown number of participants, with multiple different key characteristics and motivations. Though many social observers might dismiss some categories of participants as unimportant, each category is intricately related to the others, and therefore should not be dismissed from discussion. For example, bareback sex that occurs between two men who are both HIV positive is (to some) a nonissue. Yet these men comprise part of a community of men who serve as models to one another of acceptable standards of behavior. Their perceptions and definitions of pleasure do not occur in a vacuum and may influence others in their community. In addition, there are real dangers to the HIV-positive partners themselves who are exchanging bareback sex. Specifically, the activity provides routes of transmission for other sexually transmitted diseases, which can burden the immune system, increase viral replication, and hasten death. Finally, there is the danger that unprotected encounters with a different, more virulent strain of HIV could result in a co-infection or recombination. Such a scenario has received tentative scientific support (D'Adesky, 1997; Robertson, Sharp, McCutchan, and Hahn, 1995; Schoofs, 1997) and implies that some individuals currently responding to drug treatment regimens may cease to do so if the recombinant virus is resistant to that particular treatment.

Despite the dangers to self and others, many of these HIV-positive men consider bareback sex with other HIV-positive men to be completely acceptable, as the following statement reveals:

> It's like being thrown into jail for life and then, while serving your time, having the warden threaten to extend your sentence. The threat has no power because nothing can make a life sentence any worse. That time I got fucked by another positive guy, I felt I didn't have to fear HIV any longer. I could taunt it, challenge it by taking it into my body without being further hurt (Gendin 1997: 64).

The following statement, from a website dedicated to barebacking, lends further support for this practice:

> For years now, poz men have had to bear a double burden—the burden of the virus itself and the burden of preventing the spread of the disease. Correctly, I believe, many of us have come to the conclusion that within ourselves there is little need to practice this self imposed sexual martyrdom. . . . For us, it's too late. So why shouldn't we party? (Responses to the *Dallas Voice* Article, 1997: 5).

Another contributor to the same website defended the practice as follows:

> After all, "safer sex" is not hot sex; it's pretend sex. The need for the intimacy of actual skin contact is primal. Condoms are not just a question of sensitivity, they are a barrier to physical, emotional and spiritual communion (Responses to the *Dallas Voice* Article, 1997: 6).

Thus, this category of barebackers feels justified in continuing the behavior. Some have acknowledged the risks to self and others but still eschew safe-sex techniques. This can have important consequences for others in the gay community. As one individual noted, "If the larger negative population learned that they could have the real sex they want, if they are willing to tolerate the risks of being positive," rising infection rates could become problematic (Responses to the Dallas Voice Article, 1997: 6).

Such views are no longer automatically considered as cavalier in the eyes of onlookers, owing to the development of new drug treatment regimens that seem able to check the progression of HIV infections (Rotello, 1997; Signorile, 1997b). With these medical advances, there appears to be a portion of the gay community that is willing to risk infection to regain the sense of closeness that was lost as a result of safer sex practices. The assumption is that treatment now exists that can make the disease "manageable" over the course of a lifetime rather than an automatic death sentence. As one HIV-negative individual argued, "It's a very manageable disease with the meds today. I'd probably not die from it" (Signorile, 1997a: 86).

Furthermore, the influence of HIV-positive individuals on HIV-negative individuals should not be underestimated, when considered in context. Though for many years HIV-negative people (both homosexual and heterosexual) have stigmatized HIV-positive people as persons to be avoided (Sandstrom, 1994), there is some evidence to support the notion that those who are HIV positive are revered, almost as fighters in a holy war. "If someone has AIDS or HIV, that kind of lionizes them. It's heroic, like fighting the battle. . . . When you get with someone who has HIV, it's like being with someone greater than you are" (Peyser, 1997: 77). Gay individuals who join the HIV-positive ranks sometimes feel they are entering a selective club, receiving a benefits package that, importantly, includes community sympathy (McCoy, 1997). This can be a powerful draw to an already disenfranchised segment of the population. Thus, as only one category of bareback sex, HIV-positive couplings may serve not only as a model for the management of desires but also as a symbol of the rewards that may accrue to those members of our society who possess fatal injuries.

Other categories of barebackers coexist with this first. One category is composed of men of uncertain HIV status who refuse, for a variety of personal reasons, to use safer sex techniques. One often-cited reason is offered in the following statement:

> I would even say that the risks commensurate with the rewards [of
> bareback sex] indicates a level of trust, of cohesion, that I don't think
> is achievable when both partners are primarily concerned with pre-
> venting the exchange of bodily fluids (O'Hara, 1997: 9).

In other words, many of these barebackers are convinced that latex
simply ruins the intimacy. Some of these individuals have never been
tested for HIV, whereas others do so irregularly. HIV status is not a
major concern, in themselves or the partners they choose. In fact, some
of these barebackers insist on not knowing, acting on the old adage
"What I don't know can't hurt me." Since the acknowledgment of the
AIDS epidemic, this is the category of individuals who have been most
stigmatized (even by the gay community) as pariahs. They were seen to
be flirting with suicide, even homicide, in their refusal to incorporate
safe-sex techniques into their behavioral schemes. In terms of risk of
seroconversion, one might label them passive-aggressive. This group
continues to exist today, no less dangerous to themselves or others than
they were at the beginning of the epidemic. But they have now been
publicly joined by a group of barebackers who do not passively seek
HIV infection but, rather, actively "chase" the "bug."

It is possible, even probable, that bug chasers have existed since the
beginning of the AIDS epidemic, but that their numbers were extremely
small. As the epidemic has progressed, claiming more victims, it is likely that bug chasing increased in frequency owing to a variety of reasons, some of which are articulated below. More important, however,
than the speculated increase in frequency of participation in this activity
is the certain increase in frequency of public discourse about participation in this activity. In large part, this has occurred because of the evolution and increasing ubiquitousness of computers and the Internet in people's everyday lives. As a means of communication with others of
similar interests whom we would otherwise rarely identify, there is no
better source. Consequently, bug chasers, in their quest to ascertain
interested partners, have simultaneously made very public an activity
that heretofore has been virtually unknown by the public at large.

Bug chasing as a form of bareback sex actually involves two categories of participants (though encounters may involve more than two
individuals in each of these two categories). There are, of course, the
HIV-negative men who seek to become infected with the virus (bug
chasers), and there are the HIV-positive men who seek to share the
"gift" of HIV (gift givers; Signorile 1997a). Chasers typically advertise
for partners with statements such as the following: "Will let you fuck

me raw only if you promise to give me all your diseases like AIDS/herpes, etc. Let's do it" (Sheon and Plant, 1998: 10). Gift givers, on the other hand, typically make comments such as these:

> Traveling POZ delivery service who prefers other poz guys, but will do it with consenting and sober neg dudes who want to enlist in our ranks. . . . [I plan] to make de-poz-its in eleven cities in four countries between now and October and [am] looking for sex partners at every stop (McCoy, 1997: 2).
>
> Attention neg men! Why stay locked in a boring world of sterile sex when you can join the ranks of the AIDS Freedom Fighters? Let me give you my gift and set you free (Jackson, 1997: 2).

Becoming "bug brothers" may occur one-on-one but is just as likely to result at special marathon group sex parties that are held for the purpose of seroconverting as many HIV-negative participants as possible. That individuals would knowingly participate in such events is shocking not only to some members of gay community but also to the public at large. Especially for this newly informed segment of the population, the practice of bug chasing may seem incoherent, until considered in sociological context.

Explanations for Bug Chasing

The following explanations are focused particularly on active bug chasers, though many would also apply to the more passive-aggressive barebackers discussed earlier. Four lines of explanation have emerged from the literature and Internet data sources. Although analytically these arguments seem easy to separate, practically they are intricately connected.

Fear and Relief

For some bug chasers, the problem has been that fear of infection inhibited their behavior in the past to such an extent that their perceived quality of life had diminished to unacceptably low levels. "I think about AIDS and the possibility of contracting HIV but that fear is not nearly as strong as the fear of not being with the man I love" (Ames et al., 1995: 70). These individuals wish for the "relief" of knowing that they are infected. For them, infection is often viewed as "the great inevitable," and thus they wish to merely quicken the inevitable so that they can get on with the business of living out their lives in a more uninhibited fashion, however short that life might be. Some of these individuals, like the HIV-positive men discussed above, believe that HIV is now medically manageable. Consequently, inducing a manageable infection is perceived to be the best route to an increased quality of life.

> In a way it's a relief. I don't have to wonder anymore. That awful waiting is gone. So now, if I do find someone, the relationship can be 100 percent real with nothing in the way. That's what I want: 100 percent natural, wholesome and real. Maybe now that I'm HIV positive, I can finally have my life (Green, 1996: 38ff).

Risk Taking as Eroticism

For many individuals, regardless of sexual orientation, the most captivating quality of the sex act is its irrationality. Safe sex, many bug chasers feel, negates that possibility (Gendin, 1997). This category of bug chasers defines their behavior as part of an erotic experience filled with excitement and danger. "The thrill of going bareback makes the sex hotter" (Signorile, 1997a: 2). These individuals perceive heightened sexual satisfaction derived from high-risk sexual encounters wherein they "flirt with death." "Some appear to find a particular sexual charge in the fact that the semen they're receiving is infected" (McCoy, 1997: 2). Other forms of such high-risk activity include autoerotic asphyxiation and sadomasochistic bondage/torture activities, and even dangerous sporting events (such as skydiving and bungee jumping) have been linked to "sexual charges" (Lowery and Wetli, 1982; McCoy, 1997; Myers, 1994). Breaking the rules, for some, is simply very exciting.

> Hard as it may be to understand, some gay men have unsafe sex because they want to . . . skate close to the edge. Danger can be erotic, even the threat of contacting a deadly disease (Peyser, 1997: 77).

Loneliness and Group Solidarity

For other bug chasers, the problem is loneliness. Many HIV-negative gay men feel that they have been left behind as lovers and friends have moved on to a status they do not share. The loss of solidarity and sense of community is overwhelming, particularly for individuals ensconced in a nation already divided along heterosexual-homosexual lines. Now, there is a further split within the homosexual community between those who are HIV positive and those who are HIV negative. The HIV-negative individuals sometimes feel such isolation as a result that they wish to become members of their community again, regardless of the cost. They are willing to commit what is, in essence, suicide in order to maintain their membership in the group. "A lot of gay men feel out of place, put down, worthless. If you're HIV-positive, everybody is generous. There is a sense of community" (Peyser, 1997: 77). An important component in the makeup of that community is the new emphasis on AIDS as a form of empowerment. "Like the pink triangle that was once used by the Nazis to brand homosexuals and is now a sign of gay pride, gays have sought to transform HIV from a death knell to an empowerment tool" (Peyser, 1997: 77). The campaign to change the perception of HIV has not occurred to the exclusion of HIV-negative members of the gay community. In discussions focused on stigma-management techniques, invariably there are those present who are not infected with the virus. The messages to which they are exposed resonate a persuasive theme: embracing an AIDS identity can be empowering for HIV-positive individuals (Sandstrom, 1994; Tewksbury and McGaughey, 1997). For example, in one sample of respondents, "There is consensus that HIV can bring meaning to life—meaning that would most likely not be experienced by a non-infected individual" (Tewsbury and McGaughey, 1997: 68). Other HIV-positive individuals have noted that having the virus becomes a transforming experience:

> I now view AIDS as both a gift and a blessing. . . . You go through this amazing kind of transformation. You look at things for the first time, in a powerful new way that you've never looked at them before in your whole life (Sandstrom, 1994: 334).

AIDS, then, has become a master status not only in the larger society but in the gay community as well. But within this prominent subculture, the meaning of the status is very different. It is becoming destigmatized, resulting in a change in identity from deviant to charismatic (Warren, 1980). Some bug chasers, feeling excluded from full participation in their community, simply wish to be empowered in the same manner as that of their peers in order to obtain the "privileges of membership" (Gendin, 1997).

Political Actions

Still other bug chasers behave in this way because they see the behavior as a politically charged action in response to the larger, homophobic culture that has stigmatized gay individuals as a whole and especially HIV-positive gay individuals as outcasts. As one barebacker put it, "Anal sex is my right and damned if I'll do without it!" (Ames et al., 1995: 64). The discrimination and moral disdain to which gay men are subjected are viewed by some bug chasers as forces that literally push them to respond in such a politically charged way. To illustrate this line of reasoning, we rely on Lemert's (1951) theory of secondary deviance, where stigmatized individuals come to accept as part of their self-image the public designation of the pejorative label. On acceptance, individuals then go on to fulfill the negative prophecy, strengthening the original stigma against them. Some homosexual men, stigmatized as deviant and disenfranchised from the larger society, may become secondary deviants through the act of seroconversion. "A few men believed that [unprotected] anal sex was a 'required' part of truly gay sex and an essential part of coming out. For some of these men, continuing to engage was a political act" (Ames et al., 1995: 64).

Conclusions

This research has examined one form of sociologically unknown sexual deviance: barebackers engaged in bug chasing. This form of deviance has generated much public controversy in recent months, reflecting the larger cultural division in the United States over the complex meanings of sexual behavior. As a form of sexual deviance, bug chasing represents a sociological construct in that it has evolved distinct forms of social structures that help to sustain involvement. Most notably is the Internet forum that has developed to facilitate these behavioral exchanges. Both Forsyth (1996) and Durkin and Bryant (1995) have argued that safe-sex concerns would lead to more virtual sex through the recent advances in computer technology. Our research suggests, however, that sometimes advances in technology may lead to unsafe sex. Thus, computer access to the Internet may encourage discussions of virtual sex (whether these discussions concern voyeurism, pedophilia, or bug chasing), which may in turn lead to dangerous, exploitive, or even unsafe real sex.

We have identified in this research several key reasons why some gay men may engage in unsafe sex, even to the point of seeking infection with a deadly virus. Together, these explanations may be considered as differing expressions of the identity construction and stigma-management processes (Goffman, 1963). In response to the stigmatiza-

tion for being either homosexual (by the larger heterosexual community) or HIV-negative (by the HIV-positive community), bug chasers may
seek to manage their stigma through any of the varied routes described
in this research. In moving from their original role designation of primary deviants to the newly acquired secondary deviant status, many
bug chasers seem to have become involved in role engulfment (Schur,
1971), where both self-concept and behavior focus largely on the
deviant role of homosexual, HIV-negative man. In some sense, these
individuals could be described as politicizing the stigma attributed to
them through this master status in their bug-chasing response (Dotter
and Roebuck, 1988; Schur, 1980). In terms of individual self-concep-
tion, to the extent that the person is able to convert the stigma from that
of a personal failing to that of a political issue, a transformation occurs.
"The politicized 'deviant' gains a new identity, an heroic self-image as
crusader in a political cause" (Humphreys, 1972: 142). Consequently,
the bug chasers gain in self-respect, sense of purpose, heightened group
solidarity, and improved perception in quality of life (Schur, 1971:
323). Both personal and socially, politicizing behaviors such as these
can garner considerable rewards.

Because of the exploratory nature of this study, many questions
remain unanswered. In particular, the characteristics of the bug-chasing
population are unknown. The anonymity provided by the Internet
makes identification of these individuals for interview particularly difficult, and consequently, demographic characteristics can only be sur-
mised from user profiles, which are not always available. Furthermore,
because of the potential use of these profiles, many users may have
changed important descriptors about themselves in order to remain truly
anonymous. Nor are we able to address issues of physical attractiveness
among the bug-chasing population. For example, Ames et al. (1995: 66)
wrote of the possibility that overweight or less attractive individuals
may be more willing to risk unsafe sex owing to desperation and a lack
of interested partners. To say that this is the case among bug chasers, at
this point, would be merely speculative. Future research might seek to
address these neglected subjects.

Finally, though we have not yet located any direct comments by
bug chasers to this effect, it is possible that guilt motivates some of
their behaviors. Many in the gay community speak of "survivor's guilt,"
but bug chasers may be more willing than others to act in response to
that guilt. As Clinard and Meier (1998) noted in their discussion of
altruistic suicides, the most common form of this type of suicide is that
which "represents an attempt to achieve expiation for violation of soci-

ety's mores" (457) as atonement for perceived wrongs. For some gay men who suffer guilt for remaining HIV negative when all around them their community has been decimated by the fatal virus, the wrong that has been committed is survival. Atonement, for these individuals, may seem to require chasing "the bug."

References

Ames, L. J., A. B. Atchinson, and D. T. Rose. (1995). Love, Lust, and Fear: Safer Sex Decisions Making Among Gay Men. *Journal of Homosexuality, 3*:53–73.

Benokraitis, N. V. (1996). *Marriages and Families.* Upper Saddle River, NJ: Prentice-Hall.

Bergling, T. (1997). Riders on the Storm. *Genre 53* (October):71–72.

Clinard, M. B. and R. F. Meier. (1998). *Sociology of Deviant Behavior.* New York: Harcourt Brace College Publishers.

D'Adesky, A. C. (1997). Double Jeopardy. *Out* (October):128–130.

Dotter, D. and J. Roebuck. (1988). The Labeling Approach Reexamined: Interactionism and the Components of Deviance. *Deviant Behavior, 9*:19–32.

Douglas, J. D., P. K. Rasmussen, and C. A. Flanagan. (1977). *The Nude Beach.* Beverly Hills, CA: Sage.

Durkin, K. F. and C. D. Bryant. (1995). Log on to Sex: Some Notes on the Carnal Computer and Erotic Cyberspace as an Emerging Research Frontier. *Deviant Behavior, 16*:179–200.

Forsyth, C. J. (1996). The Structuring of Vicarious Sex. *Deviant Behavior, 17*:279–295.

Forsyth, C. and G. M. Benoit. (1989). Rare, Ole, Dirty Snacks: Some Research Notes on Dirt Eating. *Deviant Behavior, 10*:61–68.

Forsyth, C. J. and L. Fournet. (1987). A Typology of Office Harlots: Party Girls, Mistresses and Career Climbers. *Deviant Behavior, 8*:319–328.

Gagnon, J. H. and W. Simon. (eds.) (1967). *Sexual Deviance.* New York: Harper and Row.

Gendin, S. (1997). Riding Bareback. *POZ Magazine* (June):64–65.

Goffman, E. (1963). *Stigma: Notes on the Management of Spoiled Identity.* Englewood Cliffs, NJ: Prentice-Hall.

Green, J. (1996, September 15). Flirting with Suicide. *New York Times Sunday Magazine,* 38ff.

Humphreys, L. (1972). *Out of the Closets.* Englewood Cliffs, NJ: Prentice-Hall.

Jackson, J. (1997). Raw as They Wanna Be. Online. Available at: http://rampages.onramp.net/!tmike/xtremesex/brothers_f.html.

Lemert, E. (1951). *Social Pathology: A Systematic Approach to the Theory of Sociopathic Behavior.* New York: McGraw Hill.

Little, C. B. (1995). *Deviance and Control: Theory, Research, and Social Policy.* 3rd ed. Itasca, IL: F. E. Peacock.

Little, C. B. (1983). *Understanding Deviance and Control: Theory, Research, and Social Policy.* 1st ed. Itasca, IL: F. E. Peacock.

Lowery, S. A. and C. V. Wetli. (1982). Sexual Asphyxia: A Neglected Area of Study. *Deviant Behavior, 3*:19–39.

Luxenburg, J. and L. Klein. (1984). CB Radio Prostitution: Technology and the Displacement of Deviance. *Journal of Offender Counseling Services and Rehabilitation, 9*:71–87.

McCoy, J. (1997). "Xtreme" Sex: A Return to Anything Goes, or Merely Better Communication About HIV? Online. Available at: http://www5.onramp.net/~tmike/xtremesex/dallasvoice-article.html.

Myers, J. (1994). Nonmainstream Body Modification: Genital Piercing, Branding, Burning, and Cutting. In P. A. Adler and P. Adler (eds.) *Constructions of Deviance.* Belmont, CA: Wadsworth Publishing Company.

O'Hara, S. (1997, July 8). Safety First? *The Advocate, 9.*

Peyser, M. (1997, September 29). A Deadly Dance. *Newsweek*:76–77.

Responses to the Dallas Voice Article. (1997). Online. Available at: http://rampages.onramp.net/~tmike/xtremesex/brothers_f.html.

Robertson, D. L., P. M. Sharp, F. E. McCutchan, and B. H. Hahn. (1995). Recombination in HIV-1. *Nature, 374*:124–126.

Rotello, G. (1997). *Sexual Ecology: AIDS and the Destiny of Gay Men.* New York: Dutton.

Sandstrom, K. L. (1994). Confronting Deadly Disease: The Drama of Identity Construction Among Gay Men with AIDS. In P. A. Adler and P. Adler (eds.), *Constructions of Deviance.* Belmont, CA: Wadsworth Publishing Company.

Schoofs, M. (1997). Who's Afraid of Reinfection? *POZ Magazine* (May): 61–63, 78.

Schur, E. M. (1980). *The Politics of Deviance: Stigma Contests and the Use of Power.* Englewood Cliffs, NJ: Prentice-Hall.

Schur, E. M. (1971). *Labeling Deviant Behavior: Its Sociology Implications.* New York: Harper and Row.

Sheon, N. and A. Plant. (1998). Protease Disinhibitors? The Gay Bareback Phenomenon. Online. Available at: http://www.managingdesire.org/sex[panic/ProteaseDisinhibitors.html.

Siegel, K., F. Mesagno, J. Y. Chen, and G. Christ. (1989). Factors Distinguishing Homosexual Males Practicing Risky and Safer Sex. *Social Science Medicine, 28*:561–569.

Signorile, M. (1997a). In the Company of Men. *Out* (October):86–89, 146–149.

Signorile, M. (1997b). *Life Outside: The Signorile Report on Gay Men.* New York: Harper Collins.

Tewksbury, R. and D. McGaughey. (1997). Stigmatization of Persons with HIV Disease: Perceptions, Management, and Consequences of AIDS. *Sociological Spectrum, 17*:49–70.

Toolan, J. M., M. Elkins, and P. D'Encarnacao. (1974). The Significance of Streaking. *Medical Aspects of Human Sexuality, 8*:152–165.

Warren, C. A. B. (1980). Destigmatization of Identity: From Deviant to Charismatic. *Qualitative Sociology, 3*:59–72.

Weinberg, M. S. (1981a). Becoming a Nudist. In E. Rubington and M. Weinberg (eds.), *Deviance: An Interactionist Perspective*. New York: Macmillan.

Weinberg, M. S. (1981b). The Nudist Management of Respectability. In E. Rubington and M. Weinberg (eds.), *Deviance: An Interactionist Perspective*. New York: Macmillan.

West, D. J. (1987). *Sexual Crimes and Confrontations: A Study of Victims and Offenders*. Aldershot, England: Gower Publishing Company.

2

The Structuring of Vicarious Sex

Craig J. Forsyth

This paper suggests a variation in causal explanations and typology construction regarding a form of sexual deviance. This analysis focuses on a change in what is thought to be the cause of some forms of voyeurism, defined herein as watching persons who are undressing, undressed, or in the act of sexual intercourse. Voyeurism is or has been regarded by some researchers (Gagnon and Simon, 1967; Little, 1983, 1995) and clinicians (American Psychiatric Association, 1994) as pathological deviance. Bryant (1977) considers the act of voyeurism to perhaps be normal deviance:

> In our society, considerable stress is placed on the individual's right of privacy, but nevertheless unauthorized observation of personal anatomy, or sexual activities, in the form of voyeurism or peeping, occurs at various levels of intent and intensity, in the face of social normative prescriptions to the contrary. To some degree, it may be that unauthorized observation for purposes of salacious gratification, even if relatively innocuous in import, is behaviorally endemic to our population (31).

The work of Feigelman (1974) offers support for voyeurism being a normal behavior; given the opportunity, most people will "peep." Other research supports the "normality" of peeping (Drzazga, 1960; Hamilton, 1929; Kinsey, 1953; *New York Times*, 1992). Drzazga (1960) contends that society has made little effort to understand voyeurism, although it is an ancient form of sexual behavior.

Reprinted from *Deviant Behavior,* Vol. 17, No. 3 (1996), pp. 279–295. © 1996 Taylor & Francis, Inc. Edited and reprinted by permission of the publisher.

"Vicarious sexual gratification as a symbolic replacement for physical sexual fulfillment represents a socially acceptable substitute" (Bryant, 1977: 31). Voyeurism is not necessarily pathological. As Sundholm's (1977) research points out, watching sex on a movie screen is not much different, nor does it have any more or less erotic quality, than watching sex through someone's window. Safer sex in the 1990s has both suggested and legitimized the idea of viewing sex. Lower-risk sex is a national topic ("Safer Sex," 1991).

There is a fairly well developed body of literature on various sexual activities that involve what could be termed voyeurism. As the literature indicates, there are two general situations of voyeurism: one where the person or persons know they are being watched and one in which the person or persons do not know or do not want to be watched.

> Nude sunbathing, for example, incorporates a particular type of voyeurism. Voyeurism . . . poses a dilemma for the nude beach naturalists, those who share in some vague way the hip or casual vision of the nude beach . . . [V]oyeurs have become the plague of the nude scene. . . . The abstract casual vision of the beach does not see it as in any way a sex trip, but the casual vision of life in general certainly does not exclude or downgrade sex (Douglas, Rasmussen, and Flanagan, 1977: 126–127).

Some nude beachers express disdain for the "straight" voyeur, but a majority of nude sunbathers do not mind others peeping at them (Douglas et al., 1977).

> Sometimes I really feel hostile to the lookers. Obviously you can't look at people that way even if they are dressed . . . [i]t really depends on your attitude in looking (130).

But there are those on the beach who have mixed emotions about being the object of peeping.

> A group of boys had apparently entered [the nude beach] with the intention of peeking at some nudes. Since I was the only woman there, they congregated around me. This wouldn't have bothered me at all if they had been nude, too. But they remained clothed in their surfer suits. At first, this seemed a prostitution of the purpose of the beach— they were being "dirty" about it and it almost made me feel that way. But after a while I realized that if I gave them pleasure by looking at me, then that was a fine thing. If their thing is to look at nude women for a charge, I certainly am not one to stop them from doing their thing (Douglas et al., 1977: 128).

The women who exposed their breasts at the New Orleans Mardi Gras were playing to two groups of voyeurs. The attention of one type of voyeur is welcomed, and the attention of the other is not.

> I hate those fuckers [on the ground] who try to see my boobs. If I'm with some people they can look. That's okay. But those guys who seek a look—they are disgusting . . . I guess I feel sorry for them too. But I still don't like them. You know it's so obvious, they get right next to the float and then turn around. Their back is to the float. They are not watching the parade. We tell them to "get the fuck out of here asshole" and they leave (Forsyth, 1992: 400).

Other women enjoy being watched.

> Sexual satisfaction . . . I love it when they look. The more they look the more I show them (Forsyth, 1992: 400).

Bryant (1977) describes why people expose themselves to voyeurs.

> Individuals . . . expose portions of their anatomy in the presence of others, and especially others of the opposite sex, in violation of social prescription for a number of reasons, and may even justify their actions with various rationales. People may exhibit their bare anatomy out of pride, for economic purposes . . . or to even interest members of the opposite sex . . . Persons may exhibit themselves . . . to sexually stimulate the observer or as a means of sexually arousing themselves. . . . Depending on the social context, anatomical exposure may be conceptualized as . . . erotic . . . or it may also be defined and labeled as pathological (99–100).

In Weatherford's (1986) study of what he termed "porn row," much of the sex was voyeuristic. The peep show, whether viewed through a gloryhole or booth window, is voyeuristic sex (Potter, 1989; Tewksbury, 1990). The "pulp voyeur," as described by McKinstry (1974), is actually a reader of pornography and would not usually be termed a voyeur. Voyeurism has also been shown to be an explicit part of many homosexual encounters (Delph, 1978; Humphreys, 1975).

What constitutes voyeurism varies. Some authors believe that true voyeurs need an unknowing victim and are not satisfied unless they are violating someone's privacy (Langevin, 1983).

A man visiting a strip show on a business trip away from home is not a voyeur, but someone who regularly peeps into bedroom windows and masturbates is clearly a voyeur (Smith, 1976; West, 1987). Langevin (1983) cites the example of males in an office who bring binoculars to view women undressing in a nearby apartment building as not being "true" voyeurs, because their behavior is situational and they are not masturbating to orgasm. Some researchers distinguish voyeurism as perverse or abnormal when the voyeur has a preference for voyeurism over sexual intercourse (Bergler, 1957; Oberndorf, 1939; Yalom, 1960).

> Deviant sexual habits are often multiple, making a single label inadequate. Many deviant behaviors are merely exaggerated versions of familiar components of ordinary sexuality. The borderline between normal and deviant is sometimes blurred (West, 1987: 75).

As will be shown in this research, the names given to sexual deviations by those in various disciplines cover a wide range of behaviors. This paper suggests that some voyeurism can be considered, and better understood, as sociological deviance.

The Societal Production of Sexual Deviance

Some researchers (Gagnon and Simon, 1967; Little 1983, 1995) have defined three types of sexual deviance: normal, pathological, and sociological. Normal deviance is sexual behavior that is widespread and occurs with low visibility.

> A number of sexual activities are quite frequent even though they . . . offend the normative standards of most people in community. (Little, 1983: 28).

Statistically speaking, these acts are normative rather than deviant. Some researchers refer to this type of behavior as "secret deviance." Oral sex is an example of normal sexual deviance. Although many individuals consider oral sex to be deviant, a majority of adults have performed or received oral sex (Benokraitis, 1996: 147). Other behaviors that are considered normal deviance are masturbation and premarital sex.

> A basic characteristic of this type of normal deviance is that it does not give rise to a specific form of social structure organized around the deviant act or its consequences. While some forms of "normal" deviance occur in social relationships no special groups . . . are organized around this activity in order . . . to maintain people in it.

The second type of sexual deviance refers to the general case where there is a particular type of association between law, mores, and behavior. This type of deviance is labeled pathological. Pathological deviance is considered by most people to be harmful, is against the law, and is engaged in by relatively few individuals. Examples include sexual contact with children, incest, exhibitionism, voyeurism, and rape (Gagnon and Simon, 1967; Little, 1983, 1995).

> These types of deviance, unlike "normal deviance," involve very few persons, but are like it in that pathological deviance does exist without supportive group structures . . . for the actor. . . . [T]hese kinds of offenses rarely involve more than one offender who is acting alone out of particular psychological needs. While the behaviors involved represent learned responses, understanding the sources of deviant learning and the reinforcement of continued behavior generally necessitates a psychological or social-psychological perspective rather than a sociological one (Gagnon and Simon, 1967: 9).

Much of the research on voyeurism has been done within a criminal/clinical psychological framework and therefore treats voyeurism as either a sexual perversion or a sociopathic personality disturbance (Alamensi, 1960; Bergler, 1957; Coleman, 1956; East, 1946; Karpman, 1960; Oberndorf, 1939; Yalom, 1960).

The third type of sexual deviance is sociological. It consists of precisely those sorts of behavior that spawn unique forms of social structure. Social structure–generating deviance includes behavior that generates specific social structures that serve to recruit participants, train them, gather people together to perform the act, and provide social support for the actor. Examples are pornography, homosexuality, prostitution, swinging, and nudism in nudists' camps.

> Of course, any of these behavior may be explained, in part by reference to the psychological history of the participants. However, in each case, an elaborate set of ongoing relationships provided the participant with specialized knowledge to help manage interactions or clients. Through such relationships, the deviant can learn the attitudes and rationalizations that allow him or her to place the behavior in the best possible light (Little, 1983: 29).

Whereas some individuals develop a homosexual commitment and engage in homosexual behavior without having had contact with other homosexuals, most homosexuals engage in and, in many ways, depend upon contact with other homosexuals (Gagnon and Simon, 1967: 9–10; Little, 1983, 1995).

> The social structures engendered by this category of deviance are implicit when one speaks of the homosexual community with its bars, steam baths, publications, organizations, and argot (Little, 1983: 29).

The same can be said for the prostitute.

> [W]hen a female prostitute enters "the life," she becomes part of an occupational culture with an elaborate set of social networks including pimps, other prostitutes, steerers, clients, and vice officers (Little, 1983: 29).

The Generating of Voyeurism

This research contends that some voyeurism is the province of sociology rather than psychology. This voyeurism is sociologically generated because: (a) it is widespread; (b) it is little different from viewing sex on a screen; (c) a network of mutual voyeurs exists that will continue to recruit new members; (d) the need for lower risk sex has begun to legitimize this form of sexual expression/outlet; and (e) some researchers have used the term "normal voyeurism," which include such behavior as sheet-lifting orderlies or peeping construction workers on high-rise buildings (Bryant, 1982; Feigelman, 1974). The fact that it is a collective activity is at least partially responsible for its being considered normal. Using the above literature and data collected from two groups of voyeurs, this paper demonstrates that certain kinds of voyeurism are not pathological and, indeed, are sociological (Feigelman, 1974) and perhaps emerging as normal deviance.

Methodology

This research is based on data obtained from two groups of voyeurs in 1994 and 1995. Data were gathered using several means: Individuals or couples were interviewed in the home shop of the key informant; observations for the peeping activities were done on seven different occasions for Group 1 and two occasions for Group 2, so as to validate the data obtained in the interviews; and the author participated in the "after-peeping meeting" of Group 1 on four occasions. Four members of

Group 1 were interviewed individually. Because of the construction of Group 2, the author interviewed only members of this group as couples or as individuals. The author interviewed five couples. On each of these occasions, the couple, the key informant, and the author were present. The author also interviewed three individuals—two males and one female. On each of these occasions the individual, the key informant, and the author were present. The author also interviewed three individuals—two males and one female. On each of these occasions the individual, the key informant, and the author were present. Additionally, the owner of a business that sells telescopes was interviewed; this interview also took place in the home shop of the key informant. Notes were taken during the interviews.

Findings

The individuals in this research did their peeping in groups. Although some started out as solitary peepers, it became a group activity. The fact they did not act alone but rather in groups (although one functioned as a primary group and the other as a quasi group or aggregate, and there were only two types of peeping behavior detected) licenses the author to describe the actions of these voyeurs within one of the two types of groups below. As will be discussed, the two kinds of peepers differed in several ways: the awareness of the victims that they were being viewed, the reciprocal nature of the viewing, the group structure, the success rate of the group, and the history and maintenance of the group.

Group 1

This group of voyeurs had victims who were not aware they were being viewed. This group was composed of a small group of close friends having the characteristics of a primary group. There was a rather low success rate, in that there were often nights in which there were no victims to be seen. Members of this group were men who worked in buildings downtown. Each man had access to a high location near or on top of one of the buildings. All of these individuals worked at night, in jobs as janitors, maintenance men, or equipment operators. The group was more than 20 years old and had started when two of the participants worked on the same shift at the same downtown building. One of these individuals had gotten a job at another building, other coworkers became interested and got jobs at other buildings, and so on until the group grew to its current size of 9. The last member came into the group in 1992. As one of the members commented, "We now have guys at all the good buildings in the city."

The group would meet at one of the buildings, set up the telescopes and "peep." The individual with access to the building used on a particular night would have a telescope there, and others might or might not bring their own. The only restriction was that those bringing their own scopes had to break them down so that they could fit in a small carrying bag. Anyone who asked what they were doing were told that the men were in an observatory club: "They are stargazing." There were 9 men in this group, although no more than 4 were ever present at any time in the presence of the author. All of these men were White. They appeared to range in age from the late 30s to early 60s. There were a lot of "dry runs" (nothing to see) in this group. After a peeping, dry run or "wet run" (when they saw something), the men would go off to an urban neighborhood bar as a group. There they would sometimes meet other members who could not make the peep session, talk of their night's experiences, and drink beer.

On a dry night, the meetings at the buildings where the men worked would last an hour or two; on a wet night the guys would stay until the nudity and/or sex either had ended or was no longer in their view. Meetings would often begin between 9 p.m. and 10 p.m. and would end as late as 3 a.m. During these encounters, typical conversations revolved around whether the person(s) being viewed had been seen before, the anticipation of further actions on the part of the victims(s), the level of attractiveness of the victim(s), and whether the voyeurs were looking at a man. On several occasions when one person had been peeping into a hotel room, another individual would say after "taking' the telescope (their turn at looking through the scope), "That's a fucking guy, asshole." Looking at a man and thinking he is woman is one of the interesting aspects of voyeur culture. One man who had apparently made this mistake on more than one occasion was always the focus of jokes during viewing—"Make sure it ain't a man you are looking at" or "Make sure you know what the difference is." This ribbing would continue in the bar. The author was surprised by the amount of both nudity and sexual activity that could be viewed in office buildings and hotels and the fact that the victims could have easily hidden their activities by drawing curtains or turning off lights. This fact that these individuals did not attempt to obstruct the view caused the author to consider the relationship between voyeurism and exhibitionism suggested by the literature (Feigelman, 1974; Gagnon and Simon, 1967; Langevin, 1983; Smith, 1976; West, 1987).

Another characteristic of this group was the stigma attached to solo peeping. As a result of the mark attached to this behavior, none of these men admitted to peeping alone.

> Guys who look alone are jerkoffs, because they must be jerking off to the sights. Man, them fellows are sick. . . . There is a guy over in [name of building] that gets on the roof. He works the graveyard shift. He lays flat on that tar and gravel roof with his scope like a rifle, you would think he was in Vietnam or something. He looks at that same fucking hotel and office building every night. I asked him if he wanted to get with us, but he gave me some fucking excuse. A guy who works with him said he stays up there a lot.

Getting caught is always a possibility for these voyeurs.

> My boss saw my telescope in my locker and said, "Get that motherfucker out of here man—you are going to get us all fired," I brought it home, but about a week later I had it back. Shit, man, ain't nothing to do here at night. I do my work.
>
> No one has ever caught us looking at them. The only way they could see us is if they had a scope too. So what the fuck are they going to say?

As previously mentioned, the activity of this group was markedly different from the behavior of the second peeping group. The most significant of these differences is that Group 1 voyeurs had victims who were oblivious to being watched.

Group 2

In this group the "victims" were aware they were being watched; indeed, there was a reciprocal nature to the viewing. These individuals did not have the characteristic of a primary group, because not all members participated with other members, nor even knew all the members. The success rate of this group was near perfect, because mutual peeping encounters were arranged. The history of this group is very different from that of the former group. One person said this group had started in 1983, when one of the core couples answered an ad in a newspaper.

> It was a kind of swingers news or something like that. There was an ad that said something like, "Vicarious sex your thing? Do you like to

watch? Must have scope or be willing to buy. Couples Only." We answered the ad and met this one couple. We watched each other a few times, then the couple said there were others they would put us in contact with, we said yes, and here we are. . . . We ran our own ad. . . . Some of the other couples also had ads.

This group was a loose collection of individuals made up of several couples who viewed each other having sex. In a sociological sense, it was not a true group, even though dyadic arrangements were routinely constructed. "Scenes" were arranged, where one couple would have sex or appear nude where the other couple could view them. These arrangements included the use of apartments, offices, hotel rooms, and cars. Couples would set up the time and place for their performance to be viewed by another couple. One rule for such encounters was that there was supposed to be a reciprocal nature to the viewing: The viewing couple was to become the viewed on the next encounter. Another rule was that no one was supposed to talk about the encounters outside of the participants, and no cameras could be used. A final canon was that only one couple could view another couple; there could be only one couple being watched and watching. As one participant said, "There is no group sex thing here." Individuals could not participate as singles. The reasons for the prohibition against individuals viewing alone were similar to those of Group 1.

We do not allow singles to participate. I don't mean people have to be married or living together, but that there must be two couples involved. We almost let a female in once. She wanted to watch and then do something alone for us, but we decided it was too perverted. Having single individuals makes the date kind of dirty rather than sexy.

All the participants in this group appeared to be between the ages of 25 and 40. All core couples and all other participants were White. The number in this group could only be estimated, because some couples might participate once whereas others might be longtimers. Not all participating couples had participated with all other couples. There were six core couples who had remained in the group for approximately 10 years. Other couples had moved away or tired of the activity. It was estimated by the key informant and core members that 40 other couples had participated.

One of the core members described the activity:

We usually start with a call to another couple. We will arrange both dates, you know—their turn and our turn. One couple we do it with has an office by a hotel, and we reserved a certain room which is across from their office. The next time, or maybe the same night, they are watching us. We have done this a lot.

Another offered a description of another kind of activity.

Sometimes you can have a view into a building close by so they identify places where you can go and look. Other times they will park close to your home their car, although it is hard to get a good view into a car. Man, there are a million ways. Whatever you prefer, and if you can give and get a view is great.

One female participant offered an argument for her peeping:

There is nothing wrong with it. Everyone enjoys it, nothing sneaky, everything is on the up and up, it is sort of like having sex with your same partner but adding a bit of spice to it.

One woman applicant implicitly dismissed the pathological nature of her behavior by giving the following sociological account. She thought there were many people performing these voyeur roles.

There are lots of couples doing this. We met a couple at a party, and in conversation they referred to ads in newspapers, about lonely hearts and that stuff. The conversation then started about how hard is it to meet people and the rise of video clubs and love ads, and we got into a conversation about ads for watching. . . . They had done this before. . . . We have hooked up with them half a dozen times. . . . It's always great.

When asked about the specific wording, content, and the publication of these so-called "ads for watching," the following responses were given.

I remember one ad was very simple. It said "Couples with scopes," and they had an address. I never responded to an ad, nor did I ever run an ad.

The only ad I ever responded to was in a kind of booklet or newspaper the guy I later bought my big scope from gave me. It said, "Great safe high tech sex. Need a scope. Couples only. No singles."

Man, everybody is doing this. You don't even need ads; just ask your close friends. I bet they will do it. We got a buddy. He has had a

> lot of girlfriends. They all said, "Sounds great. Let's do it." This is just something different, so it is strange until you do it. It is sort of like oral sex was 20 years ago.

The key informant gave a different account of these ads.

> I have never seen these ads in any magazines. But there was a newsletter a couple of times that a customer showed me. I didn't really pay any attention to it. These people have sort of a network they end up with. You know, you meet someone, and you meet someone else through them.

I told the key informant I would like further information regarding these ads. In response to this request, he set up a meeting with an individual from whom he bought parts and supplies for his shop. It was my opinion, after this interview, that these individuals had produced a short newsletter at one point, but that it proved to be too obtrusive. It was quickly replaced by networking, although there might still be some isolated ads for other voyeur couples. The talk of ads might also be a device that served to "normalize" their sexual activity. If there are many ads, then many people do this, so it is normal. If this was indeed the case, then the talk about ads was another attempt to repudiate the pathological nature of their performances, by assigning a more normal social version.

The comments from several members of this group reinforced the views of Bryant (1977, 1982). Individuals expose parts of their anatomy in the sight of others, especially others of the opposite sex, in violation of social proscription and justify their actions with various rationales.

The key informant reinforced the comments of many of these couples regarding the normality of the voyeur in general. He believed that the telescope had become a normal part of office decor. The informant said that a large part of his business was now selling scopes to executives in high-rise buildings.

> When you go into an office, many times there is the scope standing by the window ready to be used; no longer is it hidden in the closet. It is a piece of furniture to be admired and used. There is no longer a stigma put on the activity.

An interview with an owner of a shop that sold scopes said that his shop also sold many telescopes to offices.

We have a name for them now—"office scopes." They must be functional and attractive, which means a lot of wood and brass or chrome. You know, all polished, and shiny and expensive-looking. Recently we have orders for a lot of wood. We also get a lot of work repairing these same scopes, so they are using them. They are not just part of a stylish trend, although I know a lot of this business is because the guy down the hall has one. But also caught up in this demand is that the guy down the hall is looking at this great looking lady. . . . There still may be some who look at the city and the stars, but the majority of people who need a repair or an upgrade are doing so because they cannot snoop so well anymore with their old scope.

Discussion

Some kinds of voyeurism generate specific social structures that serve to recruit participants, train them, gather people together to perform the act, and provide social support for the actor. Patterns of deviant activity, such as the kinds of voyeurism described here, cannot be explained by ascribing them to individual pathology (Feigelman, 1974; Gagnon and Simon, 1967; Little, 1983, 1995). The voyeuristic activities described herein exist because of the social structures that support them. The question of whether pathological voyeurism and nonpathological voyeurism are totally different kinds of behaviors or are to be viewed on a continuum is answered by the perspectives and predilections of individual researchers (Feigelman, 1974). This researcher suggests that pathological voyeurism and nonpathological voyeurism are indeed separate kinds of sexual behavior, which would not have the same label.

Typically, voyeurism has been addressed from a psychological perspective. However, this research has shown that sociology is of paramount importance in explaining some forms of voyeurism. Voyeurism is a product of social activity. The widespread use of telescopes for the purpose of peeping means its future is leading toward even further normality. Much like oral sex, it will soon be regarded—indeed, may have already become regarded—as normal deviance.

The voyeurs described in this paper engage in a form of sexual expression—one contractual, the other contrived. Many forms of deviance do not spread (Douglas et al., 1977), but those that do, do so because there is a sociological structure to generate them (Forsyth and Benoit, 1989; Forsyth and Fournet, 1987; Toolan, Elkins, and D'Encarnacao, 1974; Weinberg, 1981a, 1981b). Thus begins the process of normal deviance. Perhaps this research will contribute to an understanding of the etiology of both pathological and sociological voyeurism and the process of normalization.

References

Alamensi, R. J. (1960). The Face-Breast Equation. *Journal of American Psychoanalysis Association,* 8:43–70.

American Psychiatric Association. (1994). *Diagnostic and Statistical Manual of Mental Disorders.* 4th ed. Washington D.C.: American Psychiatric Association

Benokraitis, N. V. (1996). *Marriages and Families.* Upper Saddle River, NJ: Prentice-Hall.

Bergler, E. (1957). Voyeurism. *Archives of Criminal Psychodynamics,* 2:211–225.

Bryant, C. (1982). *Sexual Deviance and Social Proscription.* New York: Human Sciences Press.

Bryant, C. (1977). *Sexual Deviancy in Social Context.* New York: New Viewpoints.

Coleman, J. C. (1956). *Abnormal Psychology and Modern Life.* Glenview, IL: Scott-Foreman.

Delph, E. W. (1978). *The Silent Community.* Beverly Hills, CA: Sage Publications.

Douglas, J. D., P. K. Rasmussen and C. A. Flanagan. (1977). *The Nude Beach.* Beverly Hills, CA: Sage.

Drzazga, J. (1960). *Sex Crimes.* Springfield, IL: Charles C. Thomas.

East, W. N. (1946). Sexual Offenders. *Journal of Nervous and Mental Diseases, 103*:626–666.

Feigelman, W. (1974). Peeping: The Pattern of Voyeurism Among Construction Workers. *Urban Life and Culture, 3*:35–49.

Forsyth, C. (1992). Parade Strippers: A Note on Being Naked in Public. *Deviant Behavior, 13*:391–403.

Forsyth, C. and G. M. Benoit. (1989). Rare, Ole, Dirty Snacks: Some Research Notes on Dirt Eating. *Deviant Behavior, 10*:61–68.

Forsyth, C. J. and L. Fournet. (1987). A Typology of Office Harlots: Party Girls, Mistresses and Career Climbers. *Deviant Behavior, 8*:319–328.

Gagnon, J. H. and W. Simon. (1967). *Sexual Deviance.* New York: Harper and Row.

Hamilton, G. V. (1929). *A Research in Marriage.* New York: Albert and Charles Boni.

Humphreys, L. (1975). *Tearoom Trade: Impersonal Sex in Public Places.* New York: Aldine.

Karpman, B. (1960). Toward a Psycho-Dynamic of Voyeurism: A Case Study. *Archives of Criminal Psychodynamics, 4*:95–142.

Kinsey, A. (1953). *Sexual Behavior in the Human Female.* Philadelphia: W. B. Saunders.

Langevin, R. (1983). *Sexual Strands: Understanding and Treating Sexual Abnormalities in Men.* Hillside, NJ: Erlaum.

Little, C. B. (1995). *Deviance and Control: Theory, Research, and Social Policy.* Itasca, IL: F. E. Peacock.

Little, C. B. (1983). *Understanding Deviance and Control: Theory, Research, and Social Policy.* Itasca, IL: F. E. Peacock.

McKinstry, W. C. (1974). The Pulp Voyeur: A Peek at Pornography in Public Places. In J. Jacobs (ed.), *Deviance: Field Studies and Self-Disclosures.* Palo Alto, CA: National Press Books.

New York Times. (1992, October 16). Through a Glass Furtively: The Peephole Lawyer Takes on Holiday Inn. B18.

Oberndorf, C. (1939). Voyeurism as a Crime. *Journal of Criminal Psychopathology, 1*:103–111.

Potter, G. W. (1989). The Retail Pornography Industry and the Organization of Vice. *Deviant Behavior, 10*:233–251.

"Safer Sex." (1991, December 9). *Newsweek 118* (24):52–61.

Smith, S. R. (1976). Voyeurism: A Review of the Literature. *Archives of Sexual Behavior, 5*:585–608.

Sundholm, C. A. (1977). The Pornographic Arcade: Ethnographic Notes on Moral Men in Immoral Places. In C. Bryant (ed.), *Sexual Deviancy in Social Context.* New York: New Viewpoints.

Tewksbury, R. (1990). Patrons of Porn: Research Notes on the Clientele of Adult Bookstores. *Deviant Behavior, 11*:259–271.

Toolan, J. M., M. Elkins, and P. D'Encarnacao. (1974). The Significance of Streaking. *Medical Aspects of Human Sexuality, 8*:152–165.

Weatherford, J. M. (1986). *Porn Row.* New York: Arbor House.

Weinberg, M. S. (1981a). Becoming a Nudist. In E. Rubington and M. Weinberg (eds.), *Deviance: An Interactionist Perspective.* New York: Macmillan.

Weinberg, M. S. (1981b). The Nudist Management of Respectability. In E. Rubington and M. Weinberg (eds.), *Deviance: An Interactionist Perspective.* New York: Macmillan.

West, D. J. (1987). *Sexual Crimes and Confrontations: A Study of Victims and Offenders.* Aldershot, UK: Gower.

Yalom, L. (1960). Aggression and Forbiddenness in Voyeurism. *Archives of General Psychiatry, 3*:309–319.

PART 2

NORMAL SEXUAL DEVIANCE

Normal sexual deviance is sexual behavior that is relatively common although with limited or low-key visibility. Even though considered a "secret deviance" by most, these are sexual behaviors that are practiced by many people, if not a majority of the population. This type of deviance is not associated with any specific form of social structure; no special groups are organized to perform or maintain this behavior. It is usually an individual decision to perform this type of sexual deviance, with no implication of harm to the participant. The chapters in this section explore several forms of commonplace sexual behavior that have frequently been considered deviant.

The authors of the first article, Sprecher and Regan, explore and compare the experiences of virgin college students. Although these individuals feel that their lifestyles are normal, others perceive virginity as against the norm, and therefore conceivably consider college virginity a sexually deviant lifestyle.

Another sexual behavior that many people consider to be against the norm is masturbation. In prison, autoeroticism is not only regarded as a sexually deviant behavior, it is also usually forbidden. In the second article of this section, Hensley, Tewksbury, and Koscheski examine masturbation among female inmates in a Southern female correctional facility and present a theoretical framework to explain why masturbation occurs in this specific institutional setting.

In the third article, Forsyth's research focuses on the motivation behind female parade strippers who expose their breasts during Mardi Gras to obtain beads and trinkets from the men who ride on parade floats. The underlying theme of his work is the relationship of public nudity to deviant behavior. Incidences of mooning or streaking, for example, are considered acts that insult the normative standards of behavior. In contrast, people who spend time in nudist camps and on nude beaches feel that nudism has become routinized in the interest of a healthier lifestyle. In this context, the clothed voyeurs that often gawk at the nude individuals are considered deviant.

All three of these forms of sexual deviance—virginity, masturbation, and public nudity—are obviously fairly common practices. What the following articles focus on, then, in discussing each within a framework of deviance, are the settings, specific populations, and social contexts that provide the social norms and values leading to a definition of deviance. As you read these articles, focus on how and why the behaviors might be defined differently if they were found in a different setting and/or among a different population. For example, consider the once pathological sexually deviant act of masturbation which is now considered a normal sexually deviant act. Before the twentieth century, masturbation was not only perceived as an immoral act both culturally and/or religiously, but also as a physical and psychological disorder suffered by both men and women. It was not until the latter years of the twentieth century that masturbation was demedicalized and stripped of its myths. Masturbation has now been advocated as an alternative sexual practice to reduce the spread of HIV.

3

College Virgins:
How Men and Women
Perceive Their Sexual Status

Susan Sprecher and Pamela Regan

After the sexual revolution of the 1960s and the resulting freedom from sexual mores that promoted and glorified abstinence until marriage, it became somewhat socially gauche (and probably more difficult) for young adults to maintain their virginal status during college or the period immediately after high school (Rubin, 1990). Indeed, during the 1980s, a large majority of both males and females had made the transition to nonvirginity by the age of 19 (Miller and Moore, 1990; Sonenstein, Pleck, and Ku, 1989). However, according to the popular media, we are in the midst of a sexual "retrorevolution" in which virginity is perceived as (and actually may be becoming) a more acceptable and popular choice among older adolescents and young adults; consequently, far from being embarrassed by their sexual status, some young adults who have remained virginal are proudly proclaiming their abstinence (Fleming, 1995; Ingrassia, 1994; *New York Times*, 1994). Interestingly, there have been few empirical attempts to examine systematically this anecdotal evidence about the feelings and reactions that adult virgins have about their sexual status.

Researchers have accumulated an extensive body of knowledge about the sexuality of adolescents, including the correlates of virginal/nonvirginal status and the factors that are associated with the loss of virginity (Brooks-Gunn and Furstenberg, 1989; Christopher and Roosa, 1991; Gullota, Adams, and Montemayor, 1993; Miller and

Reprinted from *Journal of Sex Research*, Vol. 33, No. 1 (1996), pp. 3–15. © The Society for the Scientific Study of Sexuality. Edited and reprinted by permission of the publisher.

Moore, 1990). We know much less about the virginity of adult men and women, perhaps because adult virgins still represent a relatively small proportion of the larger population (Billy, Tanfer, Grady, and Klepinger, 1993; Reinisch, Sanders, Hill and Ziemba-Davis, 1992; Smith, 1991). Several researchers have included virginity as one variable among many in their studies of adult sexuality (Leite, Buoncompagno, Leite, Mergulhao, and Battiston, 1994; Murstein and Mercy, 1994; Salts, Seismore, Lindholm, and Smith, 1994). Those few who have focused specifically upon adult virgins, like those who study adolescent virgins, have explored the correlates or predictors of virginity status (Herold and Goodwin, 1981; Peretti, Brown, and Richards, 1978, 1979; Schechterman and Hutchinson, 1991; Walsh, 1991; Young, 1986). In addition, many have used samples composed solely of women (D'Augelli and Cross, 1975; Herold and Goodwin, 1981; Peretti et al., 1978, 1979). Perhaps this is not surprising; after all, literary history is replete with the tales of sexually innocent young women who see to preserve their premarital virginity and sexually knowledgeable men who seek to take it from them (Fielding, 1749/1979; Richardson, 1740/1971). However, although the majority of men (and women) are sexually active by the time they reach college age (Billy et al., 1993; Reinisch et al., 1992; Smith, 1991), adult virgins are found among both genders (Laumann, Gagnon, Michael, and Michaels, 1994).

Thus, the current research endeavor was designed to focus exclusively on the experiences of a rather unique group of individuals, specifically, on those young, unmarried adults who have not yet engaged in sexual intercourse. In particular, we wished to include both men and women in our investigation of virginity and to explore if and how virgin men differ from virgin women in their reasons for choosing to remain virginal, their affective reactions to their virginity status, and such other experiences as their perceived likelihood of becoming a non-virgin and social pressure from others to maintain or lose their virginity.

Reasons for Virginity

By the time they are in college or engaged in a post–high school vocation, most young adults either have had opportunities for sexual intercourse or have considered whether they want the opportunity. Although the first intercourse experience itself is usually unplanned (Zelnik and Shah, 1983), the decision to make the transition from virgin to nonvirgin is rarely spontaneous (DeLamater, 1989; Gagnon and Simon, 1973). Young adults weigh several factors while making this important decision about their sexual status, and some decide to postpone the transition (i.e., to remain a virgin). What are the reasons virginal men and women give for their virginity, and do they have the same reasons?

One major factor related to sexual behaviors (to have sex for the first time) is sexual standards or ideology (DeLamater and MacCorquodale, 1979). Considerable research conducted over the past few decades demonstrates that men hold more permissive attitudes toward casual (i.e., uncommitted) sexual activity than do women, whereas women are more likely than are men to view romantic love, emotional intimacy, and commitment as prerequisites for sexual activity (Oliver and Hyde, 1993; Sprecher, 1989). This gender difference has been explained from a number of theoretical perspectives. For example, evolutionary psychologists posit that men, whose reproductive success requires maximizing the number of genes passed on to the next generation, seek to engage in intercourse with many fertile partners, whereas women, whose reproductive success requires maximizing an offspring's chances of survival, confine their sexual activity to long-term relationships with partners who control many resources (Buss and Barnes, 1986). Social Learning theorists suggest that men have received more reinforcement than have women for seeking sexual activity (Mischel, 1966), and script theorists point to societal norms that dictate that sexuality is tied more to the quality of the relationship for women than for men (Gagnon and Simon, 1973; Reiss, 1981). To the extent that women are more likely than men to associate sexual activity with such interpersonal phenomena as romantic love and emotional intimacy, women should place greater importance than men on lack of love and/or an appropriate relationship partner as reasons for remaining a virgin (i.e., abstaining from initial coitus).

Indeed, there is evidence to suggest that lack of a loving or committed relationship is a major reason why abstaining women choose not to have sex. In one of the few studies that focused on virgins and their decision-making processes, Herold and Goodwin (1981) asked Canadian college and high school women to indicate the most important reason why they had not engaged in sexual intercourse. A large number of the participants gave the reason that they had not yet met the "right" person. Also rated as important reasons by women were moral or religious beliefs, not being ready to have sexual intercourse, and fear of pregnancy. However, because Herold and Goodwin (1981) did not survey men, we do not know if virgin men have similar reasons.

A study conducted by Christopher and Cate (1985) suggests that young adult men may have different reasons than young adult women for remaining virginal. For part of a larger study (Christopher and Cate, 1984) these researchers asked college age, virgin men and women to indicate how important several factors would be in their decision to have sexual intercourse with an ideal partner for the first time. Women were more likely than men to rate relationship factors (love for partner) as a salient issue, which suggests that they would be more likely than men to abstain from sex in the absence of a loving relationship.

Other researchers have looked at reasons that people (who may or may not be virgins) have for not having sex with a particular partner. For example, in a study of dating couples, Peplau, Rubin, and Hill (1977) asked members of 42 abstaining couples (18% of the total sample) to rate the importance of four reasons for not having engaged in sex. More women (22%) than men (14%) said that it was too early in the relationship, and more women (31%) than men (11%) rated moral or religious reasons as important. Almost half of both men and women rated fear of pregnancy as a major reason. A much larger proportion of men (64%) than of women (11%) said their partner did not want to have sexual intercourse at the present time. Similarly, Carroll, Volk, and Hyde (1985) found that when men and women were asked, "What would be your primary reason for refusing to have sexual intercourse with someone?" more women that men claimed "not enough love/commitment," and significantly more women than men felt that emotional involvement was "always" a prerequisite for engaging in sexual intercourse.

The first goal for this investigation, then, was to examine the reasons young adults have for maintaining their virginity status and to examine whether virgin men and women have the same reasons. As reviewed previously, research on sexual standards (Sprecher, 1989), various theoretical explanations for gender differences in sexual attitudes and behaviors (Oliver and Hyde, 1993), and research on sexual decision making (Christopher and Cate, 1985) all suggest that men and women should have different reasons for choosing to remain virgins. However, no previous investigation has documented whether such gender differences exist. In our investigation, we considered the reasons that were identified in the previous literature (moral or religious beliefs, fear of pregnancy, not being ready, not being in love enough, not having a willing partner). We also considered two other general categories of reasons that we believed might be relevant: fear of contracting AIDS and other sexually transmitted diseases (STDs) and perception of self-deficiency (i.e., the belief that one is not desirable, that one lacks desire for sex, or that one is too shy to initiate sex).

Affective Reactions to Virginity

Various emotions can be experienced as a consequence of engaging in sexual activity. DeLamater (1991) discussed four: sexual satisfaction/dissatisfaction, embarrassment, anxiety/fear, and frustration. Another negative emotion associated with sexual activity is guilt (Mosher and Cross, 1971). These emotion and others (pride), however, may also occur as a result of not having engaged in sexual activity.

Despite the recent media focus on the positive emotions ostensibly associated with virginity (Ingrassia, 1994; *New York Times*, 1994), very few researchers have focused on how virgin men and women actually feel about their virginity. In an early study on adolescent sexuality, Sorensen (1973) concluded that the sexually inexperienced teenagers were satisfied with their status. He wrote: "They are, in the main, neither defensive nor ashamed of themselves, nor are they frustrated or preoccupied with the fact they do not have sex" (154). Although Sorensen (1973) did not report whether there were gender differences in affective reactions, in a recent study of adolescent males and females, Langer, Zimmerman, and Katz (1995) found that male virgins were more likely than female virgins to report that they would feel better about themselves if they started having sex. In a study of college virgins, Young (1986) found that of 139 female virgins, 96% described themselves as "satisfied," whereas only 4% described themselves as "frustrated" by their virginity. Among the 114 male virgins studied by Young, 76% were satisfied, and 24% were frustrated by their sexual status. Thus, more virgins of both genders were satisfied than frustrated, but a greater proportion of virgin men than of virgin women was frustrated. Furthermore, Walsh (1991) presented indirect evidence that men are more likely than women to experience a negative reaction to their virginity status. He examined the relationship between self-esteem and virginal status among a group of male and female virgin and nonvirgin college students. Virgin and nonvirgin women did not differ with respect to scores on a self-esteem scale; however, virgin men had significantly lower self-esteem scores than nonvirgin men. Although these studied suggest that gender differences in emotion associated with virginity in young adulthood exist, investigators have not studied how adult virgins react to their virginity status on a variety of both positive and negative emotions (including pride and embarrassment).

Thus, our second major goal was to examine the affective reactions virgins have in response to their virginity status and to examine gender differences in these affective reactions. In our investigation of this issue, we considered a number of emotional reactions—both positive (happiness and pride) and negative (anxiety, embarrassment, and guilt)—and we hypothesized, based on previous research (Walsh, 1991; Young, 1986), that men would experience less positive and more negative affective reactions to their virginity than would women.

Associations Among Reasons, Affective Reactions, and Other Aspects of Virginity

The reasons young adults have for remaining virgins are likely to be related to their feelings about their virginity status. For example, people who choose to remain virginal because they have not found the right partner may be less likely to feel "good" about their virginity than people who refrain from sexual intercourse because of moral or religious reasons. Although this and related issues have not been empirically examined to date, one study does suggest that satisfaction with one's virginity is related to religiosity. Young (1986) found that both male and female virgins who were satisfied with their sexual status reported greater religious commitment than did virgins who were frustrated by their sexual status. Perhaps reasons for remaining a virgin that reflect moral and religious beliefs are associated with positive affective reactions to virginity (pride, happiness), whereas reasons that reflect one's inability to initiate sexual intercourse with a partner or the partner's unwillingness to engage in sexual intercourse with negative affective reactions to virginity (anxiety, embarrassment).

Furthermore, reasons, for virginity and affective reactions to virginity may be related to the perceived likelihood of becoming a nonvirgin in the near future and the amount of support received from others for being a virgin. Virginity generally has been viewed as a discrete variable (i.e., one is either a virgin or not), but some researchers have further classified virgins by their perceived likelihood of becoming a nonvirgin before marriage. D'Augelli and her colleagues (D'Augelli and Cross, 1975; D'Augelli and D'Augelli, 1977), for example, distinguished between "adamant virgins" and "potential nonvirgins." Adamant virgins have decided that they will not engage in premarital sexual intercourse, whereas potential nonvirgins are willing to consider premarital sex should they find themselves in the "right" situation with the "right" partner. These types of virgins are likely to have different reasons for remaining virgins. For example, Herold and Goodwin (1981) classified their sample of high school and college women into adamant virgins and potential nonvirgins and asked them to select from an array of reasons the single most important reason why they had not engaged in inter-course. Half (50%) of the adamant virgins but only 2% of the potential nonvirgins endorsed the category encompassing moral and religious rea-sons (i.e., against religion, parental disapproval, premarital intercourse is wrong), whereas 54% of the potential nonvirgins but only 16% of the adamant virgins endorsed not having met the "right" person as the most important reason for abstaining from sexual intercourse.

Herold and Goodwin (1981) did not examine whether the adamant and potential nonvirgins in their sample differed in how they felt about their sexual status. However, the perceived likelihood of remaining a virgin before marriage may be associated with emotional reactions to virginity. Specifically, adamant virgins may have a more positive over-all affective reaction to their virginity than do potential nonvirgins and in particular may feel prouder of their sexual status than do potential nonvirgins. Conversely, potential nonvirgins may feel more guilt, anxi-ety, and embarrassment than do adamant virgins. In fact, the negative emotional reactions some virgins have to their status may be what moti-vates them to make the transition to nonvirginity.

Another factor that may push virgins toward having sexual inter-course is external: specifically, social pressure from others to become sexually active. Young adults who receive social pressure from others to become sexually active should be more likely than young adults who do not receive such pressure to perceive that they are likely to have sexual intercourse in the near future (i.e., to be potential nonvirgins). Furthermore, virgins who receive social pressure to remain a virgin should be less likely than virgins who do not receive this pressure to say that they are likely to begin having premarital sex.

Thus, our third goal was to examine the associations between rea-sons for virginity and affective reactions to virginity and to examine how both are related to other aspects of virginity, including the likeli-hood of becoming a nonvirgin and social pressure to become sexually active vs. to remain a virgin. Because our focus was on gender differ-ences, we explored whether these associations were the same for men and women.

Changes over Time in Virginity

As societal attitudes about sexuality change, so too should the experi-ences of young adults who are virginal when most of their cohort has had sexual intercourse. If, as suggested by the popular media, we are in the midst of a sexual "retrorevolution," then feelings and perceptions that adult virgins have about their sexual status should have changed over recent years. More, specifically, fear of AIDS as a reason for being a virgin and positive reactions to virginity status have probably increased over time. Thus, our final goal was to explore the possibility that perceptions of virginity have changed over a six-year period (1990–1995).

In sum, scientists have collected very little data from adult virgins about their virginity. The purpose of this study was to examine reasons for virginity, affective reactions to virginity, and other perceptions of virginity with a sample of college age, virgin men and women obtained over a six-year period. We were particularly interested in how virgin men and women may differ.

Method

Participants

The 289 participants in this study were selected from a nonprobability sample of undergraduate students enrolled at a Midwestern U.S. university who participated in a survey study of sexual attitudes and behaviors. From a larger sample of students who completed the questionnaire between 1990 and 1995 and had valid data on relevant questions (indicated their gender) we selected a sample of virgins for analysis. To be classified as a virgin, the participant had to respond to two separate questions that he or she had not had sexual intercourse. One question preceded the questions on reasons for and reactions to virginity and was "Have you ever had sexual intercourse?" and the other question, which appeared in a later section of the questionnaire, asked whether they had ever had penile-vaginal sexual intercourse. We further selected those who indicated that they were heterosexual to a question asking about sexual orientation. The final sample of 97 men and 192 women represented 11% and 13% respectively, of the larger sample of men and women participants who were self-reported heterosexuals and had their gender identified (896 men and 1,455 women).

The median age of the virgin participants was approximately 19.5; 93% were between 18 and 21. A majority (89%) identified themselves as White. On a question about religious preference, 44% identified themselves as Catholic, 19% were Protestants, 21% chose "other," 12% chose "none," and 4% described themselves as Jewish. The demographic profile of the virgin students is very similar to that of the sexually experienced respondents from the larger sample (Sprecher, Barbee, and Schwartz, 1995).

Measures

Those participants who reported that they had not had sexual intercourse were asked to respond to several questions about their virginity.

Reasons for Virginity. The virgin participants were presented with a list of 13 reasons "that people may have for not having premarital sexual intercourse." The list of reasons was based on items used in earlier research by Herold and Goodwin (1981); however, additional items were included, including fear of contracting AIDS. Participants responded to each item on a 1 = *not at all important* to 4= *very important* response scale.

A principal components factor analysis conducted on the 13 items revealed 4 factors that collectively accounted for 63% of the total variance. The first factor was labeled *Personal Beliefs* and included the following four items (factor loadings in parentheses): "I believe that intercourse before marriage is wrong" (.87), "It is against my religious beliefs" (.83), "Fear of parental disapproval" (.73), and "I do not feel ready to have premarital intercourse" (.59). The second factor, labeled *Fear*, included three items: "I worry about contracting AIDS" (.90), "I worry about contracting another STD" (.88) and "Fear of pregnancy" (.68). *Inadequacy/insecurity* was the name we gave the third factor, which included four items: "I have been too shy or embarrassed to initiate sex with partner" (.77), "I don't feel physically attractive or desirable" (.66), "I lack desire for sex" (.56), and "My current (or last) partner is (was) not willing" (.52). The final factor, labeled *Not Enough Love,* contained two items: "I have not been in a relationship long enough or been in love enough" (.84) and "I have not met a person I wanted to have intercourse with" (.78). Four scale scores were created based on the mean of the items loading on each particular factor. The higher the score, the more important the factor (coefficient alphas were .80 for Fear, .78 for Personal Beliefs, .65 for Not Enough Love, and .50 for Inadequacy/Insecurity).

Feelings About Virginity. Participants were asked how *proud, guilty, anxious, embarrassed,* and *happy* they felt about their virginity status on scales that ranged from 1 = *not at all* to 5 = *a lot.* Because a factor analysis of the five emotions yielded one bipolar factor (with positive and negative emotions negatively correlated), we also created a summary measure, an index of *hedonic emotional tone*. The hedonic emotional tone index was represented by the difference between the mean of the positive emotions and mean of the negative emotions. A positive score on this index means that positive emotions were experienced to a greater intensity than were negative emotions; a negative score means that negative emotions were experienced to a greater intensity than were positive emotions (for a description of how this measure has been used in previous studies of emotion, see Berscheid, Snyder and Omoto, 1989: or Sprecher and Sedikides, 1993).

Other Questions About Virginity.   Participants were also asked questions assessing the likelihood that they would remain a virgin and the social pressure they received to remain a virgin versus to become sexually active. *Likelihood of becoming a nonvirgin* was measured by the following three questions: "If you were in a close relationship with a partner who desired sexual intercourse and the opportunity were available, would you engage in premarital sexual intercourse and the opportunity were available, would you engage in premarital sexual intercourse?"; "How likely are you to engage in sexual intercourse before you get married?"; and "How likely are you to engage in sexual intercourse during the next year?" (Scale response options ranged from 1 =*absolutely would not* to 6= *absolutely would*). These items were highly intercorrelated (r=.74 to .84) and therefore were summed into an overall index (coefficient alpha = .91). *Social Pressure* was measured by the following two questions: "How much pressure have you received from others (dating partners, peers) to have sexual intercourse?" (1= *not at all* to 4= *none*). We recoded both items so that the higher number indicated greater social pressure. Although it might be expected that social pressure to become sexually active would be inversely related to social pressure to remain a virgin, the two items were not correlated (r = .11 for men and *r* = .10 for women) and thus were not combined.

Procedure

Beginning in Fall 1990, during each semester the first author has administered a questionnaire on sexual attitudes and behaviors to students in a large human sexuality class. It is administered early in the semester (typically the second week), in part to avoid contamination from course information. Students are told that completion of the questionnaire is anonymous and voluntary. The number of students who choose not to complete the questionnaire is estimated to be fewer than 2%.

Results

Reasons for Remaining a Virgin

Not all reasons for being a virgin were rated as equally important. For the total sample of virgins, the mean importance of the 4 factor scores derived from the 13 reasons were: *Not Enough Love* (M= 2.91), *Fear* (M = 2.86), *Personal Beliefs* (M= 2.21), and *Inadequacy/Insecurity* (M= 1.79). A series of paired *t*-test contrasts indicated that the first two factor scores were not significantly different from each other, but all other pairs of factor scores were significantly different ($p < .001$). The first column of Table 3.1 presents the mean importance rating for each of the 13 reasons, based on the total sample.

We expected to find that men and women would differ in how they responded to many of the reasons. Overall, women rated more of the listed reasons as important than did men. For example, the mean importance rating across the 13 items was 2.16 for men and 2.43 for women, $t[273] = -3.98$, $p < .001$. Follow-up comparisons done on the individual items indicated that women placed more importance than men on both items included in this factor (not been in a relationship long enough or been in love enough and not met the right person). Women also scored higher than men on the *Personal Beliefs* factor (M= 2.35 for women vs. 1.92 for men), $t[281] = -3.87$, p .001. In particular virgin women, to a greater degree than virgin men, expressed fear of parental disapproval and stated that they were not ready. On the third factor, *Fear,* women also scored higher (M = 2.98 for women vs. 2.60 for men), $t[282] = -3.19$, $p = .002$. However, women scored significantly higher than men on only one item included in this factor—fear of pregnancy. The only factor score having a higher mean for men than for women was *Inadequacy/Insecurity* (M = 1.95 for men, and 1.71 for women), $t[278] = 2.86$, $p = .005$. Of the four items included in this factor, men scored significantly higher than women on two: too shy or embarrassed to initiate sex and partner not willing.

Affective Reactions to Being a Virgin

Participants reported experiencing a variety of emotional reaction to their virginity status. Table 3.2 presents the mean responses to each of five emotions, for the total sample and for virgin men and women. In the total sample of virgins, participants reported being both proud and anxious about their virginity status. They also reported some happiness and embarrassment, but little guilt. The hedonic emotional tone index

Table 3.1   Mean Importance of Reasons for Being a Virgin for Total Sample and for Men Versus Women

Reason	Total Sample (N = 289)	Virgin Men (n = 97)	Virgin Women (n = 192)	t
I have not been in a relationship long enough or been in love enough.	3.21 (1)	2.78 (1)	3.43 (1)	–4.80*
Fear of pregnancy	3.00 (2)	2.66 (2)	3.16 (2)	–3.75*
I worry about contracting AIDS.	2.84 (3)	2.59 (3)	2.96 (3)	–2.56*
I worry about contracting another STD.	2.73 (4)	2.53 (4)	2.83 (6)	–2.04*
I have not met a person I wanted to have intercourse with.	2.61 (5)	2.00 (9)	2.91 (4)	–5.85*
I do not feel ready to have premarital intercourse.	2.60 (6)	2.12 (7)	2.84 (5)	–5.16*
It is against my religious beliefs.	2.13 (7)	2.02 (10)	2.18 (8)	–1.07
I believe that intercourse before marriage is wrong.	2.09 (8)	1.91 (11)	2.18 (7)	–1.85
I have been too shy or embarrassed to initiate sex with a partner.	2.06 (9)	2.39 (5)	1.89 (11)	3.58*
Fear of parental disapproval	2.02 (10)	1.73 (12)	2.17 (9)	–3.22*
I don't feel physically attractive or desirable.	1.96 (11)	1.98 (8)	1.96 (10)	.15
My current (or last) partner is (was) not willing.	1.85 (12)	2.24 (6)	1.65 (12)	3.88*
I lack desire for sex.	1.33 (13)	1.31 (13)	1.35 (13)	–.43

Note: Each item was rated on a 1 (not at all important) to 4 (very important) response scale. The numbers in parentheses represent the rank order of the reasons based on a comparison of the means within the column. The exact N size in this table and in the remainder of the tables varies somewhat as a function of missing data and therefore, the degrees of freedom also vary. For the gender contrasts in the table, the degrees of freedom range from 282 to 286.

$*p \leq .004$ (significance level based on Bonferroni-projected comparisons using a familywise alpha of .05)

was positive, which indicates that positive emotions were experienced by the participants to a greater degree than were negative emotions.

As hypothesized, however, men and women differed in their emotional reactions to their virginity status. Women to a greater degree than men were proud and happy, and men to a greater degree than women were embarrassed and guilty. No significant gender difference was

Table 3.2 Mean Affective Reactions to Being a Virgin for Total Sample and for Men Versus Women

Affective Reaction	Total Sample	Virgin Men	Virgin Women	t
Proud	3.55 (1)	2.89 (2)	3.88 (1)	−6.21*
Anxious	3.31 (2)	3.49 (1)	3.21 (1)	1.66
Happy	3.16 (3)	2.44 (4)	3.52 (2)	−7.12*
Embarrassed	2.41 (4)	2.70 (3)	2.27 (4)	2.58*
Guilty	1.65 (5)	2.00 (5)	1.48 (5)	3.65*
Hedonic Emotional Tone Index	+.89	−.06	+1.37	−5.93*

Note: The response scale for each emotion ranged from 1 (not at all) to 5 (a lot). The numbers in parentheses represent the rank order of the affective reactions based on a comparison of the means within the column. The Total Hedonic Tone is the difference between the mean of the positive emotions and the mean of the negative emotions. The degrees of freedom for the comparisons between men and women ranged from 284 to 286.

*$p \leq .01$ (significance level based on Bonferroni-protected comparisons using a familywise alpha of .05).

found on anxiety, although this emotion was experienced by men more than any other emotion (pride was the primary emotion women experienced). The hedonic emotional tone index was negative for men and positive for women; this difference was significant.

Associations Among Reasons for Virginity.
Affective Reactions and Other Perceptions About Virginity

Next we examined how men's and women's reasons for virginity were related to their emotional reactions and also other perceptions our participants had about their virginity status.

Reasons and Affective Reactions to Virginity. People with different reasons for being a virgin may have different emotional reactions to their status. To examine this possibility, we correlated each of the four factor scores (representing the four types of reasons) with the hedonic emotional tone index (degree to which positive emotions were experienced more than negative emotions), for men and women separately.

As hypothesized, personal beliefs (religious reasons) for virginity were strongly associated with a positive affective reaction for both men and women. No other type of reason was associated with emotional reactions for women. For men, interpersonal reasons (i.e., not enough love) were associated with a positive reaction, whereas reasons reflecting inadequacy and/or insecurity were associated with negative reaction. The fear factor was not associated with emotional reactions.

Reasons, Affective Reactions, and Likelihood of Becoming a Nonvirgin. As noted by previous researchers (D'Augelli and Cross, 1975; Herold and Goodwin, 1981), there are different subgroups of virgins. For example, Herold and Goodwin (1981) distinguished between adamant virgins and potential nonvirgins based on participants' agreement or disagreement with the item, "I am not likely to engage in premarital intercourse." We argue, however, that *likelihood of becoming a nonvirgin* should be operationalized as a continuous variable, ranging from zero or almost no likelihood to extreme likelihood. Thus, each participant in this study received a score on *likelihood of becoming a nonvirgin* based on summed responses to the three six-point items described earlier. The scores on this index could (and did) range from 3 (absolutely would not) to 18 (absolutely would). The means were 12.24 for men and 10.94 for women, $t[284]= 2.38$, $p < .05$; thus, men were more likely than women to believe that they would become a nonvirgin in the near future. To examine how likelihood of becoming a nonvirgin was related to reasons for virginity and emotional reactions, we correlated the "likelihood of becoming a nonvirgin" score with the four factor scores and the hedonic emotional tone index.

There was a very strong correlation between the importance of personal beliefs as a reason for virginity and the perceived likelihood of becoming a nonvirgin. More specifically, the more important men and women rated personal beliefs (religious reasons) for the virginity, the more adamant they were about their virginity (the less likely they were to perceive that they would become a nonvirgin). In addition, for men only, higher scores on the Inadequacy/Insecurity factor were positively associated with the perceived likelihood of becoming a nonvirgin in the near future. Scores on the Fear and Not Enough Love factors were unrelated to the perceived likelihood of becoming a nonvirgin, for both men and women.

Emotional reactions to virginity were also related to the perceived likelihood of becoming a nonvirgin. The men and women who believed it was likely that they would become a nonvirgin in the near future had the most negative and the least positive reaction to their virginity status. Furthermore, each specific emotion was significantly associated with the perceived likelihood of losing one's virginity, with the exception of embarrassment for men.

Social Pressure.   Virgin men and women reported equal degrees of social pressure to begin to have sexual intercourse. We also considered the possibility that social pressure to remain a virgin versus to become sexually active was related to emotional reactions to virginity. Social pressure to become sexually active was negatively associated with women's hedonic emotional tone index: that is, social pressure to become sexually active was associated with a negative reaction to virginity. Conversely, social pressure to remain a virgin was associated with a positive reaction for women, as indicated by their hedonic emotional tone index. For men, a strong association was found between social pressure to remain a virgin and their positive reaction as indicated by hedonic emotional tone, however, social pressure to become sexually active was unrelated to men's emotional reactions to virginity.

Changes in Virginity over Time

Because our data were collected over a six-year period, we explored the possibility that there were changes over time in the reasons for and affective reactions to virginity. We examined this in two ways: correlational analyses and cohort comparisons.

Correlational Analyses.   For both men and women, time (which ranged from 1 = Fall semester 1990 to 10 = Spring Semester 1995) was positively correlated with the factor containing fear reasons, $r = .23, p < .05$ for men and $r = .25, p < .001$ for women. More specifically, over time both genders rated worry about contracting AIDS, $r = .22, p < .05$ for men and $r = .26, p < .001$ for women and other STDs, $r = .26, p < .01$ for men and $r = .18, p < .01$ for women, as increasingly important reasons for virginity. The importance rating of fear of pregnancy also became more important for women over time, $r = .18, p < .01$. In addition, the Inadequacy/Insecurity factor became more important over time for women, $r = .15, p < .05$.

Discussion

Perhaps because the majority of young men and women are sexually experienced (i.e., nonvirginal) by the time they reach college age (Smith, 1991), the topic of adult virginity has received relatively little systematic empirical attention. The purpose of this study was to explore and compare the experiences of those young adult men and women who do in fact choose to maintain their virginity.

Reasons for Virginity

College virgins do not abstain from sexual intercourse because of lack of sexual desire. The least important reason for virginity for both men and women was "I lack desire for sex." This finding belies the stereotype of the "frigid" virgin and certainly can be used to argue against the common beliefs that sexual desire is an inherent aspect of the male but not the female experience (Regan and Berscheid, 1995) and that men have stronger and more frequent desires than do women (Richgels, 1992; Tolman, 1991). Apparently, both men and women in our sample desired sex but abstained from it because they required an "appropriate" reason to become sexually active (the "right" person); sought to avoid some real, potentially negative consequences of sexual intercourse (unplanned pregnancy, disease); and were attempting to act in service of their personal beliefs. The reasons both men and women rated as most important had to do with not enough love or having not met the right partner. Overall, then, the relative ratings of the reasons were very similar for men and women.

However, gender differences were found in the importance ratings given to many reasons. As expected, our virgin women participants were more concerned than their male counterparts with interpersonal reasons for virginity (i.e., not enough love or not having met the right person). These results are in accord with previous research that suggest that both sexually experienced and inexperienced women are more likely than men to associate sexual activity with love and/or committed relationships (Oliver and Hyde, 1993). Virgin women also placed greater importance than virgin men on such personal beliefs as not feeling ready to engage in sexual intercourse and on parental disapproval of premarital sex. The fact that during adolescence girls are more likely than boys to have discussed abstinence and other sexual topics with their parents (Leland and Barth, 1992) may explain why young adult women are more concerned with parental attitudes toward sexual activity (i.e., they may simply be more aware of their parents' views). Not surprisingly, the women in our sample were also more concerned than the men with the potential negative consequences of sexual intercourse (i.e., pregnancy).

However, men rated reasons having to do with inadequacy and insecurity as more important than did women. More specifically, men viewed their feelings of shyness or embarrassment about initiating sexual activity with a partner as a more important reason for their virginity than did women and men were also more likely to point to their partners' unwillingness to engage in intercourse. A possible explanation for these gender differences is that the virgin men in our sample may have attempted to initiate sexual intercourse with a potential partner more often than did the virgin women; consequently, they may have experienced rejection more often than have women and may feel less inclined to (and more embarrassed about) making further initiation attempts. That is, this finding may stem from differential experiences of virgin men and virgin women. If virgin men and women perceive the male role in sexual interactions as primarily proactive and the female role as primarily reactive (Gagnon and Simon, 1973; Reiss, 1981) it makes sense that men would be more concerned than women with reasons associated with the initiation of sexual activity (partner's unwillingness, personal feelings of shyness).

Our results also indicate that the reasons young adult virgins maintain their sexual status have changed over time. Specifically recent cohorts of virgins placed more importance than earlier cohorts on their fears of contracting AIDS and other STDs. Whether young adult virgins consciously decided not to have sex based upon this reason or simply provide it as an explanation for their current sexual status is not clear; however, sexually active individuals also have grown more aware of AIDS over time and appear to have altered their sexual behaviors as a consequence (e.g., Are more likely to use condoms; Mosher and Pratt, 1993; Sonenstein et al., 1989). Another reason that became more important over time, at least for women, was "My current (or last) partner is (was) not willing." Although heterosexual partners largely continue to adhere to the traditional script of male initiation of sexual activity (O'Sullivan and Byers, 1992), recent cohorts of women may be more comfortable with the role of sexual initiator and thus more likely to have experienced a partner's refusal to have intercourse. These changes found over a six-year period may indicate that the type of person who remains a virgin is changing and/or may indicate broader changes in societal attitudes about sexuality.

Affective Reactions to Virginity

Male and female virgins reported a variety of both positive and negative emotional responses to their sexual status; however, women's experiences were more positive than negative, whereas men's were more negative than positive. With respect to specific emotional reactions, women felt greater pride and happiness than did men, and men felt greater embarrassment and guilt than did women. These gender differences may be explained by culture mandates regarding sexual intercourse that teach that sexual experience is an important aspect of masculinity (Lewis and Casto, 1978; Tiefer, 1995). Virginity—defined here as not yet having engaged in sexual intercourse—therefore may represent a greater stigma for men than for women.

However, affective reactions to virginity, for both men and women, do appear to be changing over time. In particular, although virgin men continue to feel more negatively about their sexual status than do virgin women, more recent cohorts report greater pride and happiness than earlier cohorts. We also found that more recent cohorts of women reported more pride. These changes may reflect the fact that young adults—especially young men—have a greater number of publicly visible, virginal role models to emulate (for example, the group Athletes for Abstinence includes a number of well-known male athletes; *New York Times*, 1994).

Associations Between Reasons and Affective Reactions

Men and women had a more positive overall reaction to their virginity if they viewed their sexual status as the result of their personal beliefs or values (i.e., against religious beliefs, believe that premarital sex is wrong, fear parental disapproval, not ready for intercourse). To the extent that virginity represents tangible evidence that one is living according to one's personal convictions, such positive feelings are understandable. Although we expected to find that men and women who choose to remain virgins because they have not found the right partner or been in love enough would feel less positive about their virginity status, no such association was found for women, and for men, such reasons were associated with a more positive overall affective response. Perhaps men who feel "good" about their virginity—and who are violating the stereotype of the unhappy male virgin—are also those men who violate other stereotypes (who, for example associate sex and love, which is not a stereotypically "male" response; Carroll et al., 1985). In addition, for men, but not women, reasons related to inadequacy/insecurity—a partner's unwillingness to have sex and the perception that one is unable to attract or initiate intercourse with a potential partner—were associated with a negative emotional reaction. To the extent that a man's virginity is not due to personal choice, but rather reflects an inability to overcome various individual (undesirability) and interpersonal (partner's refusal) barriers to sexual experience, it appears to engender negative affect.

Adamancy Versus Perceived Likelihood of Losing One's Virginity

Although the virgin women in our sample were more adamant than the virgin men about their sexual status, the more adamant that both genders were, the more importance they placed on personal beliefs for their virginity and the more positive their overall emotional reaction. Specifically, men and women who were more adamant about their virginity were more likely to experience pride and happiness and less likely to feel anxiety and guilt than were men and women who believed that they were likely to become sexually active in the near future. These results suggest that sexual decision making and affective reactions to virginity are inextricably interwoven. However, we do not know from these data whether individuals first make a sexual decision (i.e., to have sex) and then experience emotional reactions based on that decision or whether they have certain emotional reactions to their current situation (i.e., virginity) and then make a decision as a result of those reactions (a person realizes that he or she is unhappy about his or her sexual status, and this realization contributes to the decision to become a nonvirgin).

Social Pressure

This study represents an important preliminary step toward delineating the role that social pressure may play in informing the sexual attitudes and decisions of young adult virgins. First, we found several gender differences. Virgin men and women reported receiving equal amounts of pressure (presumably from dating partners and peers) to engage in sexual intercourse, but only women reported greater negative affect toward their virginity as the social pressure to have sex increased. Women also experienced greater pressure (presumably from parents) to abstain from intercourse than men, but both men and women felt more positive about their virginity as this type of social pressure increased.

In addition, the amount of social pressure respondents received to remain a virgin was unrelated to the amount of social pressure they received to lose their virginity, which suggests that young adult virgins may get conflicting messages from different network sectors (parents vs. friends).

Future Research Directions

The current study was designed to explore young adult virginity. Specifically we examined whether virgin men and women differed in their reasons for, affective reactions to, adamancy toward, and perceived pressure to lose their virginity, and whether these aspects of virginity have changed over the six-year period spanning 1990 to 1995. Future researchers might consider other group differences (race/ethnicity, sexual orientation, age), use additional sampling techniques, and explore continued changes over time in adult virginity (ideally with longitudinal data sets).

In addition, we believe that it is important to include other subclassifications of virginity in research on adult virgins; for example, some virgins have engaged in "everything but" sexual intercourse (Rubin, 1990), whereas others have abstained from all intimate sexual activities. It is likely that sexually active but "technical" virgins will have different reasons for and emotional reactions to their sexual status than will virgins with very little sexual experience. A related issue worth examining is the phenomenon for "second virginity." This concept, currently espoused by several social groups, refers to the notion that a sexually experienced man or woman can renew or reclaim virgin status by making the decision to discontinue further sexual activity until marriage (Ingrassia, 1994). Some researchers have in fact distinguished between "regretful nonvirgins" (those who had been sexually active but who planned to abstain from sex for a while) and other types of virgins (Schechterman and Hutchinson, 1991).

References

Berscheid, E., M. Snyder, and A. M. Omoto (1989). The Relationship Closeness Inventory: Assessing the Closeness of Interpersonal Relationships. *Journal of Personality and Social Psychology*, 57:792–807.

Billy, J. O. G., K. Tanfer, W. R. Grady, and D. H. Klepinger (1993). The Sexual Behavior of Men in the United States. *Family Planning Perspectives*, 25:52–60.

Brooks-Gunn, J. and F. F. Furstenberg, Jr. (1989). Adolescent Sexual Behavior. *American Psychologist, 44:*249–257.

Buss, D. M., and M. Barnes. (1986). Preferences in Human Mate Selection. *Journal of Social Psychology, 50:*559–570.

Carroll, J. L., K. D. Volk, and J. S. Hyde. (1985). Differences Between Males and Females in Motives for Engaging in Sexual Iintercourse. *Archives of Sexual Behavior, 14:*131–139.

Christopher, F. S. and R. M. Cate. (1985). Anticipated Influences on Sexual Decision-Making. *Family Relations, 34*:265–270.

Christopher, F. S. and R. M. Cate. (1984). Factors Involved in Premarital Sexual Decision-Making. *The Journal of Sex Research, 20*:363–376.

Christopher, F. S., and M. W. Roosa (1991). Factors Affecting Sexual Decisions in the Premarital Relationships of Adolescents and Young Adults. In K. McKinney and S. Sprecher, (eds.), *Sexuality in Close Relationships.* Hillsdale, NJ: Lawrence Erlbaum.

D'Augelli, J. F. and H. L. Cross (1975). Relationships of Sex Guilt and Moral Reasoning to Premarital Sex in College Women and in Couples. *Journal of Consulting and Clinical Psychology, 43*:40–47.

D'Augelli, J. F. and A. R. D'Augelli. (1977). Moral Reasoning and Premarital Sexual Behavior: Toward Reasoning About Relationships. *Journal of Social Issues, 33*:44–66.

DeLamater, J. D. (1991). Emotions and Sexuality. In K. McKinney and S. Sprecher (eds.), *Sexuality in Close Relationships.* Norwood, NJ: Ablex.

DeLamater, J. D. (1989). The Social Control of Human Sexuality. In K. McKinney and S. Sprecher (eds.), *Human Sexuality: The Societal and Interpersonal Context.* Norwood, NJ: Ablex.

DeLameter, J. D. and P. MacCorquodale (1979). *Premarital Sexuality: Attitudes, Relationships, Behaviors.* Madison: University of Wisconsin Press.

Fielding, H. (1979). *The History of Tom Jones, a Foundling.* 3rd ed. New York: The New American Library. (Original work published 1749.)

Fleming, A. T. (1995). Like a Virgin, Again. *Vogue* (February):68, 72.

Gagnon, J. H. and W. Simon. (1973). *Sexual Conduct: The Social Sources of Human Sexuality.* Chicago: Aldine.

Gullotta, T. P., G. R. Adams, and R. Montemayor (eds.). (1993). *Adolescent Sexuality.* Newbury Park, CA: Sage.

Herold, E. S., and M. S. Goodwin (1981). Adamant Virgins, Potential Non-virgins and Nonvirgins. *The Journal of Sex Research, 17*:97–113.

Ingrassia, M. (1994). Virgin Cool. *Newsweek* (October):59–62, 64, 69.

Langer, L. M., R. S. Zimmerman, and J. A. Katz. (1995). Virgins' Expectations and Nonvirgins' Reports: How Adolescents Feel About Themselves. *Journal of Adolescent Research, 10*:291–306.

Laumann, E. O., J. H. Gagnon, R. T. Michael, and S. Michaels. (1994). *The Social Organization of Sexuality: Sexual Practices in the United States.* Chicago: University of Chicago Press.

Leite, R. M. C., E. M. Buoncompagno, A. C. C. Leite, E. A Mergulhao, and M. M. M. Battiston. (1994). Psychosexual Characteristics of Female University Students in Brazil. *Adolescence, 29:*439–460.

Leland, N. L. and R. P. Barth. (1992). Gender Differences in Knowledge, Intentions, and Behaviors Concerning Pregnancy and Sexually Transmitted Disease Prevention Among Adolescents. *Journal of Adolescent Health, 13*:589–599.

Lewis, R. and R. Casto. (1978). Developmental Transitions in Male Sexuality. *The Counseling Psychologist, 4:*15–19.

Miller, B. C. and K. A. Moore. (1990). Adolescent Sexual Behavior, Pregnancy, and Parenting: Research Through the 1980s. *Journal of Marriage and the Family, 52*:1025–1044.

Mischel, W. (1966). A Social-Learning View of Sex Differences in Behavior. In E. E. Maccoby (ed.), *The Developmental of Sex Differences.* Stanford, CA: Stanford University Press.

Mosher, D. L., and J. J. Cross. (1971). Sex Guilt and Premarital Sexual Experiences of College Students. *Journal of Consulting and Clinical Psychology, 36*:27–32.

Mosher, W. D., and W. F. Pratt. (1993). AIDS-Related Behavior Among Women 15–44 Years of Age: United States, 1988 and 1990. *Advance Data from Vital and Health Statistics*, 239.

Murstein, B. I., and T. Mercy. (1994). Sex, Drugs, Relationships, Contraception, and Fears of Disease on a College Campus over 17 years. *Adolescence, 29*:303–322.

New York Times. (1994, June 19). Proud to Be a Virgin. 1, 6.

Oliver, M. B. and J. S. Hyde. (1993). Gender Differences in Sexuality: A Media Analysis. *Psychological Bulletin, 114*:29–51.

O'Sullivan, L. F. and E. S. Byers, (1992). College Students' Incorporation of Initiator and Restrictor Rules in Sexual Dating Interactions. *The Journal of Sex Research, 29:435–446.*

Peplau, L. A., Z. Rubin, and C. T. Hill (1977). Sexual Intimacy in Dating Relationships. *Journal of Social Issues, 33*(2):86–109.

Peretti, P. O., S. Brown, and P. Richards. (1979). Perceived Value-Orientations Toward Premarital Virginity of Female Virgins and Nonvirgins. *Acta Psychiatrica Belgica, 79*:321–331.

Peretti, P. O., S. Brown, and P. Richards. (1978). Female Virgin and Nonvirgin Psychological Orientations Toward Premarital Virginity. *Acta Psychiatrica Belgica, 78*:235–247.

Regan, P. C. and E. Berscheid. (1995). Gender Differences in Beliefs About the Causes of Male and Female Sexual Desire. *Personal Relationships, 2*:345–350.

Reinisch, J. M., S. A. Sanders, C. A. Hill, and M. Ziemba-Davis. (1992). High-Risk Sexual Behavior Among Heterosexual Undergraduates at a Midwestern University. *Family Planning Perspectives, 24*:116–121, 145.

Reiss, I. L. (1981). Some Observations on Ideology and Sexuality in America. *Journal of Marriage and the Family, 43:*271–283.

Richardson, S. (1971). *Pamela; or, Virtue Rewarded.* Boston: Houghton Mifflin. (Original work published 1740.)

Richgels, P. B. (1992). Hypoactive Sexual Desire in Heterosexual Women: A Feminist Analysis. *Women and Therapy, 12*:123–135.

Rubin, L. (1990). *Erotic Wars: What Happened to the Sexual Revolution?* New York: Harper-Collins.

Salts, C. J., M . D. Seismore, B. W. Lindholm, and T. A. Smith. (1994). Attitudes Toward Marriage and Premarital Sexual Activity of College Freshmen. *Adolescence, 29*:775–779.

Schechterman, A. L. and R. L. Hutchinson. (1991). Causal Attributions, Self-Monitoring, and Gender Differences Among Four Virginity Status Groups. *Adolescence, 26*:659–678.

Smith, T. W. (1991). Adult Sexual Behavior in 1989: Number of Partners, Frequency of Intercourse and Risk of AIDS. *Family Planning Perspectives, 23*:102–107.

Sonenstein, F. L., J. H. Pleck, and L. C. Ku. (1989). Sexual Activity, Condom Use and AIDS Awareness Among Adolescent Males. *Family Planning Perspectives, 21:*152–158.

Sorenson, R. C. (1973). *Adolescent Sexuality Contemporary America.* New York: World.

Sprecher, S. (1989). Premarital Sexual Standards for Different Categories of Individuals. *The Journal of Sex Research, 26:*232–248.

Sprecher, S., A. Barbee, and P. Schwartz. (1995). "Was It Good for You, Too?" Gender Differences in First Sexual Intercourse Experiences. *The Journal of Sex Research, 32:*3–15.

Sprecher, S. and C. Sedikides. (1993). Gender Differences in Perceptions of Emotionality: The Case of Close, Heterosexual Relationships. *Sex Roles: A Journal of Research, 28*:511–530.

Tiefer, L. (1995). *Sex Is Not a Natural Act and Other Essays.* Boulder, CO: Westview Press.

Tolman, D. L. (1991). Adolescent Girls, Women and Sexuality: Discerning Dilemmas of Desire. *Women and Therapy, 11:*55–69.

Walsh, A. (1991). Self-Esteem and Sexual Behavior. Exploring Gender Differences. *Sex Roles, 25:*441–450.

Young, M. (1986). Religiosity and Satisfaction with Virginity Among College Men and Women. *Journal of College Student Personnel, 27:*339–344.

Zelnik, M. and F. K. Shah. (1983). First Intercourse Among Young Amercians. *Family Planning Perspective, 15*:64–72.

4

Masturbation Uncovered: Autoeroticism in a Female Prison

Christopher Hensley, Richard Tewksbury & Mary Koscheski

Throughout history, the subject of sexually transmitted diseases has been of great concern. From the past "epidemics" of gonorrhea and syphilis to the present-day HIV "crisis," methods of prevention have been on the forefront of thought for both medical and correctional professionals. The media, various religions, and sex education classes have taught that abstinence was the preferred mode for the prevention of sexually transmitted diseases. However, this approach was accepted by only a chosen few. For the remaining multitudes, both in free society and behind prison walls, other "outlets" of sexual expression had to be explored. With correctional policies levying severe ramifications and penalties for persons involved in sexual activities (both coerced and consensual), the obvious, yet misinterpreted and understudied alternative is masturbation.

Only a few pioneer researchers have ignored the stigma of prison sex research and delved into this forbidden topic. Tewksbury and West (2000) noted that most sex research conducted in prisons has had obvious political overtones. Only when evidence was needed to provide support for an advocated or proposed social policy would researchers be allowed to enter a prison. Under the guise of studying sexual activities, the only arenas studied were those specified by prison officials. Even today, prison sex research continues to be frowned upon, not only by general society, but by fellow researchers and prison administrators. Tewksbury and Mustaine (2001) report that only 0.1% of all articles pub-

Reprinted from *The Prison Journal*, Vol. 81, No. 4 (2001), pp. 515–525. © 2001 Sage Publications, Inc. Edited and reprinted by permission of the publisher.

lished during the 1990s in the five leading corrections journals were concerned with the issue of sex in prison. In addition, only one of the five journals contained any information about sex in prison during the 1990s.

When the topic has been studied, penologists have typically documented the extent, the dynamics, and the roles of prison sex (Tewksbury and West, 2000). For example, males have been stereotyped as being more "sexual" and in constant need of a sexual outlet. Due to this mind set, the scant research available has primarily focused on the sexual behaviors of male inmates. Due to this mindset, the scant research available has focused primarily on the sexual behaviors of male inmates and on sexual assaults and presumed coerced sexual behaviors. Consensual sex, including autoeroticism, has been only rarely studied in male prisons (See Wooden and Parker, 1982; Tewksbury, 1989).

The small number of sex researchers who have studied incarcerated females have, in contrast to the work concerning male inmates, steered their research toward consensual same-sex sexual behavior and the establishment of pseudo-families within the prison subculture. During Ward and Kassebaum's landmark study of female sexuality in prison, Iverne R. Carter, Superintendent of the California Institute for Women in Frontera, California, pointed out that "women's prisons had not been the subject of research" (Ward and Kassebaum, 1965: vii). For example, the study of masturbation in female prisons is nonexistent. However, masturbation studies in society have existed for several decades.

One of the first researchers to study masturbation in society was Alfred Kinsey. His groundbreaking studies on both males and females of the late 1940s enlightened the public about attitudes and behaviors regarding sexuality. It was not only an avenue for those involved in the study to discuss and answer questions about different aspects of their sexuality, but it was also an opportunity for society to realize that their ideas, beliefs, and activities were shared by others. Kinsey brought to light the influence of age, education, rural-urban background, and religion on masturbation. Kinsey and his associates found that 62% of the 5,940 females studied had masturbated at some point in their lives (Kinsey, Martin, Pomeroy, and Gebhard, 1953). The study also revealed that older females (ages 35–45) masturbated at a 38% higher rate than younger females (ages 5–30).

It was twenty-four years later before another major study of sexuality was conducted. *The Hite Report* (Hite, 1976) dealt only with the subject of female sexuality. The data revealed that out of the 1,844 women surveyed approximately 82% masturbated. The results of the next significant sexual research project, *The Janus Report* (Janus and Janus, 1993), revealed that of the 1,384 female respondents, 38% were frequent masturbators and 67% viewed masturbation as a natural part of life. An age comparison of females who masturbated at least once a month revealed that masturbation was most common for women in their late 20s, 30s, and 40s. Specifically, the reported percentage of women who masturbated were 27% between the ages of 18–26, 47% between the ages of 27–38, 47% between the ages of 39–50, 36% between the ages of 51–64, and 27% for those age 65 and above. This was similar to Kinsey et al.'s (1953) findings.

In 1994, a study of 647 never-married female undergraduate students in a Midwestern residential state university was conducted by Davidson and Moore. The study revealed that 16.3% of respondents had engaged in masturbation. Also in 1994, Michael, Gagnon, Laumann, and Kolata wrote *Sex in America*. This study, conducted through the National Opinion Research Center at the University of Chicago, drew on a random sampling of more than 3,400 respondents to assess a wide range of sexual information including sexual histories and beliefs. Several assumptions about masturbation were explored in this study (Michael et al., 1994). First, the researchers found that masturbation is not rare. Forty percent of the females in the survey were found to have masturbated at least once in the last year. Adding the age differential, the data revealed that among women, fewer than four out of ten aged 18–24 had masturbated, fewer than three out of 10 over the age of 54 had masturbated, but nearly half the women in their thirties had masturbated (Michael et al., 1994). Again, these results were consistent with previous findings.

The explanation for variations across age categories is usually linked with explanations about sexual development and partner availability. More specifically, "the rates of masturbation rise and fall with the availability of sex partners suggesting that each individual has a given level of sex drive that needs to be expressed in one way or another" (Laumann, Gagnon, Michael and Michaels, 1994: 80). The assumption that masturbation is more common when one has a partnered sexual outlet was clearly advocated by these authors. Nearly 45% of the women who were living with a sexual partner reported that they had masturbated within the last year. The study concluded that white, college-educated women who were living with a partner and sexually experimental had higher rates of masturbation. Young women who did not masturbate typically were sexually inexperienced and often virgins. African-Americans, both men and women, tended to be more conservative and conventional about sexual behavior and were less likely to masturbate. The researchers observed "that the practice is so strongly influenced by social attitudes that it becomes more a reflection of a person's religion and social class than a hidden outlet for sexual tensions" (Michael et al., 1994: 168).

As previously mentioned, studies on masturbation—the misunderstood stepchild of sex research—are rare both in free society and correctional facilities. In addition, research on female sexuality in prison is both marginal and centered primarily on consensual homosexual activity and pseudo-families. By combining these two arenas, the present study engulfs two subjects that are frequently overlooked by both penologists and sex researchers.

Theoretical Perspective

The two competing theoretical foundations used to explain masturbation in correctional facilities are the deprivation and importation models. The deprivation model contends that the inmate culture is a collective response to the deprivations imposed by prison life (Sykes, 1958). When correctional administrators deny inmates heterosexual outlets, they often turn to alternative outlets such as homosexuality and masturbation.

Boredom, forced association, and lack of privacy are additional pains of imprisonment (Sykes, 1958). Intimate relationships with both family and loved ones are often diminished. These "pains of imprisonment" felt by women tend to differ from those felt by men. Since sex and companionship are needs of all human beings, women cite their absence as among the most painful aspects of incarceration. Often, women respond to this deprivation (lack of companionship) by forming ties within the prison to substitute for the former familial bonds (Pollock, 1997). Thus, the conception of the pseudo-family and myths of rampant homosexuality were created.

In contrast, the importation model explains that the characteristics and actions of individuals that predate confinement are critical factors in determining modes of inmate adjustment. This model argues that inmate conduct is an extension of the cultural and structural differences in individuals beyond the prison walls. Men and women behave differently in society and have different value systems. These socialized gender differences are brought into the prison system (Irwin and Cressey,

1962). In simple terms, sex roles, expectations, and needs from the outside affect one's behavior on the "inside."

Women who are still dependent on family roles (wife, mother, daughter, etc.) as a part of their self-identity are those most likely to become involved in pseudo-families. Talking and worrying about children and/or family on the outside can be shared and understood with the "inside" family. The female inmate can function in basically the same capacity that she did in free society (conveying previous family values, ideas, and norms). This does not displace or curtail sexual urges, but rather is theorized to provide acceptable and familiar types of outlets for sexual needs.

In addition, the emotional and physical sexual needs that females import into prison may differ greatly across individuals. Those who have previously adopted a homosexual lifestyle on the outside can be expected to continue such once incarcerated. Many females, however, resort to homosexuality to sustain the needs and emotions that remain with them after being imprisoned. What about the females who do not participate in these activities as outlets for sexual release? For some women, remaining faithful to an "outside" partner is a decisive priority. Many women in prison choose celibacy as an alternative sexual lifestyle. Is masturbation their answer? This study was conducted to address this issue.

Method

Participants

In March 2000, all inmates housed in a Southern correctional facility for women were requested to participate in the current study. Inmates were assembled in the main area of their respective units by correctional staff in order that the researchers could explain the contents of the surveys. Inmates were asked to return their completed questionnaires in a stamped, self-addressed envelope within two weeks of distribution. Of the 643 inmates incarcerated at that time, a total of 245 agreed to participate in the study, yielding a response rate of 38%.

A comparison of the prison population and the study group reveals some slight differences. For example, blacks and inmates in medium security are underrepresented in the sample. Inmates describing their race as other and maximum security inmates were overrepresented in the sample.

Table 4.1   Population and Sample Characteristics

	Prison Population		Sample	
Characteristic	*N*	%	*n*	%
Race:				
White	394	61.3%	150	61.2%
Black	247	38.4	82	33.5
Other	02	0.3	11	4.4
Security Level:				
Minimum	241	37.5%	92	40.2%
Medium	393	61.1	121	52.8
Maximum	09	1.4	16	7.0
Average Age:	35 years		34.4 years	

Measures

Inmates were asked two questions concerning their masturbatory behavior while incarcerated. First, inmates were asked, "Have you masturbated since being incarcerated?" Response categories were dichotomized so that a response of no was coded as zero and an affirmative response received a score of one. They were then asked, "How often do you masturbate?" Originally, eight response categories existed. These categories were recoded so that infrequent masturbators (less than once a month) were coded as zero and frequent masturbators (more than once a month) received a score of one. Both items served as dependent variables.

Demographic characteristics (age and race) were recorded for the study group. Data were also collected on religion (protestant v. non-protestant), time served (less than 1 year, 1–5 years, 5–10 years, and more than 10 years), security level, type of offense committed, engaging in homosexual behavior while incarcerated (touching the genitals of another female inmate while incarcerated), and education (high school or less vs. some college or more).

Results

Of the 242 female inmates that responded to the questionnaire, 66.5% had masturbated while incarcerated. Of the 161 who reported masturbating, 7% had not masturbated during the last year. More than 22% of the respondents masturbated once or a few times in the last year, and 7% masturbated every other month. Approximately 13% masturbated once a month or two to three times a month, while 10% of the respondents masturbated once a week. An additional 18.6% masturbated two to three times per week. Only 3.6% of the female inmates reported masturbating once a day. Finally, 2.9% reported masturbating more than once a day.

To examine relationships between the independent and dependent variables, correlational analysis was conducted. The most salient variable is whether the inmate engaged in homosexual behavior while incarcerated. Inmates who engaged in homosexual behavior while incarcerated were more likely to report masturbating while in prison. In addition, they were more frequent masturbators than those who did not engage in homosexual behavior while incarcerated. Inmates who committed a personal crime were also more likely to masturbate (and be frequent masturbators) than those who had committed a property or drug offense. Inmates who had served longer sentence times were also more likely to masturbate than inmates who had served shorter sentence times. Protestants were less likely to masturbate than non-Protestants. White inmates were more likely to be frequent masturbators compared to nonwhites. In addition, inmates in higher security levels were more likely to be frequent masturbators than inmates in lower security levels.

Because both dependent variables are dichotomous, a series of logistic regression analyses were performed to test if the predictor variables had an effect on the dependent variables. The most salient variable in both models was homosexual behavior in prison. Table 4.2 indicates inmates who engage in homosexual behavior while incarcerated are more likely to masturbate (and be frequent masturbators) than inmates who do not engage in homosexual behavior in prison. In other words, inmates who were sexually active while incarcerated were more likely to masturbate while in prison. White inmates and inmates in higher security levels were also more likely to report engaging in frequent masturbation. Interestingly, race and security level variables were not found to have an impact on whether or not the inmate has masturbated while in prison. Based on previous literature, we expected that age, education, and time served would have an impact on female masturbation in prison. However, these variables were not significant predictors of either dependent variable.

**Table 4.2   Summary of Logistic Regression Beta Weights (*n* = 190 and
              130 respectively)**

	Masturbation Since Incarceration	Frequency of Masturbation
Age	0.50	−0.64
Race	0.52	1.11*
Religion	0.54	0.47
Education	0.06	0.51
Amount of Time Served	0.44	−0.52
Security Level	0.28	1.84*
Type of Offense	0.19	−0.42
Homosexual Behavior	1.46*	1.40*
Pseudo R^2	0.19	0.40

Note: Coding is as follows: Age (0 = Younger than 34, 1 = 34 or older); Race
(0 = Nonwhite; 1 = White); Religion (0 = Protestant; 1 = Non-Protestant);
Education (0 = High School or Less, 1 = Some College or More); Amount of Time
Served (0 = Less than 1 Year, 1 = 1–5 Years, 2 = 5–10 Years, 3 = More than 10
Years); Security Level (0 = Minimum, 1 = Medium, 2 = Maximum); Type of
Offense (0 = Personal Crime, 1 = Other Crime); Homosexual Behavior (0 = No, 1 =
Yes).
    * Denotes statistical significance at the .05 level.

Discussion

Research on human sexuality, both in free society and in prisons, has
typically focused on the sexual behaviors of males. For example, prison
sex research has typically only delved into the topics of coerced and
consensual sex among male inmates. Free society sex research is more
common, yet some topics are clearly marginalized. Perhaps the most
obvious of these topics is masturbation. In prison-based sex research,
this marginalization is even clearer.

Previous studies on masturbation in free society have consistently
found a significant relationship between age and masturbation.
However, the present study did not find such a relationship. Although
prisons have been defined as microcosms of society, prison culture is
remarkably different than free society. Clearly, this includes differences
in sexual activities of citizens and inmates. For example, female
inmates are deprived of certain sexual outlets while incarcerated. Thus,
it appears many turn to masturbation for sexual release. Previous literature has reported that women in their late twenties to forties have the

highest rates of masturbation; the women in this study have a mean age of 34, and do report high rates of masturbation. And, age does not appear to be a significant predictor of masturbatory activities, or frequency among these female inmates. Most interesting, however, is the proportion of females reporting that they do masturbate is nearly twice the proportion of free society women so reporting in previous research. This should not be surprising, however, given the unique cultural contexts and deprivations of prison life.

The results of this investigation also suggest that religious affiliation is not a predictor of female inmates' masturbatory practices. Again, this contradicts the research on female masturbation in free society. In fact, as Michael et al. (1994) have argued in free society, religion may be the most significant predictor of masturbation. However, among this incarcerated sample of women, religion has no statistically significant effect. Again, it appears that the institutional culture outweighs other factors.

Where this research does find support for the existing literature on female masturbation is in regards to the effects of having a sexual partner. Whereas in free society the literature typically presumes that a woman's partner is from a heterosexual relationship, in prison this becomes a same-sex partner. Women who had homosexual experiences while incarcerated were more likely to masturbate than women who did not engage in homosexual activity while in prison. In addition, these same women were more likely to be frequent masturbators. Thus, it may be that there are no differences in the motivation or nature of masturbation for incarcerated and non-incarcerated women, but only differences upon whom motivation has an affect. As suggested by previous literature, individuals who are sexually active with partners are more likely to masturbate; this also holds true for incarcerated women, but cuts across age and religious categories.

As previously stated, masturbation in prison is almost always a rule infraction. However, it provides inmates an alternative outlet to release pent up frustrations and stresses. It may also possibly reduce the amount of consensual and coerced homosexual behavior behind bars. We must recommend to prison administrators that masturbation is a natural part of life. In addition, masturbation in prison, unlike consensual and coerced sex, prevents the spread of sexually transmitted diseases such as HIV/AIDS for both male and female inmates. Therefore, it is important for correctional administrators and policy makers to reconsider the definition of masturbation as a violation of institutional rules.

Most important, the justification and rationale for instructing inmates that autoerotic activities are "wrong" needs to be revisited and reconsidered. In order to do so, however, it is important that policy makers first understand the motivations, dynamics, frequencies, and characteristics of practitioners of masturbation in prison. It is our intent to provide the first important steps toward this understanding.

Research of this nature is not only important for correctional administrators, but also sex researchers in general. Sex researchers must continue to delve into these "forbidden topics." We must continue to open the eyes of correctional administrators and staff. According to Tewksbury and West (2000), "Refusal or reluctance to acknowledge that sex in prison [including masturbation] exists is one thing, but refusal or reluctance even to devote research attention to the issue is detrimental to the study of corrections, to the discipline, and to society as a whole" (377). Finally, we must strive to make changes in correctional policies which have the potential to make our prisons safer.

References

Davidson, J. and N. Moore. (1994). Masturbation and Premarital Sexual Intercourse Among College Women: Making Choices for Sexual Fulfillment. *Journal of Sex & Marital Therapy, 20*(3):179–199.

Hite, S. (1976). *The Hite Report: A Nationwide Study on Female Sexuality.* New York, NY: Macmillan Publishing Co., Inc.

Irwin, J. and D. Cressey. (1962). Thieves, Convicts, and the Inmate Culture. *Social Problems, 10*:145–147.

Janus, S. & C. Janus. (1993). *The Janus Report on Sexual Behavior.* New York, NY: John Wiley & Sons, Inc.

Kinsey, A., C. Martin, W. Pomeroy, and P. Gebhard. (1953). *Sexual Behavior in the Human Female.* Philadelphia, PA: W. B. Saunders Company.

Laumann, E., J. Gagnon, R. Michael, and S. Michaels. (1994). *The Social Organization of Sexuality: Sexual Practices in the United States.* Chicago, IL: The University of Chicago Press.

Michael, R., J. Gagnon, E. Laumann, and G. Kolata. (1994). *Sex in America: A Definitive Survey.* Boston, MA: Little, Brown and Company.

Pollock, J. M. (1997). *Prisons: Today and Tomorrow.* Gaithersburg, Maryland: Aspen Publishers, Inc.

Sykes, G. (1958). *The Society of Captives: A Study of a Maximum Security Prison.* Princeton, NJ: Princeton University Press.

Tewksbury, R. (1989). Measures of Sexual Behavior in an Ohio Prison. *Sociology and Social Research, 74*(1):34–39.

Tewksbury, R. and E. E. Mustaine. (2001). Where to Find Corrections Research: An Assessment of Research Published in Corrections Specialty Journals, 1990–1999. *The Prison Journal, 81*(4):419–435.

Tewksbury, R. and A. West. (2000). Research on Sex in Prison During the Late 1980s and Early 1990s. *The Prison Journal, 80*(3):368–378.

Ward, D. and G. Kassebaum. (1965). *Women's Prison: Sex and Social Structure*. Chicago, IL: Aldine Publishing Company.

Wooden, W. S. and J. Parker. (1982). *Men Behind Bars: Sexual Exploitation in Prison*. New York: Plenum Press.

5

Parade Strippers:
A Note on Being Naked in Public

Craig J. Forsyth

This article is concerned with the practice of exposing the female breasts in exchange for "throws" (trinkets and glass beads thrown from floats) from Mardi Gras parade floats in the New Orleans area. It has become so commonplace that the term "beadwhore" has emerged to describe women who participate in this activity. This phenomenon is compared to other related practices: nude sunbathing (Douglas, Rasmusen, and Flanagan, 1977), nudism (Weinberg, 1981a, 1981b), mooning (Bryant, 1977, 1982), and streaking (Anderson, 1977; Bryant, 1982; Toolan, Elkins, and D'Encarnacao, 1974).

Being Naked in Public

As a topic for research, being naked in public can be discussed under the broad umbrella of exhibitionism or within the narrow frame of fads or nudity (Bryant, 1977). In general, exhibitionism involves flaunting oneself in order to draw attention. In the field of deviance the term exhibitionism may also refer to behavior involving nudity for which the public shows little tolerance (Bartol, 1991; Bryant, 1977). This research, however, focuses on a form of public nudity that has a degree of social acceptance.

An extensive sociological study of public nudity was *The Nude Beach* (Douglas et al., 1977). Weinberg's (1981a, 1981b) study of nud-

Reprinted from *Deviant Behavior,* Vol. 13, No. 4 (1992), pp. 391–403. © 1992 Taylor & Francis, Inc. Edited and reprinted by permission of the publisher.

ists represents another type of degree of public nakedness. Other research has addressed the topics of streaking (running nude in a public area) (Anderson, 1977; Bryant, 1982; Toolan et al., 1974) and mooning (the practice of baring one's buttocks and prominently displaying the naked buttocks out of an automobile or a building window or at a public event) (Bryant, 1977, 1982). Both streaking and mooning were considered fads. One question considered by sociological research on nakedness is when and why it is permissible, appropriate, or acceptable to be naked in public (Aday, 1990). Researchers have also addressed some possible motivations or rationales for public nudity. Toolan et al. (1974), for example, explain motivations for streaking as follows:

> While streaking is not in itself a sex act, it is at least a more-than-subtle assault upon social values. Its defiance serves as a clarion call for others to follow suit, to show "the squares" that their "old hat" conventions, like love, marriage, and the family, are antiquated (157).

Both Bryant (1982) and Anderson (1977) say that streaking began as a college prank that spread quickly to many campuses. As a fad, it still retained parameters of time and place. Bryant (1982) contended that it was one generation flaunting their liberated values in the faces of the older, more conservative generation. Anderson (1977) said that it embodied the new morality and thus was "perceived by many to be a challenge to traditional values and laws" (232).

Mooning, like streaking, was considered a prank and an insult to conformity and normative standards of behavior. Neither streaking nor mooning had any erotic value (Bryant, 1982). Unlike streaking, mooning is still not uncommon on college campuses.

Nudism in nudist camps has had little erotic value. Instead, nudity at nudist camps has been purposively antierotic. Weinberg (1981b) believes that the nudist camp would "anesthetize any relationship between nudity and sexuality" (337). One strategy used by nudist camps to ensure this was to exclude unmarried people.

> Most camps, for example, regard unmarried people, especially single men, as a threat to the nudist morality. They suspect that singles may indeed see nudity as something sexual. Thus, most camps either exclude unmarried people (especially men), or allow only a small quota of them (337).

Nudity, in this setting, was seen as being pursued in the interest of vitality and health and incorporated in lifestyle.

> In the nudist camp, nudity becomes routinized; its attention provoking qualities recede, and nudity becomes a taken-for-granted state of affairs (Weinberg, 1981b: 341).

Nude sunbathing incorporates many rationales from voyeurism to lifestyle and in many cases has a degree of erotic value. The sexuality of the nude beach has been evaluated as situational.

> Voyeurism . . . poses a dilemma for the nude beach naturalists, those who share in some vague way the hip or casual vision of the nude beach . . . voyeurs have become the plague of the nude scene . . . The abstract casual vision of the beach does not see it as in any way a sex trip, but the casual vision of life in general certainly does not exclude or downgrade sex (Douglas et al., 1977: 126–127).

Similar to the nudist in the nudist camp, nude beachers expressed contempt for the "straight" voyeur.

> Sometimes I really feel hostile to the lookers. Obviously you can't look at people that way even if they are dressed . . . It really depends on your attitude in looking. I've even told a couple of people to fuck off . . . And some people to leave. I was thinking this would be the last time I come down here . . . there were too many sightseers . . . it sort of wrecks your time to have someone staring at you (Douglas et al., 1977: 130).

But there were those on the beach who mixed pity and pleasure from being peeped at.

> A group of boys had apparently entered (the nude beach) with the intention of peeking at some nudes. Since I was the only woman there, they congregated around me. This wouldn't have bothered me at all if they had been nude, too. But they remained clothed in their surfer suits. At first, this seemed a prostitution of the purpose of the Beach—they were being "dirty" about it and it almost made me feel that way. But after a while I realized that if I gave them pleasure by looking at me, then that was a fine thing. If their thing is to look at nude women for a charge, I certainly am not one to stop them from doing their thing (Douglas et al., 1977: 128).

The concern of this paper is now to describe the method used to analyze the most recent phenomenon of being naked in public: parade stripping.

Methodology

Data for this research were obtained in two ways: interviews and observations in the field. Interview data were gotten from an available sample of men who ride parade floats (n = 54) and from women who expose themselves (n = 51). These interviews ranged in length from 15 to 45 minutes.

Observations were also made at Mardi Gras parades in the city of New Orleans over two carnival seasons: 1990 and 1991. Altogether, 42 parades were observed. The author assumed the role of "complete observer" for this part of the project (Babbie, 1992: 289). This strategy allows the researcher to be unobtrusive and not affect what is going on.

Mardi Gras: Deviance Become Normal

On Mardi Gras day in New Orleans many things normally forbidden are permitted. People walk around virtually nude, women expose themselves from balconies, and the gay community gives new meaning to the term outrageous. Laws that attempt to legislate morality are informally suspended. It is a sheer numbers game for the police; they do not have the resources to enforce such laws.

> The greatest tradition of Mardi Gras is what was known in the old days as "promiscuous" masking. In the 1830's, 40's and 50's every Mardi Gras saw masqueraders in the street—some on foot and better heeled in carriages and wagons. There were even some organized groups such as the Bedouin Company and although Mardi Gras almost came to a halt in the 1850's because of the outrageous behavior of its participants, the custom of putting on a costume and mask on Shrove Tuesday continues to this day (Huber, 1972: 37).

Although masking is allowed only on Mardi Gras day, the idea of masking pervades the season. In a sense, the season becomes a mask for any outrageous behavior. What one does during Mardi Gras does not count as a mark on one's character.

Another of the traditions of Mardi Gras is the tossing of beads and trinkets.

The custom began in the 1830's when masqueraders in carriages tossed bonbons and dragees (sugar coated almonds) for extra fun. They also tossed little bags of flour which broke upon striking a person, showering him with a coating of white. But onlookers also armed themselves with bags of flour tossed at maskers, and one writer described certain streets in New Orleans on Ash Wednesday morning as presenting the aspect of a snow blanket (Huber, 1972: 37).

This began an active relationship between the float rider and viewer. As participants became more active, behavior became more outrageous and many residents called for an end to the festival. One offended viewer said:

Boys with bags of flour paraded the streets, and painted jezebels exhibited themselves in public carriages, and that is about all. We are not sorry that this miserable annual exhibition is rapidly becoming extinct. It originated in a barbarous age and is worthy of only such (Huber, 1972: 46).

As Mardi Gras continued, the behavior of the day started to spread to any time there was a parade. As behavior became more offensive to some, particularly in the late 1960s and early 1970s other "family celebrations" spread into the suburbs. This had the effect of removing the "censors" from the scene and both concentrating and attracting the "norm violators." Now anyone who comes into the city for parades during the Mardi Gras season experiences a different celebration.

Parade Stripping

The celebration of carnival or Mardi Gras as it occurs in New Orleans and surrounding areas primarily involves balls and parades. These balls and parades are produced by carnival clubs called "krewes." Parades consist of several floats usually between 15 and 25, and several marching bands that follow each float. There are riders on the floats. Depending on the size of the float, the number of riders can vary from 4 to 15. The floats roll through the streets of New Orleans on predetermined routes. People line up on both sides of the streets on the routes. The float riders and the viewers on the street engage in a sort of game. The riders have bags full of beads or other trinkets that they throw out to the viewers along the route. The crowds scream at the riders to throw them something. Traditionally, the scream has been "throw me something mister." Parents put their children on their shoulders or have ladders with seats constructed on the top in order to gain some advantage in catching some of these throws. These "advantages" have become fixtures, and Mardi Gras ladders are sold at most local hardware stores. It is also advantageous if the viewer knows someone on the float or is physically closer to the float. Another technique is to be located in temporary stands constructed along the parade route that "seat" members of the other carnival krewes in the city or other members of the parading krewe.

In recent years another technique has emerged. Women have started to expose their breasts in exchange for throws. The practice has added another permanent slogan to the parade route. Many float riders carry signs that say "show me your tits"; others merely motion to the women to expose themselves. In some cases, women initiate the encounter by exposing their breasts without any prompting on the part of the float rider.

Findings

The practice of parade stripping began in the late 1970s but its occurrence sharply increased from 1987 to 1991. During this study, no stripping occurred in the daytime. It always occurred in the dark, at night parades. Strippers were always with males. Those interviewed ranged in age from 21 to 48; the median age was 22. Most of them were college students. Many began stripping during their senior year in high school, particularly if they were from the New Orleans area. If from another area, they usually began in college. All of the strippers interviewed were in one location, a middle-class white area near two universities. Both riders and strippers said it was a New Orleans activity not found in the suburbs and they said it was restricted to only certain areas of the city. One float rider said:

> In Metairie (the suburbs) they do it rarely if at all, but in New Orleans they have been doing it for the last ten years. Mostly I see it in the university section of the city during the night parades.

Parade strippers often attributed their first performances to alcohol, to the coaxing of float riders, to other strippers in the group, or to a boyfriend. This is consistent with the opinion of Bryant (1982), who contended that when females expose themselves it is usually while drinking. Alcohol also seemed to be involved with the float riders' requests for women to expose themselves. One rider stated:

Depending on how much I have had to drink, yes I will provoke women to expose themselves. Sometimes I use hand signals. Sometimes I carry a sign which says "show me your tits." If I am real drunk I will either stick the sign in their face or just scream at them "show me your tits."

Data gained through both interviews and observation indicated that parade stripping is usually initiated by the float riders. But many of the women indicated that they were always aware of the possibility of stripping at a night parade. Indeed, some females came well prepared for the events. An experienced stripper said:

I wear an elastic top. I practice before I go to the parade. Sometime I practice between floats at parades. I always try to convince other girls with us to show 'em their tits. I pull up my top with my left hand and catch beads with my right hand. I get on my boyfriend's shoulder. I do it for every float . . . I'll show my breasts longer for more stuff and I'll show both breasts for more stuff.

Other parade strippers gave the following responses when asked, "Why do you expose yourself at parades?"

I'm just a beadwhore. What else can I say?
For beads. It's a challenge.
I expose myself because I'm drunk and I'm encouraged by friends and strangers on floats.
I get drunk and like to show off my breasts. And yes they are real.
For beads or cups.
Basically for beads. I do not get any sexual gratification from it.
I only did it once. I did it because a float rider was promising a pair of glass beads.
When I drink too much at a night parade, I turn into a beadwhore.
It's fun.
I expose myself for pairs of long beads only.
Shock value.
I exposed myself on a dare. Once I did it, I was embarrassed.
I exposed myself because I was drunk.

Only one woman admitted that she did it for sexual reasons. At 48, she was the oldest respondent. When asked why she exposed her breasts at parades, she said:

Sexual satisfaction. Makes me feel young and seductive. My breasts are the best feature I have.

One woman who had never exposed herself at parades commented on her husband's efforts to have her participate during the excitement of a parade.

> We were watching a parade one night and there were several women exposing their breasts. They were catching a lot of stuff. My husband asked me to show the people on the float my breasts so that we could catch something. He asked me several times. I never did it and we got into an argument. It seemed so unlike him, asking me to do that.

Float riders often look upon bead tossing as a reward for a good pair of breasts, as the following comments show:

> The best boobs get the best rewards.
> Ugly women get nothing.
> Large boobs get large rewards.

When parade strippers exposed themselves they were not as visible to people not on the float as one would think. Strippers were usually on the shoulders of their companions and very close to the float. For a bystander to get a "good look" at the breasts of the stripper was not a casual act. A person had to commit a very deliberate act in order to view the event. Those who tried to catch a peek but were either not riding the floats or not among the group of friends at the parade were shown both pity and contempt.

> I hate those fuckers (on the ground) who try to see my boobs. If I'm with people they can look. That's ok. But those guys who seek a look they are disgusting. I bet they can't get any. They probably go home and jerk off. I guess I feel sorry for them too. But I still don't like them. You know it's so obvious, they get right next to the float and then turn around. Their back is to the float. They are not watching the parade. We tell them to "get the fuck out of here asshole" and they leave.

Like a small minority of nude sunbathers who like to be peeped at (Douglas ct al., 1977), there are strippers who like the leering of bystanders. Our oldest respondent, mentioned earlier, said she enjoyed it. "I love it when they look. The more they look the more I show them" (128) she remarked.

Parade strippers most often perform in the same areas. Although parade stripping usually involves only exposing breasts, three of the interviewees said they had exposed other parts of their bodies in other public situations.

Strippers and their male companions tried to separate themselves from the crowds; they developed a sense of privacy needed to perform undisturbed (Palmer, 1977; Sommer, 1969). Uninvited "peepers" disturbed the scene and were usually removed through verbal confrontation.

Most strippers and others in attendance apparently compartmentalized their behavior (Forsyth and Fournet, 1987; Schur, 1979). It seemed to inflict no disfavor on the participants, or if it did they seemed to manage the stigma successfully (Gramling and Forsyth, 1987).

Discussion

One goal of research on deviant behavior is to fit the behavior within a larger social classification. This paper has attempted to describe parade stripping within the larger frame of public nudity. It has also examined the individual motivations for this behavior, within an existent list of "excuses" for nudity (sexual, defiance, shock value, lifestyle).

The rationales of parade strippers did not neatly fit into any of the above. Parade stripping seemed to exist because trinkets and beads were given; for those interviewed, there was no apparent sexuality attached except in one case. The beadwhore engages in a playful form of exhibitionism. She and the float rider both flirt with norm violation. The stripper gets beads and trinkets and the float rider gets to see naked breasts. Both receive pleasure in the party atmosphere of Mardi Gras, and neither suffers the condemnation of less creative and less esoteric deviants.

References

Aday, D. P. (1990). *Social Control at the Margins.* Belmont, CA: Wadsworth.

Anderson, W. A. (1977). The Social Organizations and Social Control of a Fad. *Urban Life,* 6:221–240.

Babbie, E. (1992). *The Practice of Social Research.* Belmont, CA: Wadsworth.

Bartol, C. R. (1991). *Criminal Behavior: A Psychosocial Approach.* Englewood Cliffs, NJ: Prentice-Hall.

Bryant, C. D. (1982). *Sexual Deviancy and Social Prescriptions: The Social Context of Carnal Behavior.* New York: Human Sciences Press.

Bryant, C. D. (1977). *Sexual Deviancy in Social Context.* New York: New Viewpoints.

Douglas, J. D., P. K. Rasmussen, and C. A. Flanagan. (1977). *The Nude Beach.* Beverly Hills, CA: Sage.

Forsyth, C. J. and L. Fournet. (1987). A Typology of Office Harlots: Party Girls, Mistresses and Career Climbers. *Deviant Behavior,* 8:319–328.

Gramling, R., and C. J. Forsyth. (1987). Exploiting Stigma. *Sociological Forum,* 2:401–15.

Huber, L. (1972). The Great Traditions of Mardi Gras. *New Orleans Magazine,* 6:36, 37, 46,48, 50, 52, 54, 56, 59, 60–65.

Palmer, C. E. (1977). Microecology and Labeling Theory: A Proposed Merger. In H. P. Chalfant, E. W. Curry, and C. E. Palmer (eds.), *Sociological Stuff.* Dubuque, IA: Kendall/Hunt.

Schur, E. M. (1979). *Interpreting Deviance.* New York: Harper and Row.

Sommer, R. (1969). *Personal Space.* Engelwood Cliffs, NJ: Prentice-Hall.

Toolan, J. M., M. Elkins, and P. D'Encarnacao. (1974). The Significance of Streaking. *Medical Aspects of Human Sexuality,* 8:152–65.

Weinberg, M. S. (1981a). Becoming a Nudist. In E. Rubington and M. S. Weinberg (eds.), *Deviance: An Interactionist Perspective,* New York: Macmillan.

Weinberg, M. S. (1981b). The Nudist Management of Respectability. In E. Rubington and M. S. Weinberg (eds.), *Deviance: An Interactionist Perspective,* New York: Macmillan.

PART 3

PATHOLOGICAL SEXUAL DEVIANCE

Pathological sexual deviance refers to sexual behaviors that are generally considered harmful, against the law, and engaged in by only a small number of people. These individuals act without a supportive group structure. Participants in this type of sexual behavior generally are motivated either by a psychological or social-psychological perspective rather than a sociological one. The chapters in this section address four different types of pathological sexually deviant behavior. These acts are often classified as "extreme," since a majority of society is outraged by them.

In the first article, Hale transports the reader into the world of convicted rapists in an attempt to identify and understand the gains or rewards pursued by men during the act of rape. The inclusion of direct quotes from rapists gives the reader an understanding of how these individuals rationalize their actions not only during the rape but even at the time of the study.

Further justification, rationalization, and normalization of misconstrued sexual perceptions are examined by DeYoung in the second article of this section. DeYoung discusses and assesses the philosophies of men who engage in sex with young boys, members of the North American Man/Boy Love Association (NAMBLA). As a pedophile organization active within the United States, NAMBLA supports and promotes the political, civil, and educational rights of adults to have sex with boys, despite the fact that a societal consensus exists condemning adults who have sex with children. Since such acts are generally considered abusive, victimizing, and exploitive, how does NAMBLA justify or rationalize this deviant behavior? DeYoung explores this question by reviewing three years' worth of publicly circulated NAMBLA literature.

The third article in this section, written by Zolondek, Abel, Northey, and Jordan, attempts to provide a picture of juvenile sex offenders (JSOs) and their deviant sexual behaviors, such as voyeurism. Their study suggests that many deviant behaviors intertwine, and that JSOs may require treatment different from that of adult offenders.

In the final article, Davis explores voyeurism from the perspective of preventing further sexual offenses by its participants. Expanding from the psychological aspects of voyeurism to the inclusive predisposition for planned premeditated sexual offenses, Davis presents information that connects nonoffensive fantasies with the sexually deviant behaviors that are often carried out by perpetrators.

All of the sexual behaviors discussed in this section are violations of the law. Each of these behaviors violates mainstream norms and is performed by forcing one's sexual desire or actions upon non-compliant, non-consenting persons (i.e., the victims). However, it is not due to their illegality that these are deviant acts; rather, societal intolerance of victimization defines these sexual behaviors as deviant. Their illegality is a consequence of their deviance.

6

Motives of Reward Among
Men Who Rape

Robert Hale

Rape and those who commit rape have been the focus of a range of studies since the mid-1970s. The statistical and demographic characteristics of rape have been analyzed in an attempt to better understand the circumstances of this crime. The background characteristics of men who commit rape also have been explored in an attempt to develop a composite or profile. In addition, the motivations of men who commit rape have been examined to better understand what compels the rapist. Deterrence of criminal behavior is achieved as the individual balances beliefs of potential punishment against the anticipated risk of the criminal act.

While studies of rape have a long history, Scully (1990) and Scully and Marolla (1984, 1985) have produced a progression of highly regarded works exploring the motives of reward among men who commit rape. In addition, Decker, Wright, and Logie (1992) have produced a model study of perceptual deterrence. They encourage future research that attempts to cross-validate perceptual deterrence across different types of offenses and offenders. This study will merge the ideas of rape and perceptual deterrence to a sample of men convicted for rape in an attempt to identify the anticipated gains (rewards) that motivate these men.

Reprinted from *American Journal of Criminal Justice,* Vol. 22, No. 1 (1997), pp. 101–119. © 1997 by the Southern Criminal Justice Association. Edited and reprinted by permission of the publisher.

Review of Literature

Explanations of Rape

Traditionally, the rapist is seen as compelled to rape, driven by either "uncontrollable urges" (Edwards, 1983) or a "disordered personality" (Scully and Marolla, 1984). Attributing rape to an uncontrollable impulse implies that normal restraints of self-control are reduced or erased by an innate sex drive. The major thesis is that sexual deprivation causes predisposed individuals to lose control of their behavior and force a victim into unwanted sexual relations (Symons, 1979).

The "disordered personality" approach tends to attribute rape to a mental illness or disease. Rape is thought to be a symptom of some deeply rooted abnormality, either cognitive or organic. Lanyon (1986) believes that all sexual offenders, not just rapists, are acting from the same sickness, although the sickness is not identified. Ellis and Hoffman (1990) state that a "mutant gene" may be the cause, but they do not rule out other genetic or hormonal influences. Scully and Marolla (1985) point out that the "belief that rapists are or must be sick is amazingly persistent" (298), and Lanyon (1986) asserts that this belief "tends to be the view held by the judicial system, by social service agencies, and the general public" (176). The further implication of either of these approaches is that thinking is not a part of the process of rape; this holds particular consequences for the etiology of the crime and rehabilitation of men who commit rape.

However, an abundance of research shows that thinking and choice are a part of the rapist's construction of the crime, and the learning approach is a common theme in the literature on rape. From this perspective a number of typologies of men who rape have been created (Burgess, 1991; Holmes, 1991; Knight and Prentky, 1987; Scully and Marolla, 1985). Scully (1990) and Weiner, Zahn, and Sagi (1990) identify three categories of rape; Holmes identifies five categories of rape, the same number given by Knight and Prentky; while the Scully and Marolla study (1985) describe six categories of motive for rape. Although there is some overlap between the descriptions in these studies, there are also some mutually exclusive categories. From the studies noted above and other sources, eight categories of reward for rape can be identified.

The first category originates in the work of Black (1983) and is expanded by Scully and Marolla (1985). The rapist commits his crime but views his act as a legitimate form of revenge. This view is referred to as "The Punishment Model" by Felson and Krohn (1990). In these rapes, men are seeking to hold accountable and punish a female for some action that the rapist subjectively perceives as an insult. The action may have been committed directly by the victim, or she may be a victim of "collective liability," in which the victim is a representative of a larger class of individuals (Black, 1983; Scully and Marolla, 1984).

The revenge motive is common when the victim is the primary source of the frustration, whereas punishment is often the goal when the victim is held accountable for collective liability. In these rapes, the rapist views his action as an attempt to subordinate women for an attempt to challenge male dominance. This perception comes from the rapist's belief that he has the right to discipline and punish.

The second category reflects an anger within the rapist, often emerging from his perceptions that a woman is interested in having sex with him but later refuses to fulfill his desire. This category would be comparable to the "deniers" found by Scully (1990). When seeking this type of reward, the rape becomes a means to a specific end, which is sexual satiation. The rapist believes he can seize what he desires, reflecting his belief that even if a woman declines sexual advances, rape is a suitable means to what is desired (Groth and Birnbaum, 1979; Holmes, 1991).

The third category reflects the desire of the rapist that the sex act be performed totally for his satisfaction, without regard for the feelings or emotions of the victim. Thus, the rapist can avoid feelings of intimacy and caring while having his desires fulfilled. This approach would be applicable in some respects to the impersonal, anonymous sex that often occurs in casual "one-night stands" and between prostitutes and their customers (Felson and Krohn, 1990; Russell, 1988, 1995; Scully and Marolla, 1985).

The fourth category of reward includes rapists who commit their crimes for the excitement they receive. The sex is secondary to the rush of emotion that goes along with the act. Sexual deviants do not emerge at the most severe levels of deviance or illegality: Evidence abounds that chronic sexual deviants have a history of involvement with "nuisance" sex behaviors before progressing into such crimes as rape (Holmes, 1991; Rosenfield, 1985). Some rapists have reported feelings of an intense "high" as they anticipate and then complete the rape (Knopp, 1984; Warren, Hazelwood, and Reboussin, 1991). Rapists who report this goal as a reward are seen as pushing the limits of excitement and personal enjoyment to the ultimate illegal extreme.

The fifth category includes those who rape for the adventure or challenge the act affords them. The gang rapist is typical of those included in this category. The challenges of forcing the victim to complete a sex act and of being able to perform sexually in front of other male participants and the danger inherent in attempting a rape are cited as reasons by those included in this category as reasons for rape (Holmes, 1991). This category is similar to the proving of "masculinity" observed by Russell (1989), Kimmel (1996), and Messner (1989). The danger of the act seems to be the motivating factor for these men: The danger lies either in the risk of identification and capture or in the potential inability to perform in the situation. The thrill lies in the promotion of loyalty and brotherhood among those associated with the commission of the rape.

The sixth category reflects the notion that the underlying motivation for rape is domination of the victim, rather than the sex that accompanies the rape. The goal of this type of rapist is to ensure that women are frightened and intimidated sufficiently to not challenge the power and superiority of males (Deming and Eppy, 1981; Herman, 1995).

The seventh category has its basis in the evolutionary theory of rape, which proposes that rape originates from pressures of natural selection that require men to be more aware of sexual opportunities, to have sexual relations with a wide variety of sexual partners, and to use force when necessary to fulfill their sexual desires (Quinsey, 1984; Shields and Shields, 1983; Symons, 1979; Thornhill and Thornhill, 1983, 1987).

The final category was proposed by Abel and Blanchard (1974) and is detailed by Prentky and Burgess (1991). The reward for the rapist in this category is the physical fulfillment of a fantasy. The role of fantasy has been documented as a precursor to a number of violent crimes, including serial rape (MacCullough, Snowden, Wood, and Mills, 1983; Warren et al., 1991). The consensus is that the fantasy-world beliefs of many sadistic offenders become overt behavior when the offender feels compelled to live out their fantasy.

This study will measure the motives of reward among a sample of men incarcerated for committing rape; the men will be asked to rank order their motives for committing their crime. Then, based on the motive, the men will be asked whether a low or high likelihood of arrest would deter their committing their crime. From these results, the type of men who rape that would be deterred by the risk of incarceration should be apparent.

Data and Methods

The subjects in this study were a sample of the population of men incarcerated for rape within two maximum-security state penitentiaries in the Deep South. Data were collected at two different times. First, subjects were briefed about the purpose of the study and then were asked to complete a questionnaire. This questionnaire gathered demographic information before presenting the eight categories of reward for committing rape. The men also consented to an interview, which was conducted at another time. During the interview, subjects were asked to provide details behind their motives. Subjects were selected at random to provide the follow-up interviews. The questionnaire and interviews were administered during counseling sessions and were conducted by either the leader of the counseling session or the author. Men in this study were surveyed over a three-year period that ended in 1996.

Only those convicted of rape against an adult female were included in the study. While definitions of what constitutes rape can vary, men in this study had been found guilty under statutes that required "forcible sexual intercourse" achieved "against her (the victim's) will." Those convicted of other sex offenses, such as nuisance sex offenses, sexual assault or molestation, offenses involving pornography, or pedophilia, were excluded from the analysis. Subjects must have been convicted of the charge of rape in order to be included in the final sample. This stipulation created a sample of 132 subjects. Two potential problems could arise from using this sample. One is that subjects might provide answers for which they would anticipate being rewarded in some way, perhaps with preferences for early release. To bypass this issue of validity, subjects were informed that all answers would be anonymous and that prison counselors would not know who did or did not respond to the survey. It was also stressed that no inmate would receive preferential treatment for completing the survey, just as no respondent would be deprived of benefits for refusing to participate.

A second flaw is that the entire model could be seen as speculative since all subjects are incarcerated at the time of the survey and thus cannot fully answer concerning their motivation as if they were truly free to act on their perceptions of risk and reward. Surveying men who were incarcerated might provide the better measure of cost and benefit, rather than posing artificial situations to men who are not free to act.

The group of 132 rapists had an average age of 32.6, with a range from 17 to 67 years of age. The mean educational level of the sample was 12.5 years, with a range from seventh grade to post-college graduate education. At the time of their offenses, 72% had been or were married and another 13% had been living with a woman. The majority (57%) were employed in skilled or unskilled labor positions.

The group had a lengthy involvement in sex offenses. On average, they began their sex offenses (e.g., voyeurism, exhibitionism, and scatophilia) in their early teens (mean = 13.4), and they committed their first rape on average at age 17.4. Of the sample, 85% had a prior conviction for a sexual offense, and 52% had a prior rape conviction. Most reported being heterosexual (82%), 7% reported begin homosexual, 5% reported being bisexual, and 8 of the men chose not to answer this question.

The goal of this study is to examine how men incarcerated for rape view the rewards of their actions. Subjects in this study were asked to remember a rape they had committed or had thought about committing. Each respondent was then asked to fill in details describing the crime, such as the time of day and characteristics of the setting and of the victim; the goal was to make the crime situation as real as possible to the respondent. Subjects were then presented with eight categories of potential reward and were asked to select which reward would compel them to commit the rape.

Subjects were asked to rank order the eight categories of reward that would influence them to commit rape. After the men had ordered their perceptions of the reward they anticipated, they were asked to consider how the risk of apprehension would affect the likelihood of committing rape.

The men were asked whether they would attempt to commit the rape they had visualized earlier within the context of the amount of reward anticipated and the risk of apprehension. Four responses were possible: (1) No; (2) Not Likely; (3) Likely; (4) Yes.

Results

Table 6.1 provides four types of information. The second column (Number) details how often each category was selected as the primary goal for committing rape by the 132 respondents; the third column (Percent) lists what percentage of the men are reflected by the number in column two.

Twenty-eight men (21%) answered they would rape for the reward of "Revenge and Punishment." Twenty-three of the men (17%) commit-

Table 6.1   Frequency of Selection as Primary Goal for Committing Rape

Category	Number	Percent	Cumulative Points	Average Score
Revenge/Punishment	28	21	963	7.3
Anger	19	14	1003	7.6
Impersonal Sex	9	6	726	5.5
To Feel Good	4	3	950	7.2
Adventure/Danger	18	13	831	6.3
Control/Power	23	17	752	5.7
Masculinity	14	10	946	7.2
Fulfill a Fantasy	17	12	990	7.5

ted rape "To exert control or power" while 19 (14%) committed rape to release "Anger."

The cumulative points given to each category were then calculated; these scores are derived from the addition of the scores given to each category by each of the 132 respondents. The highest possible score for any category in this column is 1,056, assuming each of the men gave that particular category the highest score of eight; as shown, "Anger" is the motive receiving the highest cumulative score, followed by those whose motive was "To fulfill or experience a fantasy" and those raping for "Revenge and Punishment."

Although the reward of "Revenge and Punishment" is the single highest category, the cumulative totals reveal that more men were raping out of "Anger" or "To fulfill or experience a fantasy." The category of "Anger" as a reward received a cumulative number of 1003 points, while the category of "Fulfill A Fantasy" received a cumulative total of 990 points. The category of "Revenge and Punishment" received 963 points and was the third highest category in terms of cumulative points.

When the rapist is seeking a reward of personal satisfaction and enjoyment, he is more likely to defy a "High Risk" of apprehension in order to commit the rape. Follow-up interviews with rapists in this category affirmed the hypothesis that the high risk of apprehension added to the satisfaction derived from the rape. According to "Vance," an inmate who fits into this category:

> The idea that she might later figure out who I was added to the thrill, at the time. . . . I had seen her around, and I'm sure that she had seen me. Plus, the place where I got her (in a car parked outside a shopping

center) was pretty open, too. I guess I picked that spot because I knew there was more chance of getting caught. But I never figured it was going to happen.

For men in this category, the attempt to commit rape in spite of a high risk of apprehension added to the pleasure of completing the act. Their satisfaction was actually the result of two separate situations.

In only two other categories of reward were the men willing to chance a high risk of apprehension, when the reward was either the danger or challenge of the rape or to fulfill a fantasy. Research points out that these rapes are often committed in front of an audience, such as instances of gang rape (Holmes, 1991; Scully and Marolla, 1984; Scully, 1990). When witnesses are present, whether or not they are active participants in the rape, the risk of apprehension increases. It is assumed that those who are willing to commit rape in front of witnesses are aware of the increased risk of apprehension. As "Larry" pointed out:

> The guys that were with me that night, we had known each other for-
> ever, we had grown up together. They had stuff on me, and I had stuff
> on them. I knew they would not talk, 'cause I could turn on them, and
> they knew it.

Thus, the rapist who is seeking an adventure in spite of a high risk of apprehension appears to believe that his accomplices will not corroborate the crime.

Those who rape in order to experience a fantasy also appear to be unconcerned when the risk of apprehension is high. Fantasy is an integral part of not only "normal" sexual relations but also of deviant and criminal sexual acts (Burgess, Hartman, Ressler, Douglas, and McCormack, 1986; Holmes, 1991; Prentky and Burgess, 1991). Fantasy is defined as a series of thoughts that preoccupy the individual into the rehearsal of the script. As the fantasy evolves, it may include feelings, emotion, and dialogue (Burgess, 1991).

The fantasy of rape provides a secondary motive for rape for many men in this study. Research has asserted that fantasies of violence are often a precursor to violent behaviors (Cohen, Garofalo, Boucher, and Seghorn, 1971; MacCullough et al., 1983; Prentky, Cohen, and Seghorn, 1985; Warren et al., 1991). These fantasies are thought to be linked to the rapist's feelings of anger, of revenge, or of danger and adventure. The rapist is motivated by these emotions and has fantasized a script that allows for their resolution.

This assumption was borne out through follow-up interviews with men who fit this classification. Typical of those who raped out of a motive of revenge was "Ken," who stated:

> I had a dream of getting even to her for the divorce. Then she remarried and I lost track of her. Even though I didn't have no interest in finding her, I still hated her for what she had done. I wished of getting back at her, but the only thing I could do was to hurt somebody like her who reminded me of her. It still wasn't enough, but I felt better after I did it (rape).

The revenge expressed by "Travis" had a longer history:

> I never felt like my own mother ever cared for me. She was always off doing her own thing, she never seemed to have time for me. Never seemed to care. The only women I ever got involved with were those I could treat however I wanted. And it was never good. I used to sit around and think of ways of getting even, when I had the chance. I figure now it goes back to my mother, I probably knew it then, but I couldn't help myself. And I'll probably do the same if I ever get out of here.

While those who raped from a motive of revenge had over time put some thought into their actions, the anger-rapist was more impulsive. His act of rape stemmed from an immediate situation that, in the perception of the rapist, was an affront that demanded a response. For "Dan," the affront was the discovery his wife was having an affair:

> When I heard this, I just lost my cool. You know, how they say a heat of passion thing, or something like that? Everything just turned red and black in my head, like something went off. . . . I looked at her and thought, "If you are giving it to someone else, then I'll take it any way I want to." I saw it as having sex, although I was forcing her to, and I knew she didn't want to. At least, not the way I was making her do it. . . . They called it rape later, but I didn't see it that way. . . . I'm not sure I see it that way even now.

Sometimes the anger-rape has nothing to do with an affront by another person. For "Doug," it was simply a combination of events, none of which were directly related to a female:

> That night I was really pissed off about a lot of things. I mean, not really a lot of things, but some things were really eating at me. I had been looking for a job, and that was not going well. Money was tight,

and I was getting hassled over the bills. I was just mad at everything in general, nothing seemed to be going my way. And then, out in the bar, I saw this girl who seemed to have it all together, who seemed to have a lot. I decided right then I was going to show her before the night was over what it was like to lose something . . . what it felt like to hurt.

Discussion

This study provides support for the idea that rape can occur for a variety of motives. Among these motives, violence is certainly an issue to consider. While definitions of violence vary, emotions of anger, hatred, and revenge, along with beliefs of punishment and privilege, are repeatedly used as descriptions. In this study, violence emerges as a leading factor in rape. More men rape out of revenge, or to punish the victim, than for any other single motive, while anger is a latent motive for many men who commit rape.

Given the amount of research detailing rape as a crime of violence, these findings are not surprising. The data add support to the contention that violence is an integral part of the link between men and rape. Evidently men who rape from a motive of revenge or anger are not considering, or affected by, the danger of committing the act. As mentioned earlier, many of the men whose primary motive was the element of danger were involved in gang rapes or were seeking personal satisfaction; revenge and anger were not part of the incident. Similarly, men who raped with the motives of anger or revenge were not concerned with the danger, but were more concerned with correcting a perceived "Wrong" (Katz, 1988).

The link between power, anger, and revenge as factors in rape has long been noted, but this study fails to provide support for it. The key variable seems to be "power," as anger and revenge have been discussed as important within this study. It is plausible that men in this study did not want to admit (either to themselves or the researcher) that they were seeking power, given that power rapists tend toward insecurity with doubts about their masculinity (Holmes, 1991; Maletzky, 1991; Scully and Marolla, 1985). It would also be that the anger and revenge felt by these men simply overshadowed the need for power, although all three sensations were present.

While the analyses in this study show that violence is a factor influencing many men to commit rape, violence is present in every case. Certainly rape is a violent act, and the control of a victim often requires that violence be used by the perpetrator. However, there are motives for rape that do not include violence. When men are committing rape "to feel good," to experience a new "adventure," or to "fulfill a fantasy," violence does not have to be part of the script. It is entirely possible that "Larry" and "Vance" committed their crimes without intending to use violence. Of course, this explanation is certainly open to debate, depending on the definition of violence and the definition of the situation; however, from the perspective of the perpetrator, there are instances when rape does occur without violence.

Responses in this study imply that the majority of rapists are not suffering from psychoses or other serious psychiatric disorders, as those from the "disordered personality" perspective would believe. Certainly, these men have a distorted perception of the role of sex and of females. This is not, however, a full sign of mental illness or other cognitive impairment. It is more a reflection of poor judgement, which is more typical of faulty social or learning skills.

References

Abel, G. G. and E. B. Blanchard. (1974). The Role of Fantasy in the Treatment of Sexual Deviation. *Archives of General Psychiatry, 30*:467–475.

Black, D. (1983). Crime as Social Control. *American Sociological Review, 48*:34–45.

Burgess, A. W. (ed). (1991). *Rape and Sexual Assault: A Research Handbook.* New York: Garland.

Burgess, A. W., C. R. Hartman, R. K. Ressler, J. Douglas, and A. McCormack. (1986). Sexual Homicide: A Motivational Model. *Journal of Interpersonal Violence, 1*:251–272.

Cohen, M. L., R. Garofalo, R. Boucher, and T. Seghorn. (1971). The Psychology of Rapists. *Semin Psychiatry 3*:307–327.

Decker, S., R. Wright, and R. Logie. (1992). Perceptual Deterrence Among Active Residential Burglars: A Research Note. *Criminology, 31*:135–147.

Deming, M. B. and A. Eppy. (1981). The Sociology of Rape. *Sociology and Social Research, 64*:357–380.

Edwards, S. (1983). Sexuality, Sexual Offenses, and Conception of Victims in the Criminal Justice Process. *Victimology: An International Journal, 8*:113–128.

Ellis, L. and H. Hoffman. (eds.). (1990). *Crime in Biological, Social, and Moral Contexts.* New York: Praeger.

Felson, R. B. and M. Krohn. (1990). Motives for Rape. *Journal of Research in Crime and Delinquency, 27(3)*:222–242.

Groth, A. N. and J. Birnbaum. (1979). *Men Who Rape.* New York: Plenum Press.

Herman, J. L. (1995). Considering Sex Offenders: A Model of Addiction. In P.

Searles and R. Berger (eds.), *Rape and Society*. Boulder, CO: Westview Press.

Holmes, R. (1991). *Sex Crimes*. Newbury Park, CA: Sage Publications.

Katz, J. (1988). *Seductions of Crime*. New York: Basic Books.

Kimmel, M. (1996). *Manhood in America: A Cultural History*. New York: Free Press.

Knight, R. A. and R. A. Prentky. (1987). The Developmental Antecedents and Adult Adaptations of Rapist Subtypes. *Criminal Justice and Behavior, 14(4)*:403–426.

Knopp, F. (1984). *Retaining Adult Sex Offenders: Methods and Models*. Syracuse, NY: Safe Society Press.

Lanyon, R. I. (1986). Theory and Treatment in Child Molestation. *Journal of Consulting and Clinical Psychology, 54*:176–182.

MacCullough, M., P. Snowden, J. Wood, and H. Mills. (1983). Sadistic Fantasy, Sadistic Behavior, and Offending. *British Journal of Psychiatry, 143*:20–29.

Maletzky, B. (1991). *Treating the Sexual Offender*. Newbury Park, CA: Sage Publications.

Messner, M. (1989). When Bodies Are Weapons: Masculinity and Violence in Sport. *International Review of the Sociology of Sport, 25(3)*:203–220.

Prentky, R. A. and A. W. Burgess. (1991). Hypothetical Biological Substrates of a Fantasy-Based Drive Mechanism for Repetitive Sexual Aggression. In A. W. Burgess (ed.), *Rape and Sexual Assault*. New York: Garland.

Prentky, R. A., M. L. Cohen, and T. K. Seghorn. (1985). Development of a Rational Taxonomy for the Classification of Sexual Offenders: Rapists. *Bulletin of the American Academy of Psychiatry and the Law, 13*:39–70.

Quinsey, V. L. (1984). Sexual Aggression: Studies of Offenders Against Women. In D. Weisstub (ed.), *Law and Mental Health: International Perspectives*. Vol. 1. New York: Pergamon.

Rosenfield, A. (1985. Sex Offenders: Men Who Molest: Treating the Deviant. *Psychology Today,* (April):8–10.

Russell, D. E. H. (1995). White Man Wants a Black Piece. In P. Searles and R. Berger (eds.), *Rape and Society*. Boulder, CO: Westview Press.

Russell, D. E. H. (ed.) (1989). Sexism, Violence, and the Nuclear Mentality. *Exposing Nuclear Phallacies*. New York: Pergamon.

Russell, D. E. H. (1988). Pornography and Rape: A Causal Model. *Political Psychology, 9*:41–73.

Scully, D. (1990). *Understanding Sexual Violence: A Study of Convicted Rapists*. Boston: Unwin Hyman.

Scully, D. and J. Marolla. (1985). Riding the Bull at Gilley's: Convicted Rapists Describe the Rewards of Rape. *Social Problems, 32 (3)*: 251–263.

Scully, D. and J. Marolla. (1984). Convicted Rapists' Vocabulary of Motive: Excuses and Justifications. *Social Problems, 31*:530–544.

Shields, W. M. and L. M. Shields. (1983). Forcible Rape: An Evolutionary Perspective. *Ethology and Sociobiology, 4*:115–136.

Symons, D. (1979). *The Evolution of Human Sexuality*. New York: Oxford University Press.

Thornhill, R., and N. W. Thornhill. (1987). Human Rape: The Strengths of the

Evolutionary Perspective. In C. Crawford, M. Smith, and D. Krebs (eds.), *Sociobiology and Psychology: Ideas, Issues, and Applications.* Hillsdale, NJ: Erlbaum.

Thornhill, R. and N. W. Thornhill. (1983). Human Rape: An Evolutionary Analysis. *Ethology and Sociobiology, 4*:137–173.

Warren, J. I., R. R. Hazelwood, and R. Reboussin. (1991). Serial Rape: The Offender and His Rape Career. In A. Burgess (ed.), *Rape and Sexual Assault.* New York: Garland.

Weiner, N. A., M. A. Zahn, and R. J. Sagi. (1990). *Violence: Patterns, Causes, and Public Policy.* New York: Harcourt Brace Jovanovich.

7

The World According to NAMBLA: Accounting for Deviance

Mary deYoung

Look tenderly on little boys
Their softness as fleeting as a flower,
The cheeks like petals such a little hour,
The deepest dimple theirs so transiently . . .
Look tenderly on little boys.

The transience of childhood innocence is an enduring theme in literature and poetry, however the "Little Boys" poem from which those
verses are taken did not appear in a literary anthology, but in the monthly *Bulletin* of NAMBLA—the North American Man/Boy Love
Association. Organized in 1978 in the wake of the arrests of 24 prominent Revere, Massachusetts professional and business men for sexual
activities with adolescent males, NAMBLA is a political, civil rights,
and educational organization that advocates and promotes adult sexual
behavior with male children. The taboo against adult-child sex indeed is
consistently and ardently held in this and other cultures (Murdock,
1949), yet when NAMBLA was formed there already was an international network of organizations of self-proclaimed pedophiles that
served as organizational models.

Inspired by their European predecessors, two pedophile organizations which predated NAMBLA also were formed in the United States.
The Rene Guyon Society, created in 1962 by a group of seven layper-

Reprinted from *Journal of Sociology and Social Welfare,* Vol. 16, No. 1 (1989), pp.
111–126. © 1989 by the Western Michigan University School of Social Work.
Edited and reprinted by permission of the publisher.

sons after attending a conference on sexuality in Los Angeles, took its name from the French jurist and Freudian psychologist who had been an outspoken advocate of adult-child sex. It also adopts his motto as its slogan: "Sex by year eight, or else it's too late." The Society advocates the abolition of statutory rape and child pornography laws, and encourages what it claims to be its 5,000 members to give their own children, and others, early sexual experiences with loving adults (O'Hara, 1981). While still maintaining a mailing address in the Los Angeles area, the Society is no longer politically and socially active in promoting its cause. Believing that affection transcends age differences, the Childhood Sensuality Circle was founded in San Diego in 1971 to champion sexual self-determination for adults and children. It also advocated the abolition of age of consent laws, promoted the early initiation of young children into sexual behavior with family members, and encouraged children to use their own standards in the selection of adult sexual partners (Davilla, 1981). The organization stopped publishing and mailing its *Nusletter* in 1984 because of the failing health of its elderly founder, Valida Davilla, a former student of Wilhelm Reich.

NAMBLA, then, is the only pedophile organization that remains active in this country, and has withstood the legal harassment that has closed down many of its European counterparts as well. Due to their beliefs and practices all of the pedophile organizations, in fact, have experienced a considerable amount of legal interference ranging from searches of their headquarters and their members' homes, to seizures of materials for evidence, to the arrests and incarceration of their members. Social stigma also has been sustained by organization members. Some have lost jobs when their organizational affiliation was discovered; others have been forced to use pseudonyms to protect their identities; and still others have been ostracized by their professional colleagues and social companions (O'Carroll, 1982).

These pedophile organizations and their members consistently have come up against an unusual degree of consensus on the part of the larger society that adult sexual behavior with children indeed should be taboo, that it is victimizing and exploitative, and that its redress properly falls within the purview of the law. Although not uniform in extent, the strength of the consensus that does exist should not be underestimated. It continually has been demonstrated in studies of attitudes toward crimes and the law held by various ethnic and socioeconomic groups in this country (Finkelhor, 1984; Rossi, 1974; Sellin and Wolfgang, 1964), as well as in cross-cultural surveys (Newman, 1976). It may very well be that in the consciousness of the larger society, quite nothing is more repugnant than the sexual abuse of children (Finkelhor, 1984).

And that raises an important question. In the light of that strong consensus that adult sexual behavior with children is victimizing and that it is reprehensible, how does NAMBLA justify and normalize its philosophy and practices? In other words, how does NAMBLA account for its deviance? It is the purpose of this paper to explore an answer to that question by reviewing the 1982 through 1985 newsletters, booklets, and brochures published for public dissemination by NAMBLA. This paper does not provide a systematic analysis of the content of these publications; rather, it utilizes a data-reduction technique (Weber, 1985) by which textual material is classified into content categories generated by a larger theoretical framework. For the purposes of this paper, that framework will be Scott and Lyman's (1968) theory of accounts.

Accounting for Deviance

Sociologists have long noted that individuals and groups can and do commit acts and hold beliefs they realize are considered wrong by others and that in doing so, they create a problematic situation that calls for resolution, or at the very least for explanation. The problematic nature of the situation arises because the behavior or the beliefs of these individuals deviate from the expected, the routine, or what the larger society may even consider the normal. In that problematic situation, then, the deviating individuals or groups are motivated to avoid or to reduce public censure and stigma by engaging in behavioral or verbal conduct that justifies and normalizes their deviance vis-a-vis the expectations of others and the norms of the larger society (Mills, 1940; Scott and Lyman, 1968).

Psychologists would refer to this conduct when it is verbal in nature as rationalization, but sociologists offer a broader framework for its interpretation. Such verbal behavior, or its correlate in written form, is considered an "aligning action" (Stokes and Hewitt, 1976). That metaphor of alignment is both descriptive and explanatory. By examining various techniques and strategies, it describes how deviating individuals and groups attempt to align their lines of conduct with others and with the norms of the larger social structure; and it explains *why* they do so. The techniques of alignment are varied, but the motivation for engaging in them is consistent: successful alignment will justify and normalize the deviant behavior or belief, thus reducing, if not eliminating, social censure and stigma.

Scott and Lyman (1968) refer to these various aligning actions as "accounts," those "linguistic devices employed whenever an action is subject to a valuative inquiry" (46), and they propose two different types. The first, excuses, are those accounts in which the individuals or group admit the behavior or the belief in question is wrong, bad, or inappropriate, but deny full responsibility for it. Excuses generally take the form of "appeals." An "appeal to accident" redefines the offending conduct or belief as the product of unforseen or uncontrollable circumstances; an "appeal to defeasibility" insists that it occurred only because the individuals or the group were not fully informed or fully aware. An appeal to "biological drives" presents the deviant behavior or belief as the product of innate drives that cannot be predicted or controlled; and an "appeal to scapegoating" blames others for it.

The second type of accounts, justifications, are those in which the individuals or group accept responsibility for the deviant behavior or belief, but deny the pejorative, or stigmatizing quality of it. This category of accounts has generated a great deal of research within the sociology of deviance. Based as it is upon the criminologic concepts of "techniques of neutralization" (Sykes and Matza, 1957), it has been used as a theoretical framework for analyzing the verbal accounts of compulsive gamblers (Cressey, 1962), social dropouts (Polsky, 1967), moral offenders (Hong and Duff, 1977), and murderers (Levi, 1981). And in recent years, it also has been used to analyze the verbal and the written accounts of sexual deviants. In two interesting studies, Scully and Morolla (1984, 1985) used the concept of accounts to examine the justifications and excuses of convicted incarcerated rapists; a similar framework was used by McCaghy (1968) with child molesters. Writings by sexual deviants also have been scrutinized through this particular theoretical lens. Taylor (1976) reviewed the works of the so-called "Uranian poets," those pedophilic writers whose ranks included such notables as F. E. Murray, W. B. Nesbitt, and Ralph Chubb, and discovered examples of the "uses of artistry as a motive-formulation resource for the justification and possible enactment of guilt-free sex" (100). In a content analysis of the publications of the three pedophile organizations in this country, deYoung (1988) found persistent themes that could be categorized as justifications.

Justifications, then as a category of accounts, have demonstrated considerable utility as a theoretical framework for the analysis of the language and writings of deviant individuals and groups. It is this framework that will be used in this paper's examination of the publications of the NAMBLA organization. Justifications generally involve six different strategies (Scott and Lyman, 1968), four of which will be used in this paper: denial of injury, condemnation of the condemners, appeal to higher loyalties, and denial of the victim. Each of these will be explained as to its style and intended purpose and will be illustrated with selections from the publicly disseminated literature of NAMBLA.

Denial of Injury

With this justification, the individuals or the group acknowledge responsibility for the deviant act or belief but insist that it is permissible because no one is injured or harmed by it. For NAMBLA, this justification involves the admission that the organization advocates adult-child sex, and that its members engage in that behavior, and the justification that neither the behavior nor the philosophy is in any way injurious to children.

This assertion is contrary, of course, to the strong consensus that adult sexual behavior with children is indeed harmful. The child sexual abuse literature is rife with empirical research and case studies that bolster that consensus (deYoung, 1985, 1987). Even the language that is part of the lexicon of both the lay public and professionals in the field—words like "abuse," "victimization," "exploitation," and "trauma"—attest to what most people believe are the deleterious effects on children of adult sexual behavior.

In the face of that strong consensus, then, NAMBLA must redefine the impact of both its philosophy and its members' behavior so as to stress the positive, rather than the injurious effects of adult-child sex. Its publications, therefore, are filled with anecdotal accounts, letters, poetry, and articles that proclaim the benefits and advantages to children of having a sexual relationship with an adult male. Some of those advantages are very specifically detailed. Accounts of children having been rescued from lives on the streets, of children finding a loving alternative to an abusive home, or of discovering in the pedophile someone to talk to or to help them during periods of distress are prominently featured in every NAMBLA publication. Yet when examples of the benefits to individual boys are set aside, the more general advantages of man/boy love are much less clear. The rather esoteric tenor of these explanations is illustrated by the following examples from NAMBLA publications:

> Man love is also something which has helped thousands of boys dis-
> cover their own sexuality and get in touch with what they really feel
> (Lotringer, 1980: 1). If sex is an expression of shared love (as
> man/boy love is), then it is beneficial to both partners, regardless of
> age . . . Nothing is more beneficial than to feel a sense of security in
> the love of another. It creates a euphoria. The (pedophile) takes the
> young boys from the streets, give them a good home and material
> needs, and loves them (*Bulletin,* April, 1985: 6).

NAMBLA, however, does acknowledge that harm may follow the
adult-child sexual encounter; in the fact of such overwhelming clinical
and case study evidence, it can do little but acknowledge that. The
organization, however, is quick to place the culpability for that harm on
others who, it insists, respond inappropriately or prejudicially to adult-
child sex. By displacing that blame, NAMBLA implies that there is
nothing deviant about the sexual behavior, per se, but only in the public's reactions to it.

> Why can't we here in America do as those in the Netherlands have
> done? That is, EDUCATE the public to see that, in proper context, a
> man/boy relationship can be of benefit to the boy and the trauma that
> the police so quickly point out as connected to such relationships are
> caused not by the relationship, but by what the police themselves sub-
> ject the boy to? (*Bulletin,* December 1984: 4). In no study known to us
> is there any suggestion that pedophile contacts are harmful in them-
> selves. But in our culture we usually cannot consider just the actual
> contacts. If they lead to *other* things there might well be a lot of dam-
> age that can be done by the parents of a child who had contact with a
> pedophile. On discovery they often react in panic. They become furi-
> ous or outraged. Such a reaction . . . is very harmful to the child . . .
> Then there is the damage caused by contact with the police and the
> courts . . . The reactions of society can cause great damage to the child
> (deGroot, 1982: 6).

Another tactic for denying injury is the publication of youngsters'
accounts of the benefits they have experienced from sexual relationships with adult males. Here are the very persons the larger society
views as victims adamantly disavowing that label and, at least by infer-
ence, rejecting the care and protection that would be afforded them
because of that status. The NAMBLA *Bulletin,* for example, featured a
column for some period of time by "The Unicorn," an eleven-year-old
self-described "faggot" whose column was a testimony to the erotic
superiority of sex with adult males as he described his various lovers
and the positive effects each has had on his physical, emotional, and

even spiritual development (*Bulletin*, November 1983: 10). The organization also published a pamphlet titled, "Boys Speak Out on Man/Boy Love" (1981) which features short anecdotal accounts by boys of the positive effects of their sexual experiences with adult males. A perusal of the titles of the selections in this pamphlet suggest the tone of the testimonials: "Thank God for Boy Lovers," "If It Weren't for Mark, I'd Probably Be Dead Today," "I Need My Lovers," and "The Best Thing That Ever Happened to Me."

The NAMBLA *Bulletin* also publishes letters from youngsters that describe the benefits they receive from sexual relationships with men.

> I am a boy of 13 and I hope you will read this letter. The spelling and stuff isn't too good . . . I wish I was one of the kids (in the stories featured in the *Bulletin*) with someone to love me like that . . . And I think it's wrong for people to bother men and boys who just want to love each other (*Bulletin,* April 1983: 3).
>
> There are enough of us young people in the country to stand up and put our foot down. To tell our feelings in the way we want to be understood and the way we want to be loved . . . What we need is communication, peace, love, joy in our hearts, and happiness for people we are in love with. (Signed) Lover Boy Joe, age 13 (*Bulletin,* September 1984: 5).

The denial of injury, then, is a justification that redefines adult sexual behavior with children in positive terms. As a rhetorical strategy, it is used to convince those of the larger society who will read its literature, that contrary to what is popular belief, no injury or harm is incurred by children from engaging in sex with adult males; that the harm that has been stressed by other sources is really due to the inappropriate and prejudicial reactions of ignorant people and systems; and that even the children who have experienced this behavior will eschew the label of victim and proclaim the beneficial effects of sexual behavior with adults if only asked. The insistence of this justification is that there is nothing really deviant in adult-child sex, therefore any censure of the NAMBLA organization and its membership is undeserved.

Condemnation of the Condemners

The second justification is the condemnation of the condemners, a rejection of those who would reject. The utility of this strategy is that in redirecting the condemnation and censure it has received from the larger society back on the society itself, NAMBLA can normalize its philosophy and the behavior of its members by demonstrating that they do not differ noticeably from that of the larger society. The condemners, real and potential, are thus characterized as hypocritical and as deserving condemnation themselves.

Since the censure given to adult sexual behavior with children is so strong, the condemnation of the condemners found in the publications of NAMBLA is equally strong. Much printed space is taken up with what are often sustained polemics against professionals in the field of child sexual abuse, and against the criminal justice and the mental health systems. Individuals are listed by name, cases are dissected and analyzed, and flaws in decision-making, and errors in judgment are highlighted, all in a tone that is more often mockingly derisive than not. The following illustration demonstrates the width and the depth of that condemnation:

> Con men who once made their living selling snake oil are now surfacing as "experts on child sexual abuse." They have deliberately confused expressions of love and affection with violent physical abuse . . . Police departments suffering from a bad public image due to internal corruption, excessive use of force, and for poor management have turned to boy-lovers as easy prey . . . District Attorneys needing a dramatic case for the voters to remember and psychiatrists needing public funds to build a private practice have turned to boy-lovers as the answer to their prayers. Demagogues in state and federal legislatures have also found the anti-boy-love hysteria tailor made for raising campaign funds and increasing name recognition through the sponsorship of laws pandering to the public's misconceptions (*Bulletin,* May, 1983: 4).
>
> (The children) continue to seduce adults and call those who reproach them for it "silly fools." The children had learned a bit about psychoanalysis. They said. "For every objection they were forced to abandon, these funny ladies and gentlemen immediately produce another. Could it be that they are really only unconsciously hiding the secrets of their own inner souls? Isn't it just that they are a little bit afraid of sex itself?" But nobody bothered to listen to what they said, for how could the truth ever be heard from the mouths of children? (*Bulletin,* March 1983: 9).

The intent of this justification strategy is both straightforward and clear: if the condemners can be reconceptualized as engaging in the same or even more victimizing or exploitative acts as those for which NAMBLA members are accused, then their censure of the members is irrelevant at best, and hypocritical at worst. The sting of any subsequent criticism from them, then, is effectively precluded.

Appeal of Higher Loyalties

The third justification that can be found in the publications of NAM-BLA is the appeal to higher loyalties, a strategy by which the organization and its members normalize their behavior and philosophy by insisting the interests of a higher principle to which allegiance is owed is being served. That higher principle, for NAMBLA, is the liberation of children from what it characterizes as the repressive bonds of society; the sexual liberation of children, then, is presented as a necessary step for achieving the larger goal. The following excerpt illustrates that point:

> Members of NAMBLA are committed to the protection and development of the young. Our beliefs and activities have their foundation in values which say that all people are important and should have the inherent right to conduct themselves as they wish as long as the rights of others are not abused. Children are our special concern. We seek their freedom from the restrictive bonds of society which denies them the right to live, including to love, as they choose (*Bulletin,* December 1984: 6–7).
>
> We recognize that children need more than sexual freedom and self-determination; they need economic self-sufficiency and the right and power to control all aspects of their lives, with help from but without interference by adults. NAMBLA favors the empowerment of young people in our society. Children should be treated as full human beings, not as the private property of their parents and the state ("What is NAMBLA?" Undated: 1).

This espoused higher loyalty has the character of what Hewitt and Hall (1973) refer to as a quasi-theory, and "ad hoc explanation brought to problematic situations to give them order and hope" (367). Because it has structure and consequence, a quasi-theory permits otherwise deviant situations and philosophies to be perceived by others as meaningful and even normal in light of commonsense notions of human behavior and social arrangements.

That children need to be treated "as full human beings," that their protection and development are preeminent concerns falls well within the rubric of commonsense and common interest. It is both meaningful and normal to hold such an ideal, and on these issues alone, NAMBLA would not expect disagreement from the larger society. That larger society also may agree on some of the fundamental objectives that must be accomplished in order to achieve that goal, such as the empowerment of children, but when NAMBLA adds what would be considered a deviant objective, the "sexual freedom" of children to that logic, the appeal to higher loyalty takes on the character of a quasi-theory. It espouses a hopeful goal, the development of children into "full human beings," and develops a structure, that is a set of objectives for achieving that goal, and includes within that set an objective that the larger society would not under other circumstances accept.

Another facet of this appeal to higher loyalties involves the affinity NAMBLA has with the goals of other, nonstigmatized organizations and with social welfare concerns. The organization, as an example, has expressed a great deal of sympathy and support for the women's movement as well as loyalty to the gay rights movement, and views its own struggle for credibility and acceptance as analogous to their struggles. NAMBLA has also taken on such social welfare concerns as sexism, ageism, racism, nuclear warfare, abortion, unemployment, and the military draft, as well as esoteric concerns such as circumcision, and clitoridectomy (*NAMBLA Journal*, 1983: 3). This partnership with other legitimate organizations and with social issues that are concerns of the larger society as well is a strategy for aligning the organization of NAMBLA and its membership with that larger society.

These appeals to higher loyalties and the affinity with the goals of other legitimate organizations and with pressing social welfare concerns, allows NAMBLA to assume a mantle of legitimacy. That mantle, if successfully worn, further protects the organization and its members from the censure of the larger society.

Denial of the Victim

The final justification found in the publications of NAMBLA is denial of the victim. Here the victim, the child in this case, is reconceptualized as having deserved or brought on the deviant behavior; due to the victim's culpability, therefore, the responsibility of offending individuals for the behavior and its consequences is diminished.

This justification involves the conceptual transformation of children from victims of adult sexual behavior into willing partners. This transformation can only occur if NAMBLA is successfully able to convince the disbelieving larger society that children are able to give full and informed consent to sexual acts with adults. But this issue of consent is a thorny one. Long after the debate about the morality of adult-child sex has been aired, and long after the uncertainties about the effects of such behavior on children has been satisfactorily addressed, the issue of consent will remain the most basic and fundamental problem that larger society has with adult sexual behavior with children (Finkelhor, 1979).

And it is a persistent and difficult problem for the NAMBLA organization as well, and one that has organization, NAMBLA has made such general statements on the consent issue as these: "If a child and adult want to have sex, they should be free to do so. Consent is the critical point . . . force and coercion are abhorrent to NAMBLA" (*Bulletin*, December 1984: 3); and, "NAMBLA is strongly opposed to age of consent laws and other restrictions which deny adults and youth the full enjoyment of their bodies and control over their lives" (*Bulletin*, September 1984: 7).

The problem, however, is not really with the definition of consent, the law spells that out quite clearly, but with the *age* at which it can be given is a free, knowledgeable, and informed manner. NAMBLA asserts that the current age of consent laws in this country which *pro forma* make its members' sexual behavior with youngsters illegal, are anachronistic and repressive. It strongly advocates for their repeal, as the following excerpt illustrates:

> NAMBLA does not simply wish to repeal age of consent laws; rather, we have never accepted the validity of the frame of reference of which such laws are based. Under the circumstances, we cannot name an age of consent . . . NAMBLA will not participate in an abstract, narrowly defined and ultimately pointless game of "pick an age" . . . Sex does not require highly developed "cognitive tools;" it ought to come naturally (*Bulletin*, April 1983: 1).

Does sex require highly developed "cognitive tools"? If the act itself does not, the consent to engage in the act certainly does, so despite the organization's resistance to engage in a game of "pick an age," the age at which a child can give full and informed consent to sexual acts must be determined if this justification is going to be successful in normalizing the behavior of NAMBLA members and avoiding public censure.

And the very debate over that age still wages within the ranks of NAMBLA. In a position paper created by the steering committee of the organization, consent was defined as "both informed (understood and accepted in advance) and with the intent and spirit of love" (Proposal, undated). Since understanding and acceptance at least imply some "cognitive tools," the committee backed off from its original insistence that it would not pick an age, and selected nine as the age of consent.

Some members argued that it should be lower. One insisted that "a five year old aware of sexual feelings can act upon them at any time of his choosing. There are many five year olds who understand the meaning of sex more than many 35 year olds" (*Bulletin*, July/August 1983: 4). Other members, perhaps predicting how the larger society would respond to these proposed ages, advocated that the age be raised to thirteen or fourteen. Even while the NAMBLA organization vehemently argued this issue, one of its founding members went on record to defend all consensual sexual relations, "regardless of the age of the partners" (Lotringer, 1980: 21).

Obviously the issue of consent and the age at which children can freely and intelligently render it continues to be a problem for the NAMBLA organization. It is for the larger society as well as evidenced by the fact that the age of consent established by law tends to vary from one state to another. While the larger society may find some value in debating whether that age should be uniform across the country, and may find some interest in deciding what that age should be, the same attitude studies that demonstrate such a strong consent that adult sexual behavior with children is harmful and exploitative, also show an increase in that consensus where very young children are concerned. In other words, the debate about whether that age should be thirteen, fourteen, or fifteen may be lively, but there is little demonstrated acceptance of lowering that age, and virtually none for removing it.

Denial of the victim, predicated as it is upon this issue of consent, is unlikely to be a successful justification; indeed, it may be this single issue of consent and the failure of this justification that will always keep the deviant label on this organization and its members, therefore keeping them out of alignment with the larger society.

Conclusion

In the face of a strong consensus that adult sexual behavior with children is abusive and exploitative, and that its effects are negative at best and traumatic at worst, the North American Man/Boy Love Association has a vested interest in justifying and thereby normalizing its philosophy and its members' practices. This paper has utilized the sociological framework of accounts, with a special reference to justifications, to examine how that process is accomplished in the publications of NAMBLA.

The use of accounts by deviant individuals and groups is an area of research that has the potential of generating insights into deviancy. And in the area of sexual deviancy, where myth and misunderstanding abound, the study of these aligning actions may increase knowledge as to how individuals and groups labeled deviant attempt to negotiate and reconceptualize their beliefs and their behavior in the face of society's censure.

If the imputation of deviance is indeed a product of an interactive process between the individuals or group so labeled and the labelers (Schur, 1979), then the study of accounts may also lead to an understanding of that process. How accounts are given in terms of their manner and their style, and how accounts are accepted and the consequences of their acceptance are researchable hypotheses, and studies designed to address these issues and others will make rich contributions to the sociology of deviance.

References

Cressey, D. R., (1962). Role Theory, Differential Association, and Compulsive Crimes. In A. Rose (ed.), *Human Behavior and Social Processes*. NY: Houghton Mifflin.

Davilla, V. (1981). *CSC Position Paper*. 2nd ed. San Diego, CA: Childhood Sensuality Circle.

deGroot, D. (1982). *Paedophilia*. Boston, MA: NAMBLA.

deYoung, M. (1988). The Indignant Page: Techniques of Neutralization in the Publications of Pedophile Organizations. *Child Abuse and Neglect: The International Journal, 12*(4):583–591.

deYoung, M. (1987). *Child Molestation: An Annotated Bibliography*. Jefferson, NC: McFarland and Company.

deYoung, M. (1985). *Incest: An Annotated Bibliography*. Jefferson, NC: McFarland and Company.

Editor and Collective. (1983). *NAMBLA Journal, 6*.

Editor and Collective. (1981). *Boys Speak Out on Man/Boy Love*.

Editor and Collective. (Undated). *What is NAMBLA?*

Editor and Collective. (Undated). *NAMBLA?*

Finkelhor, D. (1984). *Child Sexual Abuse: New Theory and Research*. NY: The Free Press.

Hewitt, J. P. and P. M. Hall. (1973). Social Problems, Problematic Situations, and Quasi-Theories. *American Sociological Review, 38*:367–374.

Hong, L. K. and R.W. Duff. (1977). Becoming a Taxi-Dancer: The Significance of Neutralization in a Semi-Deviant Occupation. *Sociology of Work and Occupations, 4*:327–343.

Levi, K. (1981). Becoming a Hit-Man: Neutralization in a Very Deviant Career. *Urban Life, 10*: 47–63.

Lotringer, S. (1980). Loving Boys. *Semiotext(E) Special*:1–5, 20–30.

McCaghy, C. H. (1968). Drinking and Deviance Disavowal: The Case of Child Molesters. *Social Problems, 16*:43–49.

Mills, C. W. (1940). Situated Actions and Vocabularies of Motive. *American Sociological Review, 5*:904–913.

Murdock, G. P. (1949). *Social Structure*. NY: Macmillan.

NAMBLA Bulletin, 6(3), April 1985.

NAMBLA Bulletin, 5(10), December 1984.

NAMBLA Bulletin, 5(7), September 1984.

NAMBLA Bulletin, 4(9), November 1983.

NAMBLA Bulletin, 4(6), July/August 1983.

NAMBLA Bulletin, 4(4), May 1983.

NAMBLA Bulletin, 4(3), April 1983.

NAMBLA Bulletin, 4(2), March 1983.

Newman, G. (1976). *Comparative Deviance: Perception and Law in Six Children*. NY: Elsevier Publishing Company.

O'Carroll, T. (1982). *Paedophilia: The Radical Case*. Boston, MA: Alyson Publications.

O'Hara, T. (1981). *Rene Guyon Society Bulletin*.

Polsky, N. (1967). *Hustlers, Beats and Others*. Chicago, IL: Aldine Press.

Rossi, P. (1974). The Seriousness of Crime: Normative Structures and Individual Differences. *American Sociological Review, 39*:224–237.

Schur, E. (1979). *Interpreting Deviance*. NY: Harper and Row.

Scott, M. B. and S. M. Lyman. (1968). Accounts. *American Sociological Review, 3*:46–62.

Scully, D. and J. Morolla. (1985). Riding the Bull at Gilley's: Convicted Rapists Describe the Rewards of Rape. *Social Problems, 32*:251–263.

Scully, D. and J. Morolla. (1984). Convicted Rapists' Vocabulary of Motive: Excuses and Justifications. *Social Problems, 31*:530–544.

Sellin, T. and W. Wolfgang. (1964). *The Measurement of Delinquency*. NY: John Wiley and Sons.

Stokes, R. and J. P. Hewitt. (1976). Aligning Actions. *American Sociological Review, 41*:838–849.

Sykes, G. and D. Matza. (1957). Techniques of Neutralization. *American Sociological Review, 22*:663–670.

Taylor, B. (1976). Motives for a Guilt-Free Pederasty: Some Literary Considerations. *American Sociological Review, 24*:97–114.

Weber, R. P. (1985). *Basic Content Analysis*. Beverly Hills, CA: Sage.

8

The Self-Reported Behaviors of Juvenile Sex Offenders

Stacey O. Zolondek, Gene G. Abel,
William F. Northey, Jr. & Alan D. Jordan

Sexually abusive behavior has traditionally been viewed as perpetrated exclusively by adult men. However, more recent crime statistics and research on sexual offenses have consistently shown that this is not the case, and in the past 15 years, sexual abuse perpetrated by juvenile sexual offenders (JSOs) has received increased attention. Conservative estimates indicate that between 15% and 20% of all sexual offenses are committed by youth younger than 18, and as many as 50% of all molestations may be committed by youth younger than 18 (Davis and Leitenberg, 1987; Furby, Weinrott, and Blackshaw, 1989). Furthermore, many adult sex offenders began their offending as juveniles (Abel, Mittelman, and Becker, 1985).

The only fairly definitive conclusion that can be drawn to date is that JSOs are a very heterogeneous group. As Weinrott (1996) noted, "There is great variation in victim characteristics, degree of force, chronicity, variety of sexual outlets (i.e., other paraphilias), arousal profiles, and motivation and intent" (20). Numerous studies and literature reviews have summarized the data about JSOs (Davis and Leitenberg, 1987; Ryan, Miyoshi, Metzner, Krugman, and Fryer, 1996; Vizard, Monck, and Misch, 1995; Weinrott, 1996), and findings have indicated that often, multiple paraphilias are demonstrated by the same individual, providing evidence that sexually exploitative behaviors may be contained within a single continuum (Abel and Osborn, 1992; Ryan,

Reprinted from *Journal of Interpersonal Violence,* Vol. 17, No. 3 (1996), pp. 279–295. © 1996 Sage Publications, Inc. Edited and reprinted by permission of the publisher.

1997). Unfortunately, this continuum, although potentially useful, is generally reduced to categorization of offenses into hands-off, hands-on, and pedophilic offenses (Becker, Harris, and Sales, 1993). A thorough description of juveniles' sexual offenses is necessary to paint a more complete picture of who these juveniles are and what they are doing.

Molestation of children is the highest-frequency offense reported in samples of JSOs and JSOs who molest children report the highest number of victims (Davis and Leitenberg, 1987; Ryan et al., 1996; Weinrott, 1996). Few studies report data on other sexual offenses perpetrated by JSOs. This may be due to the fact that other sexual offenses rarely result in arrests compared to hands-on offenses (Abel, Becker, Mittlman, Cunningham-Rathner, Rouleau, and Murphy, 1987). Ryan et al. (1996) did find that between 35% and 50% of hands-off JSOs had also sexually abused a child.

The modal age of offenders reported in studies tends to be 14 to 15 years, with a first offense most likely to occur at age 13 or 14. However, there is some evidence indicating that about 25% of JSO samples had engaged in sexually abusive behaviors before age 12 (Metzner and Ryan, 1995; Ryan et al., 1996; Weinrott, 1996). In his review of the JSO literature, Weinrott (1996) concluded that it is rare for juvenile child molesters to have both male and female victims. Victims are most likely to be female acquaintances or siblings; rarely are they strangers. In general, the victims of JSOs are at least acquainted with the perpetrator. Reports consistently indicate that more than 50% of perpetrators know their victim, and in cases of child molestation, 75% of victims were either related to or acquaintances of the perpetrator (Davis and Leitenberg, 1987). Ryan et al. (1996) reported that almost 40% of the JSOs in their national sample were blood relatives of the victims, and that sexual victimization of strangers only accounted for 6% of the cases.

Most offenses committed by JSOs are verbally coercive rather than overtly aggressive or violent (Ryan et al., 1996; Weinrott, 1996), and the intensity of the coercion may increase with the age of the victim (Becker, Cunningham-Rathner and Kaplan, 1986). Finkelhor and Dziuba-Leatherman (1994) found that only a small fraction of JSOs commit crimes that result in physical injury, and generally no more force is used than is necessary to complete the act. Although about one third of offenders blame the victim for their offense, most offenders report using some coercion, ranging from bribes and promises to some level of force to gain compliance (Metzner and Ryan, 1995).

Prevalence of conduct disorder is reportedly high among juvenile child molesters. Whereas serious delinquency, substance abuse problems, and interpersonal aggression are relatively uncommon, some researchers have reported that general delinquent behavior is often quite common pre- and post-adjudication for sexual offense. For example, nonsexual criminal activity has been reported by 29% to nearly two thirds (Ryan et al., 1996) of JSOs. Furthermore, there is a significantly greater chance that JSOs will engage in a nonsexual offense after treatment than a sexual offense (Bourduin, Henggeler, Blaske, and Stein, 1990; Brannon and Troyer, 1991; Davis and Leitenberg, 1987; Furby et al., 1989; Kahn and Lafond, 1988). Many JSOs have been exposed to neglect, abuse, family violence, and early sexualization. Ryan et al. (1996) indicated that 43% of their sample reported physical abuse, 39% sexual abuse, 26% neglect, and 63% had been witness to some form of family violence. Similar findings have been found by other researchers (Awad and Saunders, 1991; Hunter and Santos, 1990; Kahn and Lafond, 1988).

In a recent review of the literature of JSOs, Vizard et al. (1995) concluded that "there is a long way to go before we fully understand or effectively meet the needs of these young people" (749). Unfortunately, much of what is known about JSOs comes from clinical writings and from studies using small samples of offenders, which calls into question their representativeness. Furthermore, some studies use retrospective information reported by adult sexual offenders. It is unknown whether the information reported by youth differs from that given by adult offenders reporting about their youth. Few studies replicate measures used by others and instead rely predominantly on self-report or subjective clinical impressions, rarely using standardized instrumentation. The largest study to date described a sample of 1,600 JSOs. Ryan et al. (1996) described the findings of the National Adolescent Perpetrator Network (NAPN), which had requested that its members complete a standard data collection instrument in regard to characteristics of their JSOs. Because decisions about whom to include were left to program administrators, it is difficult to assess the representativeness of this sample. The NAPN questionnaire was completed by clinicians rather than by the JSOs themselves, and criteria for eliciting reports of JSOs' behaviors into the specific categories of sexual offenses found in adult samples.

The purpose of the present study is to describe a national sample of 485 male JSOs using a standardized protocol. To date, there are no studies of JSOs that use self-report data from a sample this large. This study differs from Ryan et al. (1996) in that it uses a self-report, paper-and-pencil instrument rather than clinician report. The literature suggests that adolescents report more deviant behaviors when paper-and-pencil assessments are used during face-to-face interviews (Erdman, Klein, and Greist, 1985; Ochs, Meana, Pare, Mah, and Binik, 1994; Weinrott and Saylor, 1991). The data from JSOs are also compared to adult sexual offender data. Although there is some evidence that once caught, juveniles are more likely to admit to their offenses than are adults, this assumption may be premature. Little is known about the truthfulness of information collected from JSOs and the effect that social desirability has on responding. This study also examines the utility of incorporating a social desirability to scale into measures of juvenile sexual behavior by exploring possible differences in reporting between boys high and low in social desirability.

We predict that JSOs undergoing this assessment will report a variety of sexual offenses and that their offenses will be similar to those of adult sexual offenders. Furthermore, we expect that the frequency of committing the reported sexual behaviors will be high and that JSOs will report engaging in their reported behavior several times. It is expected that juveniles who score higher on a social desirability measure will report less engagement in sexual offenses and that these JSOs will have friends who engage in similar levels of nonsexual antisocial behaviors.

Method

Participants

Participants in this study were 485 boys between the ages of 11 and 17 who were seeking either evaluation or treatment for possible sexually deviant behaviors and interests at several locations in 29 of the United States and in Canada. Of the 485 participants, 42.7% were assessed in sites in the Southeast, 19.4% were assessed in sites in the Southwest, 9.3% were assessed in sites in the Midwest, 9.1% were assessed in sites in the Northwest, 8.5% were assessed at sites in the Northeast, 4.8% were assessed in sites in Hawaii, 1.8% were assessed in sites in Canada, and 5.4% were assessed elsewhere. Forty-eight percent reported that they were assessed in treatment centers, 35.7% reported that they completed the assessment in their clinician's office, 3.7% reported that they completed the questionnaire in a detention center or jail, 3% indicated that they were being assessed because they had been the victims of sexual abuse, and 8.8% reported that they were filling out the questionnaire for other reasons. These categories were not mutually exclusive.

In this sample, 56.3% of the boys were Caucasian, 21.5% were African American, 9.8% were Hispanic, 3.8% were American Indian, 0.8% were Asian, and 7.6% were of another racial group. Participants reported that 2.5% had completed high school, 27.4% had completed some high school, 17.3% had completed junior high school through the ninth grade, 38.6% had completed the seventh or eighth grade, and 12.8% had only completed grade school. Most of the JSOs (60.2%) reported that their parents owned their homes. The JSOs in this sample mostly lived in small homes; 60.3% had between 1 and 5 rooms in their home, 28.2% had 6 to 10 rooms in their home, and only 6.6% had more than 10 rooms in their homes. According to their reports, 28% of the adults that the JSOs lived with engaged in some type of skilled labor (carpenter, painter, fireman, clerk, and skilled worker) for a living, 24.5% made a living through unskilled labor (factory, gas station, waitress, and house cleaning), 17.3% of the adults they lived with made a living as professionals (doctor, lawyer, accountant, teacher, and nurse), 10.3% owned their own businesses, 12% were unemployed and/or on welfare, and 21.1% had military occupations.

As part of the clinical assessment, the boys completed a standard self-report questionnaire (Abel, 1995).

Results

Table 8.1 shows the percentage of JSOs who reported engaging in various paraphilic behaviors, age of onset of these behaviors, mean number of victims, and the mean number of times that they engaged in the behaviors. The percentage of JSOs engaging in sexual behaviors differed from those self-reported by 5,063 adult men on a similar questionnaire (Abel and Osborn, 2000). Juveniles reported higher frequencies than adults for fetishism, obscene phone calls, child molestation, and phone sex. Fewer juveniles than adults reported engaging in zoophilia, and frequencies of exhibitionism, voyeurism, masochism, sadism, use of pornography, transsexualism, and transvestitism did not differ for juveniles and adults.

JSOs also indicated that they engage in delinquent behaviors at higher frequencies than their peers do. Furthermore, JSOs did not report engaging in high rates of substance use. With the exception of alcohol

Table 8.1   Percentage of Juvenile Sexual Offenders Engaging in Behaviors

Behavior	Percentage Reporting	Age of Onset	Number of Victims	Number of Acts
Exhibitionism	11.5	11.4	6.0	11.1
Fetishism	26.4	10.8	NA	46.0
Voyeurism	17.0	11.0	8.8	16.9
Zoophilia	5.0	10.8	Unknown	11.6
Obscene phone calls	16.4	12.3	10.0	Unknown
Masochism	1.9	9.7	NA	40.9
Child molestation	60.8	11.9	4.2	11.1
Unwanted rubbing/touching	17.0	11.7	9.1	15.4
Sadism	2.1	11.0	2.4	11.2
Transvestism	4.6	11.5	NA	9.4[a]
Phone sex	15.4	12.4	Unknown	11.7
Pornography	31.6	11.4	NA	22.9
Transsexualism	3.3	10.1	NA	NA

a. Mean number of times per month.

and marijuana, fewer than 10% of the JSOs reported that they had tried drugs or that they used drugs more than 10 times. Slightly more than half of the JSOs had never tried marijuana, and 34% reported never trying alcohol.

Juveniles were asked to self-report on who they were accused of victimizing; 8% had been blamed for touching an adult woman, 2% an adult man, 13% a girl of the same age or older, 7% a boy the same age or older, 14% a girl 1 or 2 years younger, 8% a boy 1 or 2 years younger, 15% a girl 3 or 4 years younger, 10% a boy 3 or 4 years younger, 28% a much younger girl (5 or more years younger), 24% a much younger boy (5 or more years younger), and 19% had not been blamed for touching another person. These percentages may add up to more than 100, as many JSOs were accused of more than one offense; therefore, these categories were not mutually exclusive.

Participants who reported molesting a child (n = 292) were also asked to report the degree of coercion and force used to gain compliance in sexual activities with a much younger child (5 or more years younger than the perpetrator) and to indicate all responses that applied; 14% claimed that the activity was initiated by the child; 34.9% reported that activity was mutual; 24.3% promised the child candy, money, a toy, and so on; 29.8% tricked the child; 10.3% threatened the child; 5.1%

roughed up the child, a bit; 4.1% roughed up the child a lot; and 0.2% reported that the child died.

Of those who had molested a child, 43.2% of the JSOs indicated offending against a younger sibling, 30.1% against another family member, 33.6% against a non-family member whom they knew, and 7.5% against a foster sibling. Only 8.2% of the sample reported offending against a stranger.

Juveniles were asked to indicate whether they had been blamed for molesting a child and how well the characteristics of the actual offense matched what they had been blamed for. Overall, 27.4% of the JSOs who had been blamed for molesting a child reported that the characteristics of the offense were exactly as the child had reported. However, 13.2% reported that they were blamed but had not committed the offense or been near the child; 16.7% reported that they were blamed, had been near the child, but did not commit the offense; 11.1% reported they were blamed but the child had wanted the sexual activity to occur; 17.5% reported they had been blamed but had actually done less than the child reported; and 5.6% reported that they had been blamed but had touched the child more than the child reported.

Of the 27.6% (n = 134) of JSOs who had never been blamed for molesting a much younger child, 41.5% reported that they had in fact molested a much younger child. The social desirability scores of the unblamed JSOs who reported molesting a child did not differ from those who did not report molesting a child.

During Parts 1 and 4 of the questionnaire, participants were asked to indicate how honest they had been in answering the questions. When asked in Part 1, 89.2% reported that they had been absolutely honest, 9.1% reported fairly honest, and 1.5% reported that they had not been very honest. When completing Part 4, 83.8% reported that they had been absolutely honest, 14.2% reported fairly honest, and 1.6% reported they had not been very honest. These reports differed slightly based on social desirability; participants with high social desirability scores reported more honesty in responding when questioned at the end of the questionnaire. When first questioned, 85.5% of boys with low social desirability, 90% of the boys with medium social desirability scores, and 91.1% of boys with high social desirability scores reported total honesty in responding. When questioned at the end of the questionnaire, 78% low social desirability, 76.9% medium social desirability, and 85.8% high social desirability reported total honesty in responding.

Discussion

In this study, the self-reported characteristics of a large sample of adolescent sex offenders from throughout the United States were obtained using a standardized evaluation. In this sample, JSOs reported that with the exception of quitting school and belonging to gangs, they were engaging in various delinquent behaviors more frequently than were their friends. However, many of the JSOs did report having peers who engaged in a variety of delinquent behaviors. Substance use and abuse was not high. Less than a third of the sample used marijuana or alcohol, and very few had experimented with other substances. Juvenile sexual offending could be related to an overall antisocial lifestyle; however, substance abuse does not appear to play a major role.

Molestation of children was the most commonly reported offense, endorsed by more than 60% of the sample. More than 30% of the sample reported using pornography, more than a quarter of the sample reported fetishism, and between 10% and 20% reported engaging in voyeurism, obscene phone calls, unwanted rubbing or touching, and phone sex. Zoophilia, masochism, sadism, transvestitism, and transsexualism were less common; each was reported by fewer than 5% of the sample. The proportion of juveniles engaging in fetishism, obscene phone calls, child molestation, and phone sex was higher than that of adults. Hands-off offenses including fetishism, voyeurism, and pornography use had a higher mean number of acts than hands-on offenses such as child molestation and unwanted rubbing and touching. In this sample, child-molesting juveniles had fewer victims than JSOs engaging in voyeurism, exhibitionism, and unwanted rubbing or touching.

Although participants overwhelmingly reported that they had been honest in their responding to the items on the questionnaire, participants who demonstrated greater concern with reporting socially desirable responses also reported engaging in fewer paraphilic behaviors. In addition, more participants with high social desirability scores reported total honesty. This may be an example of giving a socially desirable response. In studying sexual offenders, this highlights the importance of assessing and controlling for social desirability. Self-reports of honesty in responding may be confounded by a desire to provide socially desirable responses and may not provide an accurate measure of how honest JSOs actually are. Because of socially desirable responding, self-report data obtained from juveniles are probably minimal values. JSOs who respond in ways that they perceive as socially desirable on the social desirability scale may also be responding to other questions in this manner, and our data indicate that they are less likely to admit to engaging in paraphilic behaviors. When assessing JSOs, it is crucial to perform an assessment that takes into account socially desirable responding and denying or minimalizing behaviors. Results of studies with juvenile offenders must be anchored to a measure of social desirability, or researchers must approach JSOs in such a way that they are able to obtain more accuracy in collection of data, such as using a certificate of confidentiality, which has been shown to increase reporting of paraphilic behaviors in adult samples (Abel et al., 1987).

Molestation of children tends to involve younger siblings or known nonfamily members, and JSOs tend to coerce or trick rather than threaten or rough up the child. This indicates that JSOs select victims who are easily accessible with whom they have a relationship. Whereas most of the JSOs in this sample had molested children, more than a quarter of the JSOs had not been blamed for molesting a child, and 20% of the boys in the sample had never been blamed for a hands-on offense. However, of the quarter that had not been blamed for molesting a child, 42% indicated that they had in fact molested a child. Many JSOs engage in behaviors that go undetected. Therefore, to understand the full nature of the JSOs' presenting problem, it is important to assess JSOs for paraphilic behaviors other than their index offenses.

The average age of onset of the various behaviors ranged from 9.7 to 12.4 years, which is considerably younger than what is reported (Abel et al., 1985; Weinrott, 1996). However, previous studies have relied heavily on retrospective reports of adult offenders. Therefore, it is possible that either the adolescents are beginning their sexual offending careers earlier, adult offenders may not accurately recall the age at which they began their sexually abusive behavior, or some combination of both. In either instance, the current study highlights the importance of gathering information from juveniles as soon as they are identified. On identification, JSOs are likely to have committed several offenses with several victims. When investigating age of onset of sexual behaviors, clinicians and researchers must be careful to go back to preadolescent years. Deviant sexual patterns exhibited in preadolescent boys must be taken seriously to prevent later sexual offending and to understand the etiology of paraphilic behavior.

References

Abel, G. G. (1995). *The Abel Questionnaire for Boys.* Available at: Abel Screening, 1280 Peachtree Street NW, Suite 100, Atlanta, GA 30309.
Abel, G. G., J. V. Becker, M. S. Mittlman, J. Cunningham-Rathner, J. L.

Rouleau, and W. D. Murphy. (1987). Self-Reported Sex Crimes of Nonincarcerated Paraphiliacs. *Journal of Interpersonal Violence, 2*:3–25.

Abel, G. G., M. S. Mittelman, and J. V. Becker. (1985). Sexual Offenders: Results of Assessment and Recommendations for Treatment. In H. Ben-Aron, S. I. Hucker and C. D. Webster (eds.), *Clinical Criminology.* Toronto, Canada: M. M. Graphics.

Abel, G. G. and C. Osborn. (2000). The Paraphilias. In M. G. Gelder, J. J. Lopez-Ibor, Jr., and N. C. Andreasen (eds.), *New Oxford Textbook of Psychiatry.* New York: Oxford University Press.

Abel, G. G. and C. Osborn. (1992). The Paraphilias: The Extent and Nature of Sexually Deviant and Criminal Behavior. *Clinical Forensic Psychiatry, 15*:675–687.

Awad, G. A. and E. B. Saunders. (1991). Male Adolescent Sexual Assaulters. *Journal of Interpersonal Violence, 6*:446–460.

Becker, J. V., J. Cunningham-Rathner, and M. S. Kaplan. (1986). Adolescent Sexual Offenders: Demographics, Criminal and Sexual Histories, and Recommendations for Reducing Future Offenses. *Journal of Interpersonal Violence, 1*:431–445.

Becker, J. V., C. D. Harris, and B. D. Sales. (1993). Juveniles Who Commit Sexual Offenses: A Critical Review of Research. In G. C. Nagami Haall, R. Hirschman, J. R. Graham, and M. S. Zaragoza (eds.), *Sexual Aggression: Issues in Etiology, Assessment, and Treatment.* Washington, D.C.: Taylor & Francis.

Bourduin, C. M., S. W. Henggeler, D. M. Blaske, and R. J. Stein. (1990). Multisystemic Treatment of Adolescent Sex Offenders. *International Journal of Offender Therapy and Comparative Criminology, 34*:105–113.

Brannon, J. M. and R. Troyer. (1991). Peer Group Counseling: A Normalized Residential Alternative to the Specialized Treatment of Adolescent Sex Offenders. *International Journal of Offender Therapy and Comparative Criminology, 35*:225–234.

Davis, G. and H. Leitenberg. (1987). Adolescent Sex Offenders. *Psychological Bulletin, 101*:417–427.

Erdman, H. P., M. H. Klein, and J. H. Greist. (1985). Direct Patient Computer Interviewing. *Journal of Consulting and Clinical Psychology, 51*:760–773.

Finkelhor, D. and J. Dziuba-Leatherman. (1994). Victimization of Children. *American Psychologist, 49*:173–183.

Furby, L., M. Weinrott., and L. Blackshaw. (1989). Sex Offender Recidivism: A Review. *Psychological Bulletin, 105*:3–30.

Hunter, J. and D. Santos. (1990). The Use of Specialized Cognitive-Behavioral Therapies in the Treatment of Adolescent Sexual Offenders. *International Journal of Offender Therapy and Comparative Criminology, 34*:239–247.

Kahn, T. J. and M. A. Lafond. (1988). Treatment of the Adolescent Sexual Offender. *Child and Adolescent Social Work, 5*:135–148.

Metzner, J. L. and G. D. Ryan. (1995). Sexual Abuse Perpetration. In G. P. Sholevar (ed.), *Conduct Disorders in Children and Adolescents.* Washington, D.C.: American Psychiatric Press.

Ochs, E. P., M. Meana, L. Pare, K. Mah, and Y. M. Binik. (1994). Learning About Sex Outside the Gutter: Attitudes Toward a Computer Sex Expert System. *Journal of Sex and Marital Therapy, 20*:86–102.

Ryan, G. (1997). Juvenile Sex Offenders: Defining the Population. In G. D. Ryan and S. L. Lane (eds.), *Juvenile Sexual Offending: Causes, Consequences, and Correction.* San Francisco: Jossey-Bass.

Ryan, G., T. J. O. Miyoshi, J. L. Metzner, R. D. Krugman, and G. E. Fryer. (1996). Trends in a National Sample of Sexually Abusive Youth. *Journal of the Academy of Child and Adolescent Psychiatry, 35*:17–25.

Vizard, E., E. Monck, and P. Misch. (1995). Child and Adolescent Sexual Abuse Perpetrators: A Review of the Research Literature. *Journal of Child Psychology and Psychiatry and Related Disciplines, 36*:731–756.

Weinrott, M. R. (1996). *Juvenile Sexual Abuse: A Critical Review.* Unpublished manuscript.

Weinrott, M. R. and M. Saylor. (1991). Self Report of Crimes Committed by Sex Offenders. *Journal of Interpersonal Violence, 6*:286–300.

9

Voyeurism:
A Criminal Precursor and Diagnostic Indicator to a Much Larger Sexual Predatory Problem in Our Community

Joseph Davis

Sexual assault is one of the most serious and fast growing violent crimes in the United States. The National Victim Center, located in Bethesda, Maryland, reported that more than 700,000 women are raped or sexually assaulted annually (American Medical Association, 1995). Furthermore, there is the growing concern regarding serial rape and sexually related homicide (Prentky, Burgess, Rokous, Lee, Hartman, Ressler, and Douglas, 1989). All sexual acts, paraphilias, and sexually related crimes, organized or disorganized, begin with fantasy, and when an individual suffers from sexual aberrations or perversions, the fantasy and corresponding behaviors often take on a deviant sexual nature (Freud, 1938; Hazelwood and Warren, 1995a). Considerable care should be taken in identifying and isolating the antecedent behavioral predictors of sexual offenders (McCall, 1993). Paraphilias, particularly voyeurism, are common to sexual offenders. By recognizing these public order sexual offenses that contribute to and reinforce violent sexual fantasies, the early identification of, intervention with, and potential prosecution of these offenders can occur prior to any future sexual offenses being committed (Davis, 1996; Hazelwood and Warren, 1995a).

Reprinted from *Current Perspectives on Sex Crimes*, edited by Ronald Holmes and Stephen Holmes (2002), pp. 73–84. © 2002 Sage Publications, Inc. Edited and reprinted by permission of the publisher.

Gender Identity Disorder and the Paraphilias

Diagnostically, a paraphilia is a compulsive condition responsive to, and predicated and dependent upon, an unusual and personally or socially unacceptable stimulus that is perceived in the visual imagery of fantasy for optimal initiation and maintenance of erotosexual arousal and the facilitation or attainment of orgasm (University of Washington, 1996). Furthermore, a paraphilia ("para," meaning the intended object or type of deviant behavior attached to, and "philia," meaning next to, beyond, or close to love) is a perversion of behavior (usually a sexual deviancy). In the clinical nomenclature, a paraphilia (e.g., voyeurism) is typically considered to be associated with unusual or bizarre sexual practices and attachments. The essential diagnostic features of a paraphilia (considered a sexual and gender identity disorder) as determined by the *Diagnostic and Statistical Manual of Mental Disorders, Fourth Edition* (DSM-IV) (American Psychiatric Association, 1994), are (a) recurrent, intensely sexually arousing fantasies, sexual urges, or behaviors; (b) the possible involvement of nonhuman objects; (c) the involvement of real or imagined suffering or humiliation of one's self or one's partner; and (d) the possible involvement of children, adolescents, or other nonconsenting partners.

The paraphilias listed in the *DSM-IV* include exhibitionism, fetishism, frotteurism, pedophilia, sexual masochism, sexual sadism, transvestic fetishism, telephone scatology or scatologia, voyeurism (Peeping-Tomism, inspectionalism, scoptophilia), and atypical paraphilias not otherwise specified (DSM-IV NOS), such as necrophilia, autoerotica (also referred to as asphyxophilia, hypoxphilia, psychosexual asphyxia, sexual asphyxia, autoerotic asphyxia fatality, Kotzwarraism, and Susanna Hill Syndrome), and even cannibalism. The most predominant paraphilias treated in psychiatric forensic inpatient clinics or hospitals are voyeurism, exhibitionism, and pedophilia (American Psychiatric Association, 1994). Abel et al. (1988) (as cited in Hazelwood, Dietz, and Warren, 1995) documented that people tend to suffer from multiple paraphilias, and that individuals identified as having one paraphilia generally suffered from two or three additional forms of sexual deviation (Hazelwood and Warren, 1995a). These fantasy-derived, paraphilic-related behaviors, often referred to in the law enforcement community as public order offenses, are commonly acted out and exhibited during sexual crimes (Hazelwood and Warren, 1995b).

Voyeurism as a Paraphilia

Yalom (1960, as cited in Lester, 1975) defined the term *voyeurism* as an "exaggerated desire to see by stealth, a member of the opposite sex (generally) in some stage of undress, redress, in a sexual act or the act of excretion" (22) and "a wanton desire which is so intense that it surpasses in importance the sexual act" (23) often driven by obsession and compulsion. Davis (1992) viewed voyeurism as an "ego-syntonic" compulsion (meaning in the desired direction of thinking that is acceptable to one's ego) that an individual does not object to, but only yields to, in terms of a compulsive or ritualistic abreaction or action (a psychological excitement and subconscious intrapersonal thrill of "acting out a peeping fantasy on an unsuspecting victim" without getting caught). Furthermore, according to Davis (1992), voyeurs rarely, if ever, seek out psychiatric or mental health services on their own. Many voyeurs who receive treatment typically do so as a direct result of a public safety issue and police involvement as it relates often to court-mandated or enforced treatment in an outpatient or inpatient forensic mental health setting (Davis, 1992, 1996; Yalom, 1960).

The paraphilic focus of voyeurism involves the achievement of sexual stimulation and pleasure through seclusion while in the unsuspected act of looking. In the clinical vernacular and nomenclature, voyeurs and voyeurism are often referred to as Peeping Toms, Peeping-Tomism, or inspectionism (Bartol, 1995). Due to the attainment of intrapersonal pleasure through a clandestine act of peeping (i.e., typically young male heterosexuals looking in women's windows), peepers experience sexual gratification through covertly (by stealth) observing unsuspecting individuals. Usually targeting female strangers, voyeurs enjoy viewing women who are in the process of disrobing, those who are partially nude or nude, and those who are about to engage in consensual sexual activity. Generally, the voyeur obtains most of his sexual gratification through the act of looking and does not seek out real sexual activity with the observed person (American Psychiatric Association, 1994; Forrest, 1994). However, the voyeur will fantasize and imagine having compulsory sexual relations (often leading to imagined or real masturbation and a climax with the unsuspecting victim) as represented in the postcognitive fantasy process of the perpetrator on or after leaving the victim's personal property (Forrest, 1994).

The essential diagnostic features to determine voyeurism, as outlined by the *DSM-IV*, are (a) a pattern of exhibited behavior no less than

6 months in duration; (b) recurring and intensely sexual arousing fantasies, sexual urges, or behaviors involving the act of observing an unsuspecting person who is naked, in the process of disrobing, or engaging in sexual activity; and (c) fantasies, sexual urges, or behaviors that cause clinically significant distress or impairment in social, occupational, or other important areas of functioning (American Psychiatric Association, 1994). However, Hazelwood and colleagues (Hazelwood et al., 1995; Hazelwood and Warren, 1995a, 1995b) noted that even though the first two clinical features outlined here are represented, serial voyeurists often feel very little distress or impairment other than an "excitatory autonomic physiological response" from viewing. Furthermore, voyeurists show habitual patterns of ritualistic behavior much like those of drug addicts in performing ritualistic or routine peepings while trolling through targeted neighborhoods for unsuspecting victims (Davis, 1992, 1996). Some had referred to voyeurism as an addiction of activity or an activity addiction involving a ritual of routine behavior that has some gratification attached to it (Davis, 1992, 1996; Hazelwood et al., 1995).

Voyeurism is a form of compulsion—a behavioral pattern that stems from the thoughts of extremely sexually perverse acts, termed obsessions. Many crimes that appear to be sexually motivated or related have their origins in such obsessive-compulsive, ritualistic behaviors. Obsessions are often irrational or unwanted cognitive thoughts that relentlessly persist and are forced into the individual's stream of consciousness and psyche. Furthermore, the voyeurist may develop a maladjusted lifestyle as a direct result of the relentless obsessions (Reese, 1979). Voyeurs feel compelled to peep by engaging in this sexually deviant behavior repeatedly (much like a ritualistic process).

Voyeuristic behavior is often accompanied by autoerotic, masturbatory activities during the voyeuristic process or in a latent response to the cognitive trace memory of the visualized and directed sexual arousal and subsequent excitement witnessed (Forrest, 1994).

Voyeurism and other sexual deviations have been established and traced through impressions received during psychosexual development in childhood. Conditioning, reinforcement, and overlearning as factors contribute to the early development of voyeurism (Forrest, 1994). Sigmund Freud (1938) concluded that there is something inherent or congenital (possibly biological) about voyeurism. He also believed that many sexual deviations in certain individuals are a direct result from being predisposed to perversions as they are brought into prominence by powerful maternal and paternal influences during abnormal psychosexual development. Moreover, he stated that many people have these perversions, and that the internal substrate of all perversions or sexual deviations is demonstrable in childhood. (Although all impulses manifest themselves in moderate intensity, many never reach a level that involve breaking the law.) Later in life, sexual deviates fail to repress (a protective ego defense mechanism) their primary process-centered or -oriented thinking and their impulses, and they are believed to either conserve the infantile state of their sexuality or regress to it sexually (Fenichel, 1945; Freud, 1938). Forrest (1994) also indicated that voyeurism is an infantile or childhood sexual fixation. Based on this theory of psychosexual regression, the experiences during the infantile state and childhood pertaining to the process of sexual development should be examined (Freud, 1938).

Demographic Profiles of the Voyeurist Paraphile

Davis and Bernstein (1996) completed a review of the psychiatric and medical literature on sexual deviancy. Davis (1992), Gebhard, Gagnon, Pomeroy, and Christensen (1965), and Yalom (1960) established demographic backgrounds and profiles of the voyeurist.

In 1984, the Office of Juvenile Justice and Delinquency Prevention funded a study focusing on serial rape. The research and study were a collaborative effort by the Federal Bureau of Investigation's National Center for the Analysis of Violent Crime (NCAVC) and Ann Wolbert Burgess, a professor of mental health and nursing science at the University of Pennsylvania. Forty-one incarcerated serial rapists who were responsible for 837 rapes and more than 400 attempted rapes were clinically interviewed. The psychosexual development of the subjects (one of the primary interests and foci of the study) determined that voyeurism was the predominant past or present sexual behavior in these predators (68%), which began during their childhood or adolescence (Hazelwood and Warren, 1995b).

Case # 1

Troy, one of the subjects, began window peeping at the age of 14. At 17, he spied on a 24-year-old woman and found her especially appealing sexually. He began to focus his voyeuristic activities on her and eventually observed her making love to her boyfriend. This so enraged him that he decided to rape her. After she had gone to sleep one evening, he entered through an unlocked window and jumped on her. She awoke and began screaming. In a panic, he grabbed a handful of tissues from the bedside table, pushed them in her mouth, and accidentally suffocated her. Five days later, he was arrested for voyeurism in the same neighborhood. He was not questioned about the death because he was "just a peeper." Seven years later, he confessed to the unsolved crime, but he was not believed until he gave information about the death scene that only the killer would have known (Hazelwood and Warren, 1995b).

Voyeurs are frequently detected by law enforcement or the person or people being watched (Forrest, 1994). Because of repetitive masturbation, voyeurs are often arrested for indecent exposure or public indecency (a lewd exposure of the body done with the intent to arouse or to satisfy the sexual desire of the voyeur) (Reese, 1979). Moreover, voyeurism is also considered an invasion of privacy, which tends to cause emotional distress to many victims, as compared to exhibitionism (Posner, 1992). Sexual offenses such as voyeurism, exhibitionism, fetishism, and obscene phone calls are referred to in the law enforcement community as nuisance or public order offenses. However, because of the nature of voyeuristic activities, serial or repetitive voyeurism is correlated with violent behavior. Despite the correlation with violent behavior, voyeurs are rarely psychopaths or sexual predatory criminals. However, voyeurism does include an element of sexual related sadism (Forrest, 1994).

Similar to voyeurism, the conception of sadistic sexual behavior occurs during childhood. Freud (1938) stated that when children witness sexual acts between adults and cannot understand the acts, they conceive of the sexual act as maltreating or overpowering. This childhood impression contributes to the sadistic disposition toward the sexual instinct. The sexuality of most men shows aggression—the desire to subdue their sexual object by any means other than normal courting—and suggests that sadism would then correspond to the aggressive component of the sexual instinct (Freud, 1938).

In a study assessing aggression in violent offenders, Dr. Dewey Cornell and colleagues at the University of Virginia determined that aggression was correlated with criminal psychopathology and a history of violent offenses (Cornell, Hawk, and Warren, 1996). Furthermore, Serin and colleagues (Serin, Malcolm, Khanna, and Barbaree, 1994) found in their study of 81 incarcerated sexual offenders that a significant relationship existed between psychopathy, as defined by the Hare Psychopathy Checklist—Revised (Hare, 1980), and deviant sexual arousal. Additionally, Hazelwood and Warren (1995a) stated that aggression, sex, and power are the underlying motivations for sexual assault and are expressed in complex sexual fantasies.

Case # 2

> As a teenager, one sexual sadist peeped throughout his neighborhood, masturbating as he watched women undressing or having sex. At home, he masturbated repeatedly to fantasies in which he incorporated what he had seen while peeping. As a young adult, he made obscene phone calls, which lead to his first arrest when he agreed to meet a victim (who had informed the police prior to the meeting). He later exposed himself to a series of victims, which he eventually explained was for the purpose of eliciting their reaction of "shock and fear." He followed women home from shopping malls, determined how much cover was available for peeping and entering the home, eventually raped a series of women. In his early rapes, he depended on weapons of opportunity, but later carried with him a rape kit, which consisted of adhesive duct type, handcuffs, precut lengths of rope, and a .45-caliber semiautomatic handgun. He became progressively more violent in his sexual assaults, torturing his victims by beating, burning, or pulling their breasts. His violence escalated to the point that he pummeled one victim so severely that she lost both breasts. He forcibly raped more than 50 women and was actually contemplating murder when he was finally apprehended (Hazelwood et al., 1995).

Courtship disorders directly refer to the underlying disturbances involving voyeurism, frotteurism (rubbing or touching), preferential rape, and exhibitionism. A study by Freund (1990) determined that men with courtship disorders did not differ from rapists in their responses during phallometric testing. Additionally, these authors found that 57% of their subjects (n = 195), rapists, admitted to engaging in a paraphilic act of voyeurism, frotteurism, sadism, or exhibitionism. Furthermore, Abel and colleagues (see Hazelwood et al., 1995) reported that 53% of their sample population also showed paraphilic behavior (Seto and Kuban, 1996). Investigators should not be misled by the fact that the sexual sadist usually has a history of nuisance offenses (Hazelwood and Warren, 1995b).

Voyeurs usually operate in a circular pattern, close to or near the neighborhood in which they reside. They tend to develop a pattern or route in which they patrol the neighborhood. Often, voyeurs operate or troll at the same time each evening (Reese, 1979). In a recent study conducted at the University of Virginia's Institute of Law, Psychiatry and Public Policy in Charlottesville, Virginia, in collaboration with the

Federal Bureau of Investigation's Behavioral Science Services Unit and NCAVC, on the temporal sequencing and cognitive mapping of serial rapists, the researchers and agencies reported that the majority of their subjects (n = 108) attacked victims within a half-mile of the subjects' homes. Furthermore, the rapists who lived in one city and committed the crime of rape or attempted rape generally lived within 3.14 miles of their offenses and did not travel further than 4.93 miles (Warren, Reboussin, and Hazelwood, 1996).

Fantasy and Behavior

Sexual acts, whether considered normal or perverse, originate in fantasy (Hazelwood and Warren, 1995a). Although deviant sexual fantasies are common to even normal individuals, these individuals usually repress (as a defense mechanism) their instinctual impulses and, instead, abide by contrived cultural and socially acceptable behaviors (Forrest, 1994; Freud, 1938; von Krafft-Ebing, 1965). Furthermore, the sexual offender disregards society's rules and acts freely upon his sexual impulses and desires (Freud, 1938).

Similar to an artist whose visualizations, as expressed through a certain artistic medium, are transformed from an abstract mental image to a tangible and real creation, voyeuristic behavior originates in visualizations and fantasies. This suggests an element of creativity (in an aesthetic sense) in the cognitive processes of the voyeuristic offender (Gendel and Bonner, 1984). Just as a killer leaves his signature at a crime scene, I believe that the sexual offender's fantasy is "painted with his own brush," meaning that the design and construction of his fantasy is as unique to him as were the often distorted and abstract creations of artists like Pablo Picasso or Salvador Dali (Lewin, 1996). No matter which medium the offender chooses to transfer his unique and personal interests, the crime is usually the product of the voyeuristic offender's fantasy (just as the painting is the product of an artist's visualization).

The cognitive-behavioral relationship between fantasy and the resulting behavior—whether voyeurism, serial rape, or sexual homicide—is bidirectional. The internal fantasy sets the parameters for such behaviors. Also, the procedural steps to follow along with the prescribed acts to be done (symbolically done in fantasy), as well as the actual behaviors when carried out, help to redefine, refine, improve, and vividly vitalize the fantasy, eventually leading to an acting-out (abreaction) on that fantasy as a crime. Much time is spent on developing and ruminating in fantasy, often leading the offender to harbor such deviant sexual desires and instincts since his childhood (Freud, 1938; von Krafft-Ebing, 1965). Most often, in the initial phase of fantasy development, the future offender will spend time thinking about and rehearsing the sexual act itself. The victims of the acts are often just imaginary and faceless. As the compulsion amplifies, the faceless victims often no longer suffice. The offender begins to eroticize his fantasy by acting out his craving through compulsory behavior to see real, unsuspecting people in their homes. Usually, the first real people he places in his fantasy are those around him, in his neighborhood, workplace, or school. For the first time, the offender begins to look at people as objects and not as human beings (Holmes and Holmes, 1996). This is similar to Freud's concept of the "libidinal sexual object," with the exception that there is no intention at all of any normalcy in the relationship created within the fantasy (Freud, 1938; von Krafft-Ebing, 1965). The offender is almighty and omnipotent with each successful peep. He is the one in control as the object (unsuspecting victim) is provided for his pleasure, to do with as he desires (Holmes and Holmes, 1996). As an example, early in his criminal career, a young Ted Bundy prowled local neighborhoods, looking at unsuspecting women in the midst of their sexual acts or while undressing. Subsequently, these images and developmental stages helped fuel Bundy's need to further his violent fantasies, which would later be used as an internalized cognitive script for his own sexually driven sadistic crimes (Davis, 1996).

Paraphilias are fantasy-driven behaviors (Hazelwood and Warren, 1995a). As the voyeur observes his victims, he actively fantasizes about joining in sexual activities with them. A voyeur will often fantasize over having one or more sexual experiences with the observed person, but in reality, his observations are a replacement for his own unmet sexual needs and acts (Davis, 1992; Forrest, 1994; von Krafft-Ebing, 1965). Prentky et al. (1989) defined fantasy as an elaborate set of cognition or thoughts, characterized by mental preoccupation, rehearsal, and an anchored emotion originating in semilucid daydreaming. As previously mentioned, voyeurism, as reported by Freud (1938) and von Krafft-Ebing (1965), is the fixation of a prescribed, precursory sexual aim; an aim toward fulfilling the ungratified sexual instinct and drive. Deviation to the sexual aim in voyeurs can be seen as an artistic sublimation (a defense mechanism to protect the violated, fragile ego state). In the same way an artist is influenced by his or her surroundings to create the image that he or she sees, so too is the voyeur. The deviant sexual excitations, developed by the process of sublimation, are manifested, used, and acted out in other areas of the voyeur's life (Freud, 1938; von Krafft-Ebing, 1965).

It is well reported in the literature that violent sex offenders fantasize about their crimes well in advance of acting out on them
(Hazelwood et al., 1995; Hazelwood and Warren, 1995a, 1995b;
Holmes and Holmes, 1996; Prentky et al., 1989; Ressler, Burgess, and
Douglas, 1988; Serin et al., 1994). In a study involving sexually sadistic
serial murders, Dr. Janet Warren, a professor at the University of
Virginia, and her colleagues (Warren et al., 1996) reported that 85% of
the subjects (n = 20) revealed consistent violent fantasies—featuring a
ritualized, repetitive core fantasy—in addition to multiple paraphilic
behaviors. The fantasy provided an internal script that they followed
during the offenses (Hazelwood and Warren, 1995a).

Case # 3

> Sam, a 24-year-old male, preselected his victims through peeping
> activities. He then watched his victim's home to establish a pattern of
> behavior. After deciding to commit rape, he waited until the victim
> had gone to sleep, entered the home, and placed his hand over her
> mouth. He advised the victim(s) that he did not intend to harm them if
> they cooperated. He raped more than 20 women before he was appre-
> hended (Hazelwood and Warren, 1995a).

Voyeurism places real people into the offender's mind, and from
that point, they are his; he owns them. If he wants to rape, he will, and
if he wants to murder, then he will (Holmes and Homes, 1996).
Although a correlation does not mean a certain causation, research on
serial rapists and sexual murderers has shown that a majority of the perpetrators studied have histories of voyeuristic-type behavior. Through
the investigation of serial sexual offenders and sexually related murderers, research has shown a high correlation between fantasy and serial
rape or sexually related homicide (Hazelwood et al., 1995; Hazelwood
and Warren, 1995b). The fantasy acts as a script, which these types of
offenders follow to the last detail. Moreover, the criminal behavior dis-
played in these offenses provides investigators with an astute insight
into the violent fantasies harbored within the offender's psyche
(Holmes and Holmes, 1996).

Conclusion

Overall, voyeurism does not always generalize to serial rape or sexual
homicide, but such fantasy-driven behaviors are common to a majority

of serial rapists and sexual murderers (Hazelwood et al., 1995; Hazelwood and Warren, 1995b). Although correlation does not mean a certainty of causation, such characteristic behaviors, like voyeurism, should be considered, both clinically and legally, red flags for other sexually deviant offenses. Considering that voyeurism is classified as a *DSM.*, Axis-I Gender Identity Disorder in the *DSM-IV* (American Psychiatric Association, 1994), the offender should be evaluated psychologically by also identifying, in addition to voyeurism, other potential mental disorders as outlined in the *DSM-IV*, such as Axis-II, Personality Disorders. Instead of treating the voyeur as a nuisance, public order, or misdemeanant sex offender, the voyeur should be assessed for probable dangerousness and future predatory threat, as well as the potential to commit a physical act of violence upon another person. Although individuals who are diagnosed with a mental disease, defect, or illness are not statistically noted to be violent per se (about 1% of the mental health population is recognized to be potentially violent), such a condition could exacerbate violent behavior for individuals with a propensity toward violence (Bartol, 1995; Davis, 1992, 1996; Lewin, 1996).

By recognizing the antecedent events that contribute to the development and reinforcement of deviant sexual fantasies, early identification and intervention with potential and actual offenders (i.e., treatment, incarceration, or both) is imperative in order to limit or decrease "first-strike" offenses or additional strike offenses from being carried out (Davis, 1996; Hazelwood and Warren, 1995a). Finally, as the projected frequency of public order offenses increases, more aggressive legal sanctions and penalties in terms of punishment must be legislatively orchestrated, designed, and implemented into our current system of justice. Also, an early identification system identifying potential offenders—both first-time and repeat offenders is pertinent and instrumental to the prevention of future sexually related offenses.

References

American Medical Association. (1995). *Sexual Assault in America.* Online. Available at: http://www.ama-assn.org/public/releases/assault/action.html.

American Psychiatric Association. (1994). *Diagnostic and Statistical Manual of Mental Disorders*. 4th ed. Washington, D.C.: American Psychiatric Association.

Bartol, C. R. (1995). *Criminal Behavior: A Psychosocial Approach*. Englewood Cliffs, NJ: Prentice Hall.

Cornell, D., G. Hawk, and J. Warren. (1996). *Assessment of Aggression in Violent Criminal Defendants.* Online. Available at: http://ness.sys. virginia.edu/ilppp/airaved.html.

Davis, J. A. (1996). *Criminal Investigative Analysis: Criminal and Psychological Profiling* (Lecture). San Diego, CA.

Davis, J. A. (1992). *Forensic Psychology, Psychiatry and the Law: The Public Order Offenders* (Lecture). San Diego, CA.

Davis, J. and M. Bernstein. (1996). *Prevalence of Voyeurism in San Diego County.* Unpublished report.

Fenichel, O. (1945). *The Psychoanalytic Theory of Neurosis.* New York: Norton.

Forrest, G. G. (1994). *Alcoholism and Human Sexuality.* Northvale, NJ: Jason Aronson.

Freud, S. (1938). Three Contributions to the Theory of Sex. In A. A. Brill (ed.), *The Basic Writing of Sigmund Freud.* New York: The Modern Library.

Freund, K. (1990). Courtship Disorders. In W. L. Marshall, D. R. Laws, and H. E. Barbaree (eds.), *Handbook of Sexual Assault: Issues, Theories, and Treatment of the Offender.* New York: Norton.

Gebhard, P. H., J. H. Gagnon, W. B. Pomeroy, and C. V. Christensen. (1965). *Sex Offenders.* New York: Harper & Row.

Gendel, W. S. and E. J. Bonner. (1984). Gender Identity Disorders and Paraphilias. In H. H. Goldman (ed.), *Review of General Psychiatry.* Rockville, MD: Lange.

Hare, R. D. (1980). *The Psychopathy Checklist—Revised.* Victoria, BC: Author.

Hazelwood, R. R., P. E. Dietz, and J. I. Warren. (1995). The Criminal Sexual Sadist. In R. R. Hazelwood and A. W. Burgess (eds.), *Practical Aspects of Rape Investigation: A Multidisciplinary Approach.* Boca Raton, FL: CRC Press.

Hazelwood, R. R. and J. I. Warren. (1995a). The Relevance of Fantasy in Serial Sexual Crime Investigation. In R. R. Hazelwood and A. W. Burgess (eds.), *Practical Aspects of Rape Investigation: A Multidisciplinary Approach.* Boca Raton, FL: CRC Press.

Hazelwood, R. R. and J. I. Warren. (1995b). The Serial Rapist. In. R. R. Hazelwood and A. W. Burgess (eds.), *Practical Aspects of Rape Investigation: A Multidisciplinary Approach.* Boca Raton, FL: CRC Press.

Holmes, R. M. and S. T. Holmes. (1996). *Profiling Violent Crimes: An Investigative Tool.* 2nd ed. Thousand Oaks, CA: Sage.

Lester, D. (1975). *Unusual Sexual Behavior: The Standard Deviations.* Springfield, IL: Charles C. Thomas.

Lewin, B. R. (1996). The Assessment of the Cognitive and Affective Antecedent Conditions to Assist in the Prediction of Aggression and Violent Behavior. Unpublished manuscript, California State University, San Diego.

McCall, G. J. (1993). Risk Factors and Sexual Assault Prevention. *Journal of Interpersonal Violence, 8(2)*:277–295.

Posner, R. A. (1992). *Sex and Reason.* Cambridge, MA: Harvard University Press.

Prentky, R. A., A.W. Burgess, F. Rokous, A. Lee, C. Hartman, R. Ressler, and J.

Douglas. (1989). The Presumptive Role of Fantasy in Serial Sexual Homicide. *American Journal of Psychiatry, 146(7)*:887–891.

Reese, J. T. (1979). *A Treatise On The Medical Jurisprudence of Insanity.* 2nd ed. Boston: William D. Tickner.

Ressler, R. K., A. W. Burgess, and J. E. Douglas. (1988). *Sexual Homicide: Patterns and Motives.* Lexington, MA: Lexington Books.

Serin, R. C., P. B. Malcolm, A. Khanna, and H. E. Barbaree. (1994). Psychopathy and Deviant Sexual Arousal in Incarcerated Sexual Offenders. *Journal of Interpersonal Violence, 9(1)*:3–31.

Seto, M. C., and M. Kuban. (1996). Criterion-Related Validity of a Phallometric Test for Paraphilic Rape and Sadism. *Behavior Research and Theory, 34(2)*:175–183.

University of Washington. (1996). *Sexual Dictionary.* Online. Available at: ftp://ftp.u.washington.edu/public/sfpse/sex/sexdict.txt.

von Krafft-Ebing, R. (1965). *Psychopathia Sexualis.* New York: Scarborough.

Warren, J., R. Reboussin, and R. Hazelwood. (1996). The Temporal Sequencing and Cognitive Mapping of Serial Rapists. Available online at: http://ness/ sys.virginia.edu/ilppp/serialrape.html.

Yalom, I. D. (1960). Aggression and Forbiddenness in Voyeurism. *Archives in General Psychiatry, 3*:305–319.

PART 4

SOCIOLOGICAL SEXUAL DEVIANCE

Sociological sexual deviance alludes to sexual behaviors that individuals participate in within a specific, social support structure. Associates recruit other members, socialize them regarding proper deportment, engage others to participate in the acts, and provide support for those involved. Comparable to pathological deviance, sociological deviance violates many cultural and religious ideals. However, even though these acts are usually condemned by conventional society, these actions, depending on the locale, are not always considered criminal acts. These behaviors are widely practiced with general knowledge of their existence by the general public. The chapters in this final section examine six types of sociological sexually deviant behavior, including the participants and the contexts in which these deviant sexual behaviors are pursued.

The first article by Sweet and Tewksbury examines characteristics and activities of women who earn their living as strippers. Motivation, interaction, and the challenge of a "deviant" lifestyle are investigated to understand the occupational and organizational norms of strippers. While a majority of society may in fact deem exotic dancing a degrading vocation, others see it as a lucrative profession.

The "oldest," and probably most controversial, money-making profession that has been considered sexually deviant is prostitution, the subject of the second chapter in this section. Rochelle brings the reader into the world of the female streetwalking prostitute. Although individual circumstances and commonalities among these women are examined, no "profile" could be compiled to explain why women, in general, would choose to prostitute themselves. However, it is obvious to these women, their families, and those who encounter them, what they do for a living. The fact that their "deviance" is well known and managed points to the sociologically interesting aspects of such behaviors.

In an interchange of gender and circumstance, the third chapter of the section investigates the most visible of male prostitutes, the juvenile, male street hustler. Not only does the reproach of being a prostitute exist for these individuals, but so does the stigma of being termed a homosexual. These males differ from their female counterparts in that they are more cautious in their exposure of being in "the life" and are highly concerned with social or familial ostracism. The majority of the juveniles in this study became male hustlers through peer introduction. Friends introduce them to hustling, provide instructions, support their motives, and furnish them with various techniques to successfully carry out this behavior. In other words, this is a socially supported activity, although the support is very different from that provided to women.

In contrast to the first three chapters, the subsequent pieces address sexually deviant interactions that are more formally structured by their participants. In the fourth article, written by Tewksbury, the social and sexual interactions of gay bathhouses are defined, discussed, an deconstructed. Condemned by society for being a deviant gathering place of homosexual males, and additionally denounced as a breeding ground for HIV, these "social clubs" or "health clubs" provide a discreet, organized, erotic environment for men to seek socialization with other gay men and to participate in same-sex activities. The sociological focus is the mix of setting, individuals, and activities that create this unique social structure.

Gay bathhouses are not the only type of establishment or "club" that caters to a distinctive set of individuals considered sociologically sexually deviant. Practitioners of sadomasochistic sexual pursuits, as presented by Moser in the fifth chapter of this section, not only have encounters in established "clubs" but participants in this behavior also have "parties" in rented facilities or within the privacy or their own homes. Although the types of S/M gatherings may differ (male/female, female/female), each is highly structured with rules of etiquette that are expected to be followed by all participants and observers. The general theme of these "parties" is the exhibition of, and the receiving or giving of, various S/M behaviors. Orgasm and/or sexual gratification is not necessarily the goal of the individuals who participate or observe, unlike most individuals involved in sexually deviant activities.

The final chapter in the section visits the world of the swingers. Presented by Bruce and Severance, this chapter demonstrates the ongoing popularity of participation in swinger clubs. Once thought to be a thing of the past, the Internet has allowed swingers to become more organized, recruiting others and promoting their behavior. Generally considered adulterous, these individuals have sex with others with the full knowledge and consent of their spouse and/or mate. Again, the issue for sociologists is the way in which social structures make possible or inhibit these sexual encounters.

All six of these articles address various forms of alternative sexual activities that society deems sexually deviant. While the first three articles deal with unconventional occupations, the last three deal with specific group interactions. All the individuals interviewed for these articles chose to participate in the given activity. As you read these articles, think about what makes an act sociologically sexually deviant. Is it the individual, the action itself, the setting and supportive social structure, or society's concept of the behavior?

Can the categories of these behaviors shift over time? Prostitution, for example, was once considered a totally pathological sexual behavior. However, it is now considered a sociological sexual behavior in many societies. In the United States, prostitution has been legalized in Nevada. As public attitudes progress and change, will society accept prostitution as a normal sexual deviant behavior?

10

"What's a Nice Girl Like You Doing in a Place Like This?" Pathways to a Career in Stripping

Nova Sweet and Richard Tewksbury

Among the most "deviant" occupational and career options available in contemporary society are jobs in the illicit drug economy, politics, and participation in the sex industry. However, within each of these occupational fields the specific jobs available vary widely in both their degree of acceptability and income potential. Within the sex industry, there are a number of occupational choices one may choose: prostitution, performing in pornographic movies, erotic writing, and stripping. This research is concerned with the stripping aspect of the sex industry and the characteristics that are associated with women who choose to enter the industry.

Despite being a part of the sex industry, stripping is widely considered a rather impersonal occupation. Those involved do not know each other, yet they understand one another's needs and implicitly accept the nature and structure of involved transactions. Thus, the "deviant act" becomes much easier to perform for the dancer, becomes more acceptable for patrons, and becomes something that can be engaged in and then forgotten by both customer and dancer as soon as it is over. Notwithstanding the acceptance of strippers by the customer-participants, strippers are widely viewed as "bad" by nonparticipants (and sometimes even by participants) because they challenge all social decorum by the removal of their clothes (Bell, Sloan, and Strickling, 1998; Boles and Garbin, 1974; Carey, Peterson, and Sharpe, 1974; McCaghy and Skipper, 1969; Peretti and O'Connor, 1989; Ronai and Ellis, 1989;

Reprinted from *Sociological Spectrum*, Vol. 20, No. 3 (2000), pp. 325–344. © 2000 Taylor & Francis, Inc. Edited and reprinted by permission of the publisher.

Salutin, 1971; Skipper and McCaghy, 1970, 1971; Thompson and Harred, 1992).

Although investigation of stripping is a relatively fresh area of research, there have been a number of researchers who have developed insightful and informative findings about female strippers and the industry. Researchers have outlined motivational factors (Barron, 1989; Boles and Garbin, 1974; Carey et al., 1974; McCaghy and Skipper, 1969, 1972; Reid, Epstein, and Benson, 1995; Ronai and Ellis, 1989; Salutin, 1971; Skipper and McCaghy, 1970, 1971; Thompson and Harred, 1992), means by which interactions with customers are experienced and managed (Bell et al., 1998; Boles and Garbin, 1974; Forsyth and Deshotels, 1997; Prus and Irini, 1980; Reid et al., 1995; Ronai and Ellis, 1989; Sijuwade, 1995; Thompson and Harred, 1992), as well as occupational and organizational norms of strippers (Bell et al., 1998; Salutin, 1971; Boles and Garbin, 1974; Carey et al., 1974; Enck and Preston, 1988; Forsyth and Deshotels, 1997; Mullen, 1985; Peretti and O'Connor, 1989; Ronai and Ellis, 1989; Thompson and Harred, 1992). On the basis of these studies there is an understanding of who strippers are, and how and why they perform their jobs. However, gaps remain in our understandings; the present research sought to add to our base of understanding regarding the backgrounds and developmental characteristics of women who work in the stripping industry.

Several common background factors have been identified among strippers. Factors associated with women's eventual entrance into stripping include early physical maturity and early sexual experiences, early independence and departure from home, absence of the father from the home prior to adolescence, average educational levels, and a relationship between exhibitionistic behavior and previous job experience (Peretti and O'Connor, 1989; Prus and Irini, 1980; Ronai and Ellis, 1989; Salutin, 1971; Skipper and McCaghy, 1970; Thompson and Harred, 1992).

The majority of strippers reach puberty at an early age and have this accompanied by a significant degree of emotional and social stress. Early physical maturity also tends to bring about heightened sexual attractiveness. Consequently, when these women later become adults they are accustomed to using these attributes to get special and/or extra attention. As long as strippers can remember, their bodies were objects for talk, staring, and sexual passes. Even though these experiences are often humiliating, these women come to the conclusion—usually at some point in their teens—that because their bodies attract men their bodies can bring them money (Peretti and O'Connor, 1989; Prus and

Irini, 1980; Ronai and Ellis, 1989; Salutin, 1971; Skipper and McCaghy, 1970; Thompson and Harred, 1992).

In addition, strippers' backgrounds often show a relationship with their ordinal position in the family. Patterns appear consistent: Firstborn women often seek the company of others outside the family to meet their need for affection, nevertheless, there is no evidence of causal linkage between stripping and ordinal position. However, strippers who were firstborn tend to have experienced broken family ties by age 18, and to have been raised in broken and unstable homes, where they received little attention and affection (Carey et al., 1974; Peretti and O'Connor, 1989; Prus and Irini, 1980; Ronai and Ellis, 1989; Salutin, 1971; Skipper and McCaghy, 1970; Thompson and Harred, 1992). The absence of a male figure appears related to the willingness of women to participate in stripping; such work allows for "special" male attention. If a stripper did have a father present in her childhood home he typically had a disintegrating influence on family relationships (Skipper and McCaghy, 1970). Although firstborn women tend to demonstrate independent qualities and to have experienced broken family ties, and strippers customarily encountered similar circumstances, this is not to imply that firstborn girls without a father in the home are destined to become strippers.

Women who strip are often thought of as being uneducated and "stupid" (Prus and Irini, 1980; Reid et al., 1995; Ronai and Ellis, 1989; Salutin, 1971). Therefore, the educational background of strippers has been, and still is, a relevant arena of inquiry. Research conducted in the 1960s and 1970s suggested that strippers had, on average, an educational level of only Grade 7 or 8. This fact was read to imply that these women did not possess skills suitable for the labor market (Salutin, 1971). More recent research (Reid et al., 1995), however, has indicated that strippers in the 1990s have significantly more education; strippers typically are high school graduates, often with some college experience.

The literature has also suggested congruence between the content of previous jobs and stripping (however, see Lewis, 1998). Strippers have frequently held previous jobs in which the display of their physical attributes was an integral part of job success. These jobs included work as singers, models, actresses, and waitresses/barmaids (Peretti and O'Connor, 1989; Prus and Irini, 1980; Ronai and Ellis, 1989; Salutin, 1971; Skipper and McCaghy, 1970; Thompson and Harred, 1992). Thus, a pattern of exhibitionism is apparent in the strippers' career choices. Although this does not suggest that stripping is the next logical step in a career trajectory, it does suggest that when an opportunity to strip arises, such past job experiences may facilitate women's perceiving stripping as an acceptable occupational alternative.

Although prior research has identified numerous common factors in the backgrounds of strippers—including prior jobs that include the display on one's body, and early physical maturity—it remains unknown whether one factor is more influential than another, or how these factors are related. Discussions in numerous studies attributed the lack of attention and /or absence of a father figure in these women's lives as the foundation for detrimental behaviors and attitudes, including low self-worth, low self-concept, and early sexual experiences. Regardless of what is at the core, it is rather clear that childhood and adolescent experiences, and characteristics of young adulthood, facilitate or attract women to the "deviant" career of stripping. Although informative, the existing literature is, nonetheless, incomplete. The present study seeks to add to this body of knowledge by further assessing both these and additional childhood and young adult experiences of female strippers.

Methods

The present research is based on in-depth, qualitative interviews conducted with a sample of women currently employed as strippers. All interviews were conducted between August and December 1998.

Description of Sample

The twenty women in this sample were, for the most part, experienced strippers. Only 15 percent of the interviewees had been dancing for less than 1 year, 70 percent had between 1–4 years of experience and 15 percent had more than 4 years' experience. These women lived and worked in a variety of cities, including Chicago, Boston, Atlanta, Las Vegas, New York, Tampa, Orlando, St. Louis, Phoenix, San Francisco, Charlotte, Houston, and Louisville. A few women worked in several cities, traveling on a weekly basis; however, most of the sample worked in only one city. The sample ranged in age from 18 to 34 years old. The majority of the sample was Caucasian (60 percent), while the other 40 percent of the sample identifies as African American, Asian, Hispanic, and mixed race. Most (60 percent) of the sample was between 5'0" and 5'4" while the other 40 percent were between 5'6" and 5'11". Most of the sample reported hazel/green eyes and brown hair.

Of the 20 women interviewed, 50 percent were mothers; 60 percent of these women became mothers during their teenage years. At the time of the study, most of the sample were in some kind of relationship; 60 percent reported having a steady boyfriend, 20 percent reported being single/never married, 10 percent had a steady girlfriend, 5 percent were married, and the other 5 percent were divorced.

Research Process

All interviews were conducted by Nova Sweet, who solicited interviews through the course of her work dancing in strip clubs throughout the continental United States. No requests for interviews were denied, although several women who initially volunteered were unable to schedule time.

Interviews were conducted in hotel rooms, homes, automobiles, and by telephone; scheduling constraints and privacy considerations guided the choice of locale. Interviews ranged from 1 to 2 hours in length. A semi-structured format was used, all interviews were audiotape recorded, and analysis was based on verbatim transcripts.

Findings

Overall, this study supported the general patterns, norms, characteristics, and motivations regarding female strippers currently available in the literature. More important, in combination with these factors, we found four additional common issues in the backgrounds and experiences of strippers. We offer four additional issues common to the background of female strippers: athletic background, entertainment background, childhood abuse, and the "ugly duckling syndrome." First we review the support for previously identified factors found in our data and conclude by discussing these four newly identified background factors.

Previously Established Factors

As discussed above, prior researchers have established that women who work as strippers generally both begin sexual activity and physically mature at an early age. Among the women in this sample, two-thirds report their first sexual experience at age 15 or younger, one in three at age 13 or younger. Elaine remembered when she lost her virginity, and what a relief it was to her; "I was like eleven, in the cornfield with Brian. What's so funny is that he actually said afterwards, 'well at least I know you're not gay.' And I was thinking, 'yeah, oh God, thank God.'" Most strippers who become sexually active this early did not recall their early sexual experiences as positive, however. In fact, two of the women reported their early in life, first sexual experiences as rape. Monica recalled that,

> My first sexual experience was when I was fifteen. I was volunteering at a hospital, and my boyfriend at the time brought me down to the basement which was where his office was located, he forced me into a dark cluttered storage room, and that's where I involuntarily lost my virginity.

On the issue of early physical maturity, our data were somewhat less conclusive. Nearly one-half of the women reported having physically matured "faster than other girls." It appears safe to conclude that women who strip share patterns of engaging in sexual experiences at an early age, however they do not necessarily identify as having physically matured at an early age.

Other researchers (Peretti and O'Connor, 1989; Prus and Irini, 1980; Ronai and Ellis, 1989; Salutin, 1971; Skipper and McCaghy, 1970; Thompson and Harred, 1992) have suggested that because many strippers physically mature at an early age they begin to unconsciously use their bodies and looks to get what they want from people. This behavior typically develops into early sexual experiences for these women. However, the existence of such a relationship is not strongly supported by this sample. Although the majority of these women had early sexual experiences these do not appear to be directly connected to their physical maturity. The fact is, many of our women in our study experienced sex at an early age, before having fully matured physically.

Previous research has also suggested important commonalities among strippers regarding their ordinal family position, early independence from home, and the absence of a father figure from the home prior to adolescence. On these issues we found strong support for a relationship with work as a stripper during young adulthood

The majority of women in this research were either firstborns (50 percent) or only children (10 percent). Of the firstborns, nearly all reported early independence from/in home, between 14 to 16 years of age. These women were either teenage mothers, had to join the work force to help a single parent with bills, suffered from sexual, mental, or physical abuse and left home, or were left at home unsupervised to do as they pleased. Among those women who reported being only children, early independence from home was not reported, but rather was primarily focused inside the home. As Brenda, an only child, reflected on her childhood, she recalled that

> My mom was putting herself through med school when I was growing up, I was an only child at that time, and she wasn't home a lot. I took care of myself; I was old enough to stay home by myself for a few hours, so she wasn't there a lot. Med school took up a lot of her time. I strongly feel that somewhere in my childhood I invented this story that I wasn't an okay person, and ever since then I've been doing things to try to prove to myself that I was okay, and dancing was one of those ways.

Sara's situation, as a firstborn child, was very different, but nonetheless focused on early independence. Sara left home at a young age, and explained her reasoning as

> I ran away from home when I was fourteen because I was bored with life. When I turned fifteen I met a guy and got pregnant. I told my parents, they asked me if I was going to get married. I was like I'll just stay with him. So I did, and I had my baby.

Early independence, not ordinal family position, appears to be the more influential factor related with a subsequent career in stripping. Where this becomes most clear is in the fact that for all varieties of women (only children, firstborns, and "others") early independence from home—usually between 12 to 15 years of age—was very common. Women with siblings reported the most traumatic reasons for independence. All of these women indicated they received "absolutely no" parental guidance, stability, or guidelines during adolescence. Common issues in their stories included deadbeat parents; alcoholic and drug abusing parents; physical, mental and sexual abuse by parents, relatives, or friends of parents; being frequently moved from one home environment to another; teenage pregnancy; and being homeless. Early independence for these women, then, can be seen as essentially inevitable. For some women, early independence was essentially forced on them. Jessica reflected on her entry to stripping, pointing out that it was less of a choice than it was the only way she perceived being able to survive.

It was a week before my 18th birthday when I started dancing. I was homeless, I had a one year old son, and I needed to survive. I've been dancing for four years now. . . . I only want to dance long enough to go back to school. I'm thinking I'll be done in about two more years.

Or, as Sable recalled, her family problems revolved around a lack of authority and guidance, "I moved into a aunt's house for a few months, I actually kind of moved around a lot, I was never really welcomed and secure in one spot for very long, and I was given way too much freedom."

Eight of the strippers reported their parents were still married or had at least one or both parents who had died; most commonly, strippers reported their parents had divorced and been remarried. For these women, coming from a "broken home" created important, often detrimental, consequences, beyond pushing them into early independence. Depending on which parent was present and/or active in their lives, developing issues revolved around competition for the attention, affection, acceptance, and praise of the parental figure who was not in the picture. Brenda reflected on the consequences of being raised by a single mother and its effects on her: "I didn't see my mother have very many healthy relationships with men when I was growing up. She's been married four times, my father's been married five times." Of the women who reported growing up in single-parent homes, most were raised by their mothers. Those strippers whose mothers were not their primary caregiver indicated their mothers were either not around, not active or completely uninvolved when it came to their childhood. According to Sara, money, not love, was the reason her father kept custody: "When my parents got divorced my dad took me because he had more money, there was no way my mom could support us." Of the women who were raised by their mothers, the majority reported some kind of ongoing contact with their father. However, although contact may have been maintained, most often these relationships were negatively affected by drug and alcohol abuse, and/or mental/physical/sexual abuse. As Phoebie explained, when her stepfather came into her life everything changed.

My whole life changed when my step-dad came in the picture. He was very abusive mentally, physically, he beat on my mother and my sister and I, and he would never touch my brother. That's what really deterred me from being at home. He wouldn't let us be children, I went from a straight-A student up 'til high school. All of a sudden my sophomore year I started making Fs. I was scared to go home, that's how bad it was.

Although Victoria's father did not sexually abuse her, she recalled a painful childhood:

> My father was both mentally and physically abusive. As long as he never touched my little brother it seemed all right because that's how I was raised. When I was sixteen he about hit my brother but I stepped in the way and stood up to him. Instead of hitting me his punishment was inviting my uncle to the house the next day. I had told him that my uncle tried to molest me, but he didn't care.

Alcohol and drug abuse by parents was one of the most common themes in these strippers' childhoods. Three of every four strippers reported one or both of their parents abused alcohol and fully one-half had at least one parent who abused drugs. Deidra remembered her father's involvement with drugs and his abuse towards her:

> My father has done drugs, he used to deal them. I hate him; he's a piece of shit that doesn't deserve to be able to speak to me. He's done a lot of mean things to me, every abuse possible.

As Veronica recalled her mother, she expressed the strong belief that her mother's lifestyle was a significant influence on her life. "My mother was an alcoholic, she was also a dancer. I think that had a lot to do with how I turned out."

Tying these issues together, the absence of a responsible and caring male figure in a young girl's life coupled with parents who abused both substances and their daughters sets up the scenario from which women moved to employment in the sex industry. Stripping allows for, and facilitates, the pursuit of special attention, especially attention from men.

A second typical characteristic found in the literature on strippers is that strippers have very low levels of education (Prus and Irini, 1980; Ronai and Ellis, 1989; Salutin, 1971). More recent research (Reid et al., 1995) has challenged this finding, showing that a majority of strippers in the 1990s are high school graduates and some have college experience. Our findings parallel this challenge; all but one of the women in this research had graduated from high school. In fact, the slight majority of the women in this sample had some college education. However, only one woman actually held a college degree; most of these women, did however, indicate an intention or desire to return to college.

A third pattern reported in previous research is the association between exhibitionistic behavior and previous jobs held. The literature

(Peretti and O'Connor, 1989; Prus and Irini, 1980; Ronai and Ellis, 1989; Salutin, 1971; Skipper and McCaghy, 1970; Thompson and Harred, 1992) has suggested that women who strip have always been accustomed to using their bodies, good looks, sex appeal, and personalities in their everyday lives, especially in employment. The experiences of this sample reaffirm this finding. The vast majority of these women identified themselves as having exhibitionist tendencies and enjoying being in the spotlight, showing off their bodies. Sophie explained her perspective on showing off, "If there's an opportunity and I'm around people I'll probably take my clothes off. I like the shock value." In relation to prior employment, three-quarters of these women reported being a waitress prior to stripping. Other jobs reported included professional career or management positions, retail, telemarketing, grocery store cashier, legal research, horseback riding instructor, and hospital volunteer. Hence, this sample was consistent with prior research samples in which prior jobs involve the use of their bodies, good looks, and personalities to be accepted and successful.

More interesting details about exhibitionistic behavior and employment were evident in the job aspirations reported by these women. The most common response to inquiries about childhood career aspirations was a desire to be a model. In American society modeling is associated with beauty, popularity, fame, acceptance, praise, and money. There are clear similarities and overlap between aspirations of modeling and the fact that these women strip for a living. Basically, stripping offers everything modeling offers, except for the societal acceptance. Interesting as well is that only one half of these women stated they had a desire to become a dancer when they were young (although for them this did not mean stripping). Rather, these women dreamed of dancing in ballet, music videos, and for backup groups. Only two women stated that stripping was somewhat glamorized in their lives so they had thought about it specifically. Marty is one of these women; as a little girl stripping was glamorized and she was perhaps guided toward stripping.

> When I was little, my grandmother used to come in the room with just her towel and dance around, it was glamorized to me. She used to tell me when I turned eighteen that I could go see male strippers, it was always glamorized to me.

Many women also aspired to own their own businesses. Some envisioned operating an adult entertainment club; others desired more mainstream businesses (beauty salon, or some kind of shop [novelty, coffee, and clothing]). A few women had other aspirations for professional careers (medicine, law, psychology) or other skilled occupations (glass blowing, graphic arts, massage therapist, commercial acting, police officer, or motherhood).

In summary, there is significant evidence offered in this study that supports prior research findings regarding a congruence between the content of previous jobs and stripping. It is true of this sample that most women held previous jobs or participated in activities, that required the display and use of their physical attributes and personalities. The question remains, then, what other factors may be common in the characteristics and backgrounds of female strippers? It is to this issue that discussion turns next.

Previously Unidentified Factors in Strippers' Backgrounds

Prior research has been consistent and supportive of similar factors and characteristics among women who strip for a living. It seems, however, that there are more specific and detailing issues that could add light to, and describe more specifically, the reasons why women embark on a career in the sex industry, as strippers.

In addition to issues previously identified in the literature as relevant, we also assessed qualities we presumed to be prevalent among exhibitionist women, factors we suspected would be related to sex industry employment. These qualities include being outgoing, independent, creative, motivated, and competitive. With these in mind, we hypothesized what other common activities would encourage such behavior. As a result, questions pertaining to a stripper's prior involvement in athletics and mainstream entertainment, as well as histories of abuse were included in interviews. These areas of inquiry, somewhat surprisingly, have not been thoroughly discussed in previous research.

Both athletic and entertainment backgrounds were common in the lives of the women in this sample. Among these strippers, 75 percent had participated in athletics. Athletic backgrounds in order of most to least frequent included: track/cross country, cheerleading, gymnastics, softball, dance (ballet or dance team), volleyball, swimming, soccer, basketball, tennis, Tai Kwon Do, and saddle-breaking horses; one woman performed as a college mascot.

Also, a majority of the sample indicated previous involvement in the entertainment industry. Here the most frequently reported areas of involvement were participation in theater arts, followed closely by modeling, then singing, dancing, and lastly work as an artist. Taken together, these factors suggested something about women who strip and commonalties of earlier life experiences. Generally speaking, these women tend to be very outgoing, independent, creative, motivated, and competitive. These qualities are a necessity when it comes to athletics and entertainment, as well as being critical to success as a stripper.

Therefore, the question arises, Did these women, especially as teenagers, become so accustomed to using their bodies for achievement, or being outgoing in different activities, that when the option and opportunity of stripping was presented, did it seem "natural" to participate? Or, were these women so desperate for attention, affection, and acceptance that when stripping was an option, the attraction was irresistible? This study suggests the answers are between these extremes. An athletic/entertainment background is good for building confidence, attitude, and independence, all excellent qualities of a dancer. However, these women's personalities have been shaped by experiences that create deeper issues regarding attention and affection. Together these characteristics facilitate entry into the life of stripping. Illustrating this point, Monica explained that ever since she could remember, she wanted to be a model and believed a modeling career would give her attention and proclaim her beauty.

> I love having my picture taken. I don't think I was that pretty when I was a little girl and I didn't play with make-up, or Barbie dolls, and I didn't watch Miss America. I didn't think of doing anything like that, I just wanted to model, I wanted the attention.

A second issue not (directly) addressed in the literature is the frequently implied relationship between childhood abuse victimization and subsequent sex industry employment. However, as our research shows, it is not abuse in and of itself that correlates with stripping. Rather, it is abuse victimization and the consequential lowering of self-esteem that is critical. In recollections of childhood and adolescence, two of strippers' most common themes centered on some sort of mental, physical, or sexual abuse and self-descriptions emphasizing a lack of self-confidence, self-worth, or self-esteem. On the basis of our initial contacts— and previous involvements with strippers—we queried these women in detail about their childhoods, looking for indications of all three forms of abuse as well as issues pertaining to self-esteem. What we quickly discovered was that our initial impressions were substantiated, and that strippers experienced a particular variety of low self-esteem, which they repeatedly referenced as the "the ugly duckling syndrome."

Sexual abuse or molestation as a child was reported by one-third of the sample; however, an additional one-third of the sample indicated they had suffered from what they labeled mental and/or physical abuse, rape, and forms of self-inflicted sexual abuse (being promiscuous or "sleeping around" for love and acceptance). These negative experiences were, at least in the minds of these women, directly related to later decisions to enter into stripping. Victoria remembers the negative reinforcement of being unsatisfactory in her father's eyes:

> I think I get my low self-esteem from my childhood. My father and I never had a good relationship at all. I haven't spoken to my dad in five years. Everyday it was like you're not pretty enough, you're not smart enough, and you're not skinny enough. I was never good enough. When you're dancing, everyone thinks you're pretty. You get all kinds of compliments.

The sexual abuse reported by women most often involved molestation by a family member, usually an older male relative (father, stepfather, uncle, or mother's boyfriend); when the abuse was not a family member, these women reported their molesters as a male neighbor. In most cases sexual abuse took place between the ages of 7 to 10 years old, although for some it began as early as age 4 or as late as age 13. Melanie, whose experiences are highly representative of women in this sample, reflected on her recurring molestation experiences as a child:

> The first time I was about 7, and then again when I was about 9. It was different people, family, friends, neighbors, and other people's parents. When I was 7 I had a friend and his dad, who was a teacher, sent him outside to play, I didn't know. I never told my mom until several years later. There's probably been at least three other times it happened during my childhood. I wasn't much for telling people because it was embarrassing to me.

Or as Veronica recalled,

> My first sexual experience was not by choice. It was with an old man who was about sixty, I was eleven. It was actually one of my mother's clients, she was on drugs at the time and so she sent me to sleep with this guy so she could get money. I knew what was going on, and I did have sex with the guy, but I ran away afterwards, and I never did that again.

Finally, clearly showing her belief in the connection between sexual abuse victimization and her current work as a stripper, Brenda recalled her childhood,

> I had no self-esteem when I was growing up. My stepfather sexually molested me, and I had a lot of bad issues with my mom, and her entire family. I just didn't like myself, I didn't think very highly of myself, I didn't think I was an okay person. I didn't have any self-esteem until dancing. You take your clothes off for money, and men look at you like you're a goddess, they tell you how beautiful you are, and it's like a temporary fix for your own inferior issues.

What about those women who did not suffer abuse, but grew up with little self-esteem or a false sense of self-confidence? How did they develop low self-esteem, and in what areas of their lives was it focused? The ugly duckling syndrome illustrates childhood struggles among women who at some point while they were growing up felt awkward, ugly, uncoordinated, or "geeky." As children, many of these women did not feel especially feminine or attractive. One in four indicated that they grew up as tomboys, and four of every five believed that they suffered from the "ugly duckling syndrome." A young woman who feels ugly may turn to stripping for personal validation and confirmation that she has grown to be a beautiful and sexy woman. Ferrah recalls her childhood as extremely unpleasant, largely because of others' reactions to her size. "When I was in high school I was so chubby, I was wicked unpopular. They used to call me Horse Lady because I was so chunky. I was five foot tall and a hundred and forty pounds." Sophie explained her struggle with a memorable childhood experience where she felt taken advantage of.

> I fall into that percentage of dancers who've had some sort of sexual issues, not necessarily abuse. I think the biggest reason I became a dancer was because there was this boy in high school and he got me at my junior prom. I sweared no guy would ever break my heart, and I would be the queen of knowing what men want, and I would use my sexual power to get what I wanted.

Jessica also reported a childhood that had a disintegrating influence on her self-esteem. However, rather than sexual issues, for Jessica her lack of confidence in herself, especially her femininity was related to her appearance and choice of activities.

> I was pretty much a tomboy my whole younger years. Not hard core, but all my friends were boys. I played soccer, softball; I was on the swim team for several years. I do remember being geeky and awkward when I was in elementary school.

During adolescent years negative reinforcements by parental figures and peer groups left these women with low self-esteem and a strong sense of not being physically appealing. For those "ugly ducklings" beauty was simply an unattainable dream. Hence, with maturity and age these girls worked to develop into beautiful women who desired to have their appearances accepted and they found an arena—the strip bar—that would allow for the ultimate praise and worship.

Unfortunately, childhood experiences, such as sexual, mental, or physical abuse as well as being a tomboy or feeling like an ugly duckling, touched the lives of over three-quarters of the women in this sample. The women who suffered due to these factors were deeply scarred. As children they were oppressed, their role models and peers constantly denigrated them, they were told they were not good enough, they were taught they were not appealing physically, their families and peers exposed them to adult behaviors (sex, drugs, alcohol), and they were generally socialized to believe they were flawed or less valuable than others. When these girls became adult women their feelings of being less than adequate did not go away, their feelings were not expressed and these women did what felt natural. They sought out the acceptance of others, especially men. The strip club provided them with the ultimate stadium of acceptance. Strippers never run out of customers who show their approval in so many ways.

Conclusion

Nobody grows up consciously wanting to be an outcast from the mainstream. People enjoy and strive for acceptance and approval from their peers and society. A stripper does not make a carefully thought out decision to enter a world in which she will be bombarded by negative judgements, disgust, negative attitudes, shame, disgrace, and stereotypes. Rather, women's backgrounds and experiences facilitate their initiation into a career in the sex industry by providing them with negatively imbued statuses and self-perceptions.

As this analysis of women in the stripping industry showed, there are identifiable, specific characteristics associated with women who pursue stripping as an occupation. As shown in our data, the factors that influence and facilitate a woman's decision to become a stripper include:

- Early physical maturity and early sexual experiences
- Ordinal position, absence of a father in the home, early independence from/in home
- Average educational levels
- A relationship between exhibitionistic behavior and previous job experience
- Athletic and entertainment backgrounds
- Childhood abuse
- The ugly duckling syndrome

These findings clearly add to the body of literature that identifies and summarizes characteristics among women who choose to strip for a living (Carey et al., 1974; Forsyth and Deshotels, 1997; Lewis, 1998; Peretti and O'Connor, 1989; Prus and Irini, 1980; Reid et al., 1995; Ronai and Ellis, 1989; Salutin, 1971; Skipper and McCaghy, 1970; Thompson and Harred, 1992). Most important, however, the present research advances our understanding by adding to the list of previously identified shared qualities.

What stands as the apparently most influential predisposing factors that lead one to stripping include the absence of a father figure during adolescence; a link between exhibitionist behavior, prior job experience, athletic and entertainment backgrounds; childhood abuse, and the ugly duckling syndrome. These factors all share a common link to women's self-esteem and self-confidence. Contrary to common assumptions, strippers are not necessarily strong and confident individuals with high self-esteem. These qualities are typically present in dancers, but they are not qualities that lead women into stripping.

References

Barron, K. (1989). Strippers: The Undressing of an Occupation. Unpublished manuscript, University of Kansas.

Bell, H., L. Sloan, and C. Strickling. (1998). Exploiter and Exploited: Topless Dancers Reflect on Their Experiences. *Affilia, 13*(3):352–368.

Boles, J. and A. P. Garbin. (1974). The Strip Club and Stripper-Customer Patterns of Interaction. *Sociology and Social Research, 58*:136–144.

Carey, S. H., R. A. Peterson, and L. K. Sharpe. (1974). A Study of Recruitment and Socialization into Two Deviant Female Occupations. *Sociological Symposium, 11*:11–24.

Enck, G. E. and J. D. Preston. (1988). Counterfeit Intimacy: A Dramaturgical Analysis of an Erotic Performance. *Deviant Behavior, 9*:369–381.

Forsyth, C. and T. Deshotels. (1997). The Occupational Milieu of the Nude Dancer. *Deviant Behavior, 18*(2):125–142.

Lewis, J. (1998). Learning to Strip: The Socialization Experiences of Exotic Dancers. *The Canadian Journal of Human Sexuality, 7*(1):51–66.

McCaghy, C. and J. Skipper. (1972). Stripping: The Anatomy of a Deviant Life Style. In S. Feldman and G. Thilbar (eds.), *Life Styles: Diversity in American Society*. Boston: Little, Brown and Company.

McCaghy, C. and J. Skipper. (1969). Lesbian Behavior as an Adaptation to the Occupation of Stripping. *Social Problems, 17*:262–270.

Mullen, K. (1985). The Impure Performance Frame of the Public House Entertainer. *Urban Life, 14*:181–203.

Peretti, P. O. and P. O'Connor. (1989). Effects of Incongruence Between the Perceived Self and the Ideal Self on Emotional Stability of Stripteasers. *Social Behavior and Personality, 17*(1):81–92.

Prus, R. and S. Irini. (1980). *Hookers, Rounders, and Desk Clerks*. Salem, WI: Sheffield Publishing Company.

Reid, S. A., J. A. Epstein, and D. E. Benson. (1995). Does Exotic Dancing Pay Well but Cost Dearly? In A. Thio and T. Calhoun (eds.), *Readings in Deviant Behavior*. New York: Harper Collins College Publishers.

Ronai, C. R. and C. Ellis. (1989). Turn-Ons for Money: Interactional Strategies of a Table Dancer. *Journal of Contemporary Ethnography, 18*(3):271–298.

Salutin, M. (1971). Stripper Morality. *Transaction, 8*:12–22.

Sijuwade, P. O. (1995). Counterfeit Intimacy: A Dramaturgical Analysis of an Erotic Performance. *Social Behavior and Personality, 23*(4):369–376.

Skipper, J. and C. McCaghy. (1971). Stripteasing: A Sex Orientated Occupation. In J. Henslin (ed.), *Sociology of Sex*. New York: Appleton-Century-Crofts.

Skipper, J. and C. McCaghy. (1970). Stripteasers: The Anatomy and Career Contingencies of a Deviant Occupation. *Social Problems, 17*:391–404.

Thompson, W. E. and J. L. Harred. (1992). Topless Dancers: Managing Stigma in a Deviant Occupation. *Deviant Behavior, 13*:291–311.

11

Exposing the "Pretty Woman" Myth: A Qualitative Examination of the Lives of Female Streetwalking Prostitutes

Rochelle L. Dalla

A prostitute, by definition, is one who exchanges sex or sexual favors for money, drugs, or other desirable commodities (Overall, 1992). The past decade has witnessed a substantial increase in attention focused on the sex industry, and on women who engage in prostitution specifically. To address the needs of governmental funding sources, recent investigation have often focused on drug-related (e.g., drug or alcohol addictions and abuse) or associated risk-taking (e.g., HIV/AIDS knowledge and condom use) behaviors. Consequently, rich details of the lives of prostituting women are sparse in the available literature. Little is known about these women, as individuals with unique histories and developmental trajectories. Moreover, although diversity between types of prostitution is commonly recognized (i.e., streetwalking, escort services, call-girls, strippers) similarity among women engaged in any particular type (e.g., streetwalking) is often erroneously assumed. Assumptions of homogeneity result in false stereotyping and broad, ill-fitted categorizations (Scambler, 1997). Certainly, recognizing patterns of commonality among prostituted women has significant social and policy implications. Additionally, however, acknowledging the uniqueness that exist among women engaged in similar forms of prostitution (e.g., street-level) has equal utility and application for informing policy and outreach efforts.

A dichotomy exists in the portrayal of women working the streets.

Reprinted from *The Journal of Sex Research,* Vol. 37, No. 4 (2000), pp. 344–353. © 2000 The Society for the Scientific Study of Sexuality. Edited and reprinted by permission of the publisher.

At one extreme are popular images depicted in movies such as *Pretty Woman* (with Julia Roberts), *Leaving Las Vegas* (with Elisabeth Shue), and *Taxi Driver* (with Jodie Foster) of the young, beautiful prostitute who meets a "prince" and is "saved" (the "Pretty Woman" myth). In sharp contrast, at the other extreme exists images of women walking busy thoroughfares late at night, wearing high heels and black fishnet stockings, working for abusive pimps.

Neither of these portrayals, it was assumed, accurately represents the reality of the lives of streetwalking prostitutes or the phenomenon of street-level sex work. The purpose of this investigation therefore, was to examine, in depth, "the game" known as streetwalking prostitution. This study was meant to expand previous work by (a) introducing the reader to the personal, unique developmental experiences of women involved in street-level prostitution: in conjunction with (b) describing broad-based themes common to many women engaged in streetwalking. Previous research informs the present investigation.

Childhood correlates of later prostitution have been well documented. Investigation of women who prostituted themselves on the streets have revealed systematic (and lifelong) patterns of abuse, exploitation, and degradation at the hands of men, including fathers, brothers, intimate partners, clients, and pimps (Earls, 1990; Miller, 1993; Nandon, Koverola, and Schludermann, 1998). Estimates of the percentage of female prostitutes who have experienced early sexual abuse vary considerably, from 10% to 50% (Russell, 1988), to 60% (Silbert and Pines, 1983), to 73% (Bagley and Young, 1987). Unclear and open for further debate are the causal paths linking childhood sexual abuse with prostitution. Two models have been proposed. The first suggests that early sexual abuse is directly linked to later prostitution. James and Meyerding (1977) argue, for instance, that childhood sexual abuse results in separation between emotions and sexual activity. They contend that a young girl's self-concept changes as a result of sexual abuse, in that she begins to view herself as debased, thus facilitating her identification with prostitution. Likewise, Miller (1986) argues that early sexual victimization provides training in emotional distancing, which is reenacted during sexual activities with clients, thus allowing one to more easily engage in sexual servicing.

In contrast, Seng (1989) and others (Simons and Whitbeck, 1991) report that the causal link is indirect, mediated largely by runaway behavior. Likewise, in a Canadian study, Nandon et al. (1998) compared prostitution-involved teenagers with sexually abused youth who were not involved in the sex industry. They found similarity in reports of sexual abuse. However, the youth involved in prostitution were more likely to be or to have been runaways. The researchers contend, "The current findings . . . indicate that, when in appropriate comparison group is used, known precursors of prostitution *fail* (italics added) to discriminate between the prostitution and nonprostitution groups" (207).

Theories to definitely understand prostitution entry have been elusive, despite persistent attempts. Potterat, Phillips, Rothenberg, and Darrow (1985) sought to examine two concepts (susceptibility and exposure) in a model examining women's reasons for entering prostitution. The susceptibility model contends that psychological characteristics (e.g., alienation, feelings of worthlessness) in conjunction with traumatic events (e.g., incest), make some women vulnerable to the lure of prostitution. The exposure model predicts that interpersonal contact with, and inducement from, others involved in the sex industry leads to personal involvement. Interviews with prostitution-involved women and a comparable control group were conducted. Few differences were found with regard to running away from home, experiencing physical or sexual abuse, feelings of alienation and worthlessness, mental breakdowns, drug use, or arrest records.

Other precursors to prostitution, such as economic necessity and drug abuse, have been examined. Economic vulnerability, some argue, forces women in the streets. Hardman (1997) reports, "Because of the restricted access to financial and material resources, some women may resort to prostitution as a resistance or response to poverty" (20). Prostitution in other words may be viewed as an active coping strategy in the face of privation. Likewise, Delacoste and Alexander (1998) maintain that, lacking viable alternatives, female sex-work remains consistently available.

Drug addiction has been widely examined in relation to female prostitution. Crack cocaine, specifically, and its use by street-level prostitutes has garnered much recent attention. Graham and Wish (1994) examined 164 female arrestees in order to examine female drug use in relation to deviant behavior. Approximately 60% of the participants tested positive for cocaine; 50% had a history of prostitution. Interestingly, despite the role of drug use in the continuation of prostitution, Graham and Wish report that drug use did not always precede prostitution work. Drug use, they contend, may evolve as a coping strategy among street-level sex workers. In a more recent investigation however, Potterat, Rothenberg, Muth, Darrow, and Phillips-Plummer (1998) examined the sequence and timing of prostitution entry and drug use among prostitution involved women and a comparable control group.

They found that (a) drug use was more common among the prostitution-involved women than the control group, (b) drug use preceded sexual activity in both groups, and (c) injecting drug use preceded prostitution. Within the prostitution group specifically, 66% had used drugs prior to entering prostitution, 18% began drug use and prostitution activities concurrently, and only 17% reported drug use following their entry into prostitution. The participants were interviewed again after one year; similar reports were made.

Despite the frequency with which particular antecedents to prostitution have been identified in the extant literature, inconsistency and contradictory evidence have emerged. According to Bullough and Bullough (1996), "when all is said and done, no single factor stands out as causal in a woman becoming a prostitute" (171). Nandon et al. (1998) similarly conclude that "background factors may be *necessary but insufficient* (italics added) conditions to justify prostitution activity" (219). Undoubtedly, entry into prostitution and continued work in the sex industry results from the cumulation of multiple interdependent personal and contextual factors; none of which may exist in the same form or to the same degree for all women who prostitute themselves. A "profile" of the prostituted woman (or one who will eventually turn to prostitution) does not exist.

Method

Participants

Forty-three women comprised the final sample. Participants ranged in age from 19 to 56 (mean = 33.37). Most identified themselves as White (n = 20) or Black (n = 18); five were Native American. The majority lived in shelters (n = 16) or were incarcerated (n = 14). Others lived alone or with their children (n =4), with a parent (n =2), with friends (n = 1), or with their partners/husband (n = 6). Years of education ranged from seven to college experience (mean = 9.3 years). Most (n = 40) of the women were no longer involved in prostitution-related activities, although length of time since the last incident of prostitution varied dramatically, from less than 6 months (n = 17), to 6 months to 1 year (n = 13), to 1 or more years (n = 10). The majority (n = 41) reported that they had been addicted to drugs; drugs of choice included alcohol and crack cocaine. Length of sobriety largely corresponded with length of time since last incident of prostitution.

Procedure

This investigation was conducted in a midsize Midwestern city. All data were collected by the Principal Investigator (PI). Inclusion required that participants be female, involved in or have former experience in street-walking prostitution, and be at least 18 years of age. The majority of participants were located through an intervention program designed to keep women off the streets. The program offers weekly group meetings and one-on-one counseling. Most group attendees were transitory, attending group for several weeks then disappearing for weeks or months, and then perhaps (but not always) returning. Some participants attended group on their own accord, others were court ordered to attend. With support of the Program Director and approval from group members, the PI attended weekly group meetings for a period of 17 months, beginning in the spring of 1998. Each week that a new participant attended group, investigation goals were explained. Following groups, new attendees were approached and their participation was requested. The remaining participants were located while incarcerated (n = 14) and by word of mouth (n = 3). Responses to request for interviews were overwhelmingly positive (47 women were approached, 3 declined to participate and 1 did not show up for a scheduled appointment and never responded to attempts to be reached).

Results

A brief biography of five female participants is presented. Results from data analyses including the entire sample of 43 are then discussed in three segments: (a) historical events culminating in prostitution entry, (b) life in the game, and (c) looking ahead.

Part One: Images of Individuality

Barb was petite, 30 years old, and pregnant with her seventh child when she was interviewed. Beginning early in their lives, she and her older sister were molested by their mother and her male friends (Barb believed it started when she was 2). Although other family members were aware of the abuse, no one stepped in to protect her. When asked her feelings about it she commented, "I don't need to cry about it the rest of my life; if it happened, then it happened. Apparently it didn't have any impact on my life that I know of." When her parents divorced at age 12 her mother promised Barb and her sisters that she would be back for them, but her mother never returned. Barb ran away at age 13 because she was "in love"; she prostituted for the first time at age 15. In that same year she was also raped by her sister's husband and had her first child. By the time she was 19 she was shooting Ritalin and prostituting on a daily basis to support her habit and that of a boyfriend. Most of her clients were Sugar Daddies or regulars, and condom use was infrequent. She had never been married, but noted always "(having) a boyfriend." Relationships with male partners were consistently characterized by violence. None of her children lived with her; the four oldest were in foster care and the younger two lived with their respective fathers. She had not spoken to her parents in years and contact with her sisters was sporadic and infrequent. She explained, "When I was emancipated (at 15), as far as family went, I really didn't have one." She had stopped prostituting "recently," had not used in 7 months, and was living with a male friend who "is not supportive of prostitution, at all."

Amy was 34 and the mother of two boys. Although her children were living in foster care, she had recently completed all state-ordered requirements to regain full custody. When interviewed, she was living in a shelter and working at a fast food franchise. She had never been married, although she had been involved with a man for 12 years. She was the youngest of eight children. Her parents died within a year of one another when Amy was 12. She lived with older siblings, family friends, foster families, or boyfriends until she turned 18. Her parents were alcoholics. When asked to describe her most significant childhood memory, Amy replied,

> I remember my dad beating the shit out of my mom one night and he ripped her shirt open and she had a white shirt and a white slip. She sat in the kitchen and her lip was bleeding and she had a butcher knife to her chest and after that I made up my mind that a man would never, ever hit me, because I would kill him.

She knew little about her siblings, as it had been years since she had seen or spoken to any of them. One of her older sisters was a prostitute and heavily addicted to drugs. With reference to her older sister, Amy stated, "I never thought at the time I would become one of her—I did become one of her." At 18, she tried prostitution for the first time, was arrested, and spent 30 days in jail. She would frequently bring "dates" to her home and send her children to the store down the street; many of her clients were regulars so condom use was intermittent. For several years she was addicted to crack cocaine and alcohol, although she commented, "I never did it (prostitution) for drugs, it was always for the money." She was determined to "break the cycle" and introduce normalcy into her children's lives.

Sam at 39 was living in a shelter and working as a waitress. She had four children, ranging in age from 12 to 18, none of whom lived with her. She came from a family that was "very well-off, but very disorganized." When she was 6 months old, her father left her mother and took Sam and her brothers to another state. Sam was told that her mother had run out; she and her mother were recently reunited for the first time. Sam's father was a workaholic and an alcoholic and she and her brothers were frequently left in the care of an uncle who, for years, sexually abused them all. She began running away at the age of 10 and spent several years living intermittently with various family members, foster families, and in group homes. By age 24 she had two children, was involved in her second marriage, and being ". . . beaten quite a bit, on a weekly basis." The marriage lasted two years. At age 31, Sam became involved with several prominent businessmen (Sugar Daddies) who took care of her and her children financially. She tried crack for the first time at age 37 and was immediately addicted; it was then that she started working the streets and truck stops because the Sugar Daddies "didn't want nothing to do with me anymore." Her daughter, her oldest child, had worked the truck stops with her for a period of several months. She had been drug- and prostitution-free for 8 months when she was interviewed.

Trina was 35 and came from a family of 10 children. She described her family as "real dysfunctional"; her father physically and verbally abused her mother, and both parents physically abused the children. Because Trina was "the pick" she escaped the physical assaults suffered by her siblings. She became pregnant the first time she had sex, at age 17; the child's father was shot and killed by his cousin when she was 4 months pregnant. She described their relationship as "like a puppy love thing, we were real close." At the time, her mother had told Trina, "You're pregnant, so what, that's not my fault. You knew better—go to school." She completed high school and a year of college; she had planned on becoming a nurse. Her second child was born when Trina was 20. When the infant was 3 months old, she left the child's father because he had cheated on her. Five months later she was involved in a car accident that left her in a coma for 3 weeks; she was not expected to walk again. The accident caused a miscarriage, although she had not known she was pregnant. At age 21 Trina was a single mother of two and economically strapped. She was propositioned by a bar owner who promised that "(I) wouldn't have to leave my kids, or work 11–7 and he would buy me this and do that for me." The relationship "worked out real well" for her and lasted 1 year, until she met Greg who introduced her to street prostitution and became her pimp and the father of her third child. She described still mourning the death of her first love. For her, prostitution was ". . . the perfect relationship. I didn't have to fall in love, I didn't have to be heard." Trina explained how she and Greg traveled "all over . . . to Canada, Michigan, Minneapolis, South Dakota . . . catching hoes." At one point Greg had seven other women working for him. They made a lot of money, drove Cadillacs, and lived in an upper-class neighborhood. Trina commented, however, "Fast money don't last long." One night, on a paranoid high, Greg held a gun to Trina's head and forced her to try crack to prove she was not a police informant. She became addicted. After 5 years Trina left Greg because "I got tired of him beating me up." On her own again, Trina became "real wild . . . I didn't have a supervisor anymore." Her children were eventually placed with relatives while she ". . . went selling dope and selling (myself) . . . I'd sell anything." She married a man within a year, after knowing him 1 month. The marriage lasted 1 year, although much of that time she had spent in jail "with 178 injuries to my record." It was while in jail that she met her current partner, a detention officer. Trina was interviewed in an apartment they shared; she had been drug- and prostitution-free for 3 months.

At 56, Chancey was the oldest woman participating in the investigation. She was raised in a small, rural community where her parents, she emphasized, were very strict, Lutheran, and pillars of the community. She was extremely articulate and had completed 2 years of college. She had two older siblings and a sister 15 months her junior. Chancey explained, "My mother should have only had two children. I should have probably never been born." She was also the mother of five children, one of whom was an accountant. Prostitution for her began, she felt, at age five when she was given money in exchange for oral sex by the chief of police in the town where she was raised. Those exchanges continued for approximately 3 years. In addition to the police chief, Chancey had been sexually molested by several other individuals during her childhood, including her father. Her experiences on the streets began at the age of 14: she was hospitalized at the age of 15 for a drug overdose. At age 17 she married a man who became her pimp. And although she worked in the labor market intermittently and had been the executive director of a health agency at one point, her evenings were often consumed with prostitution. She explained being "addicted to the danger, to the risk, the excitement," and continued ". . . it was like a high to get home alive a lot of times." Although she had been addicted to heroin, prostitution continued for years after she became clean. She met her second husband in treatment; they were married for 7 years. He was the first and last man with whom she had ever been "in love." During 12 years of her adulthood Chancey had not worked the streets or engaged in any type of sex-work. However, within the last 2 years, she had "relapsed" into prostitution and was again seeking help. Work in the sex industry had been a defining factor of her life for over 30 years.

Part Two: The Larger Perspective

The description of the lives of these five women provides a starting point for examining the reality of streetwalking prostitution. Despite their personally unique experiences threads of similarity bind these women in the world of streetwalking known as the game. Exploration of those similarities is described below.

Harsh Beginnings.　Sexual abuse is repeatedly identified in the extant literature as a correlate to later prostitution. These data concur; sexual abuse consistently emerged in the majority of participants' life histories. The majority of participants (n = 27; 63%) reported being sexually molested during their formative years. Family friends, fathers, stepfathers, brothers, and uncles were most often mentioned as perpetrators. Several women were molested by more than one person and two of the participants were impregnated by their sexual perpetrators; one by her brother, the other by her father. When asked if they reported the abuse, the majority (n = 18) of those who had been sexually abused answered negatively, explaining that they feared the consequences. Of the remaining nine women who sought help by reporting the abuse, seven were ignored or not believed, thus resulting in continued victimization. Sexual abuse lasted an average of 4.9 years; six of the women reported being sexually abused for 10 or more years.

Abandonment, either literal or symbolic, emerged as a second defining characteristic and was evident in the lives of 28 of the female participants. Literal abandonment, such as that described above by Amy, Barb, and Sam, occurred most typically through parental death or desertion. Parental alcoholism, drug abuse, mental instability, and severe domestic violence resulted in feelings of emotional (or symbolic) abandonment, as well. Symbolic abandonment also comprised instances when sexual abuse was reported but ignored. When she told her mother her stepfather was sexually abusing her, for instance, one participant explained, verbatim, her mother's reaction: "That's between you and him." Similarly, after disclosing sexual abuse from her uncle, another participant was told by her mother, ". . . sometimes things happen and you just have to let them go." Because of parental death, domestic violence, or drug abuse, nine of the women were removed from their families of origin and placed in foster care. Many moved from one foster home to another; these situations rarely provided a sense of stability or cohesion. One of the participants, for instance, noted having been in 27 different foster homes by the age of 18. Three reported being sexually abused with their foster homes.

Not surprisingly, leaving home appeared more attractive than staying for many of the women. Seventeen of the women ran away from home (or their foster homes) before or during early adolescence (ages 11–13). Several of the women reported running away to be with their boyfriends, others simply hitched rides with truckers and other strangers to unknown destinations. Five of the women noted traveling from one state to another, never staying in any one place more than a few months. One young woman described spending several years traveling intermittently with various carnivals. She felt the strongest interpersonal connections with street people and carnival friends, stating "Just because you have (family) doesn't mean they're going to be there for you . . . sometimes you have to learn to detach to save yourself."

Life in the Game.   The average age of entry into prostitution was 19.4 years. Length of time involved in prostitution activities varied. Seven women reported short-term involvement (ranging from 5 months to 3 years; mean = 1.6 years: mode = 1 year). Thirty-six reported long-term involvement (3.1 to 41 years; mean = 12.9 years; mode = 15 years). Drug abuse and economic necessity were described as the primary reasons for entering the sex industry.

Forty-one of the participants reported drug abuse (drug usage as routine part of their lives). Sixteen of those women were drawn to prostitution to support an established drug habit; eight reported that prostitution entry and drug abuse occurred simultaneously. Crack cocaine was the drug of choice, although heroin, alcohol, and marijuana were also used frequently. One participant explained her addiction to crack by stating, "One hit is too many, one thousand hits are not enough." Several reported "There's no reason to be out there if not for the drugs." Still, 41% reported entering prostitution out of (real or perceived) economic necessity. Nine runaways exchanged sexual services for rides, shelter, and food. Twelve others reported that income generated from prostitution paid their rent and fed their children. Amy, described above, was a single mother of two, lacking familial support, education, and marketable skills when she began regular prostitution activity. She engaged in street-level work because "I needed it (the money) to survive." She explained further, however, "It's [Prostitution is] quick and easy money, tax free, but it could cost you your life, and it does cost you your self-worth." Others simply enjoyed the lifestyle they were afforded through prostitution-related activities. "The money," noted one participant, "is more addicting than anything else." Despite economic need propelling these women into prostitution, they were not necessarily drug free. Fifty-three percent reported recreational drug use before prostitution entry, and 76% reported becoming regular users following prostitution entry. Interesting also is that, following routine and consistent drug use, these women often reported that their rates for sexual services declined precipitously (an ironic twist), findings which parallel those described by Feucht (1993).

All 43 participants worked the streets. For some, their only involvement with prostitution came from streetwalking, although many participants engaged in other forms of prostitution as well, including working truck stops (n = 6), escort services (n = 7), massage parlors (n = 4), and as stage dancers (n = 4). Chancey, for instance, worked in a residence specializing in sadomasochistic sexual services, and 2 participants had made pornographic movies. With regard to their street clientele, 10 of the participants reported having "regulars" whereas others explained seeing each client only once—"dating" the same clients on a regular basis personalized the work to a level beyond which they were comfortable. Finally, 4 of the women, including Sam and Barb, reported being supported by Sugar Daddies before they began working the streets. Barb described meeting her Sugar Daddies before they began working the streets. Barb described meeting her Sugar Daddy at age 14; he was quite wealthy and paid her extremely well. She explained, "So basically, I just did not go through a lot of the street problems that a lot of my friends experienced." Nine of the women reported becoming emotionally involved with clients or former clients.

Despite the popular image of streetwalking prostitutes' lives controlled by pimps, less than half of the women (n = 17) reported involvement with a pimp. One of the women began working for her pimp when she was 15 years old, and he was 40. Eight participants reported that their boyfriends or partners forced them onto the streets to pay for their own drug habits. Five women had children with men whom they described as their pimps. And another noted that her brother had been a pimp, but had "reformed" and was now a minister. Similarities between partners/boyfriends and pimps, included that both were prone to physical violence and abuse, fathered children of the women, were aware of the women's prostitution and drug-related activities, and often introduced the women to the streets. Yet, distinctions were also made in that (a) pimps "required" their women to make a certain amount of money; (b) took all of the women's earned income and in turn provided shelter, clothing, food, and protection (e.g., from dangerous clients); and (c) the pimps often had several women working for them at once (known as a "stable"). Finally in asking whether they had worked for a pimp or not, three participants responded, "the rock [crack] was my pimp."

Condom use by the majority of the women was intermittent at best. Some reported using condoms when with strangers only, never with their regular clientele, their pimps, or their partners. Some never used protection. Several noted that their clients did not want to use condoms because ". . . they take away the feeling," whereas other clients would pay extra in order to have unprotected sex. When asked their feelings about condom use, many stated that simply "didn't care" whether they used them or not; becoming pregnant, or being subjected to a sexually transmitted disease or a life-threatening virus such as HIV was not typically of concern, particularly when abusing drugs. Five of the women reported becoming pregnant by clients.

Of the 43 female participants, 38 had born children (number of children ranging from one to seven: mean = 2.4); only 5 still lived with their children. Many children had been placed in temporary foster care (n = 9), although some lived with their fathers (n = 6) or other family members (n = 6) (e.g., grandparents, aunts). The remaining children had been adopted. The women's contact with their children was sporadic. Sixteen participants saw or spoke with their children weekly, others (n = 5) saw their children monthly or several times a year (n = 4). Nine of the women had severed all ties with their biological children and had terminated their parental rights.

Most (n = 22) of the women were involved in prostitution-related activities prior to having children. For these women, life largely proceeded without interruption. They worked the streets while pregnant, picked up dates, and fed their addictions to drugs and alcohol. Ill effects on their children, of the prenatal abuse and later exposure to parental prostitution, was difficult to document. Some had not seen their children in years; only six women reported having children with symptoms of Fetal Alcohol Syndrome or born addicted to crack cocaine or other substances. Most of the participants, however, reported a conscious awareness that their activities had, ultimately, transferred a legacy of abuse and abandonment, similar to what they had experienced as children, to the next generation.

Others (n =16), in contrast, became involved in prostitution-related activities after their children were born. Regarding prostitution one commented, "It was so much against my morals years ago. I wanted my kids raised so perfectly and then I just turned, it's like I gave up." Some of the women reported that their children were aware of their prostitution activities and some had brought tricks to their residences. Amy, for instance, would send her sons to the store when "Tony," a regular arrived. She described a typical encounter with him: "He'd say 'two minutes and I'll give ya $20.' Okay, fine, so I'd turn on the radio and I'd do two commercials and a song, or I'd do four commercials . . . and that was two minutes. Every Thursday." Amy explained, "It was always for the money back then." It wasn't until her children were taken by the state that her addiction to crack surged. She stated, ". . . I just didn't want to feel the pain and I didn't want to admit that they were in foster care so I just used and used and used." Amy's reaction was reiterated by others; losing their children became the impetus for the most severe addictive frenzies among many.

Street prostitution is inherently dangerous. As explained by one participant, "There were times when the only way out of a situation was by the grace of God." Most of the participants (n = 31) relayed incidents of severe abuse suffered at the hands of their boyfriends, clients, and/or pimps. Many reported having been raped, beaten with objects, threatened with weapons, and abandoned in remote regions. One young woman reported having her teeth knocked out by her boyfriend and being raped at knifepoint by a trick. When asked to explain how she returned to the streets after being raped, she explained. "I just looked at it as not getting paid," and another explained, ". . . you just give them what they want and pray they don't kill you." When asked to describe her feelings of being beaten with a tire iron and left for dead. Sam responded, "I didn't care. I didn't think about it. I got 150 stitches and was back on the streets the same day." Another participant was sold rat poison instead of crack: she spent 10 days in a coma and was back on the streets the day she was released. When asked if they reported the crimes, their responses were often incredulous. One participant

explained her belief that "society and law enforcement consider a prostitute getting raped or beat as something she deserves. There's nothing
that you can do."

Steps taken to protect themselves from potential harm were
described, including relying on intuition in determining the "safety" of
a client, meeting clients in designated areas and not traveling with
them, and making exchanges in visibly parked cars. Three participants
reported jumping from moving vehicles after sensing danger, others
carried weapons (e.g., box cutter knife). Physical safety, however was
not guaranteed. One woman remarked, "Every time I got in a car I knew
my life was in danger; I didn't care."

Leaving the Streets.   What factors or experiences propel women who
have spent much of their existence in abusive, exploitative relationships, living day-by-day without regard for their futures or their lives,
into the unfamiliar terrain of sobriety and goal setting? Participants
were asked to explain their motivation for leaving the streets. Their
responses varied. It is important to note that not all of the women had
self-selected themselves out of prostitution, one third (n = 14) were
incarcerated when interviewed. These women did not seek out respite
from the streets; they were forced out of prostitution at least temporari-
ly, through legal action. The majority (n = 26), however, were actively
seeking assistance through an intervention program, although their
involvement in the program was sporadic at best. The final three participants left the streets on their own accord, without legal intervention or
programmatic support. In discussing the participants' motivation to
change, data are presented separately for the incarcerated women versus
those who attended the intervention program or left the streets on their
own accord.

The average length of time the incarcerated women had spent in
prison was 1.2 years (range = 3 months to 4 years). Several had been
in and out of prison; one woman had spent 13 1/2 years in prison with
intermittent time on the streets and her daughter was in the same peni-
tentiary for prostitution. Crimes leading to imprisonment included
prostitution, drug use, larceny, robbery, parole violation, and extortion.
The predominant theme characterizing the incarcerated women's motivations to change centered around their remaining sober, which
imprisonment had demanded. In addition, prison provided opportunities to obtain job skills (e.g., computer work) and education (e.g.,
GED) which these women felt would assist them in finding ways to

stay away from the streets. Several reported simply being exhausted (physically and emotionally). Yet the incarcerated women, specifically, were less certain than the others that their efforts would be met with success. They expressed concern that the "old playgrounds and playmates" would prove too tempting to abandon entirely. And one remarked, "I'm not done selling drugs": the work, she felt, was just too lucrative.

Participants who were not forced out of prostitution due to incarceration reported attempts to leave the streets between the ages of 19 and 55 (mean = 33.3; mode = 32). Time spent engaging in prostitution-related activities varied greatly, from short term (n = 4; range = 5 months to 3 years; mean = 1.6 years) to long term (n = 22; range = 3.1 to 41 years; mean = 14.7; mode = 15 years) involvement. Three factors were described. Intervention-involved women reported hitting bottom (e.g., being homeless, being jailed, nearly dying) as a primary reason for seeking help. One stated, "It wasn't until I faced death that I realized there was a reason to live." Regaining physical custody of children was also frequently mentioned. One participant explained, "I wasn't there for my kids when they were little; I just keep telling myself that they will need me even more in the future." Faith in a higher power and the desire for spiritual healing was also described by intervention-involved women as influencing their decision to attempt lifestyle change.

Among those who left the streets without intervention, reasons given included the fear of AIDS and the increasing danger and decreasing income associated with street-level prostitution. Due to widespread crack use, the tricks were getting cheaper; contemporary street prostitutes, it was explained, are eager to please for little in return. One of these women succinctly stated, "I'm not giving it away . . . I'm no $10, $15 ho."

Generally, whether involved in the intervention program or not, the participants shared similar dreams for their futures, including providing for their children, marrying, finding steady work, owning a home, and living a "normal" life. Several planned to go to school, with hopes of counseling other women and troubled adolescents. One participant, when asked what she hoped to have in the future, responded simply, "Serenity and peace of mind." In contrast, a few participants described a conscious effort not to think about the future; their goals centered on daily successes. Finally, rather than discussing what she hoped to have in the future, another participant stated explicitly what she did not want: "No alcohol, drugs, men, or marriages."

Discussion

Although their reasons for entering prostitution may differ, streetwalk-ing women have similarly decided (either consciously or not) to engage in life-threatening, abusive, exploitative activities where, according to O'Neill (1997), they "participate in their own annihilation," (19). The purpose of this investigation was to examine the unique developmental trajectories of women involved in streetwalking prostitution, in con-junction with illuminating greater understanding may facilitate an open dialogue and greater awareness of the women comprising the subculture of streetwalking prostitution.

The brutal realities which nudge, or as Cole (1987) would argue, force, women into the streets were relayed in bitter detail by Barb, Amy, Sam, Trina, and Chancey. Despite their individual circumstances, they simultaneously shared common experiences of abandonment, abuse, loss, and exploitation. Childhood sexual abuse was described by the majority of participants as were literal (e.g., through desertion) or sym-bolic (e.g., through parental alcoholism/neglect) abandonment. Other themes included removal from, or intentionally leaving (i.e., running away from), their families of origin.

Involvement in prostitution for many began out of economic neces-sity, or was due to drug addiction. Interestingly, however, drug use, par-ticularly as an addiction rather than as a recreational activity, began for many after entering the sex industry. In addition to supporting their own drug habits through prostitution, many participants reported supporting the habits of their partners as well. And, in contrast to Barry's (1995) findings that 80% to 95% of all prostitution is pimp controlled, only 39% of the participants reported working for a pimp.

Leaving the streets was a conscious decision made by the majority of participants. They had actively sought help through an intervention program aimed specifically at women involved in streetwalking prosti-tution. Nonetheless, program attendance was sporadic, and their success in leaving the streets was expected to be tenuous at best. For the remainder of the participants, exiting the sex industry was a conse-quence of incarceration. Yet, given their time away from the streets, many hoped to continue their progress after being released. These women, specifically, voiced concern regarding their ability to abandon entirely the illegal activities from their pasts.

The women who participated in this investigation reported never imagining that they would one day be engaging in prostitution activities: none reported *prostitute* as a long-term career goal. Prostitution and drug addiction, it is commonly believed, represent symptoms of larger systematically related issues. O'Neill (1997) writes, "Issues of sexual politics are entwined with economic and political issues . . . to create a catch-22 situation for women who may not have freely chosen to work as prostitutes but nevertheless pragmatically have decided that it is the best option available to them" (19). O'Connel Davidson (1998) further reports, "We do not hear stories about (women) giving up their careers in order to become prostitutes" (3). Which begs the question: If presented with viable and equally lucrative options, would the streets continue to lure women and girls? According to Amy, "Anybody that says that they like doing it (prostitution) is in denial." Still when asked, participants explicitly reported personal responsibility for choices made.

Undoubtedly, entry into prostitution results from the cumulation of multiple interdependent personal and contextual factors. Efforts at teasing apart those variables, and the relative significance of each, have left many questions unanswered and uncertainties remaining. Specifically, what is abundantly clear is that many women are exposed to life experiences similar to those commonly reported by prostitution-involved women (e.g., childhood sexual abuse, domestic violence, drug use), a large majority of whom never engage in prostitution-related activities (Bullough and Bullough, 1996). Potterat et al. (1998) argue for a paradigm shift; research emphases on external circumstances (e.g., environmental context), they argue, have left pervasive gaps in our understanding of internal mechanisms (i.e., psychological factors) which likely influence, to an as-yet-unknown extent, female entry into the sex industry.

Popular images presented on the big screens often portray prostitution as a temporary course of action, where in the end the heroine finds love and happiness and suffers few, if any, enduring scars from her brief stint on the streets. Reality rarely mimics the movies; Prince Charming does not materialize and save the pretty woman working the streets. For the majority of streetwalking prostitutes, the movie reel continues, days turn into months and months turn into years; there are few, if any, ways out.

References

Bagley, C. and L. Young, (1987). Juvenile Prostitution and Child Sexual Abuse: A Controlled Study. *Canadian Journal of Community Mental Health,* 6:5–26.

Barry, K. (1995). *Prostitution and Sexuality.* New York: New York University Press.

Bullough, B. and V. Bullough (1996). Female Prostitution: Current Research and Changing Interpretations. *Annual Review of Sex Research, 7*:158–180.

Cole, S. G. (1987). Sexual Politics: Contradictions and Explosions. In L. Bell (ed.), *Good Girls/Bad Girls: Sex Trade Workers and Feminists Face to Face.* Toronto, Canada: Women's Press.

Delacoste, F. and P. Alexander. (1998). *Sex Work: Writings by Women in the Sex Industry.* San Francisco: Cleis Press.

Earls, C. M. (1990). Early Family and Sexual Experience of Male and Female Prostitutes. *Canada's Mental Health,* December:7–11.

Feucht, T. E. (1993). Prostitutes on Crack Cocaine: Addiction Utility and Marketplace Economics. *Deviant Behavior: An Interdisciplinary Journal, 14*:91–108.

Graham, N. and E. D. Wish. (1994). Drug Use Among Female Arrestees: Onset, Patterns and Relationships to Prostitution. *The Journal of Drug Issues, 241*:315–329.

Hardman, K. (1997). A Social Work Group for Prostituted Women with Children. *Social Work with Groups, 20*:19–31.

James, J. and J. Meyerding. (1977). Early Sexual Experience and Prostitution. *American Journal of Psychiatry, 134*:1381–1385.

Miller, E. M. (1986). *Street Women.* Philadelphia: Temple University Press.

Miller, J (1993). Your Life Is on the Line Every Night You're on the Streets: Victimization and the Resistance Among Street Prostitutes. *Humanity and Society, 17*:442–446.

Nandon, S. M., C. Koverola, and E. H. Schludermann. (1998). Antecedents to Prostitution: Childhood Victimization. *Journal of Interpersonal Violence, 13*:206–221.

O'Connell Davidson, J. (1998). *Prostitutes' Power and Freedom.* Ann Arbor, MI: The University of Michigan Press.

O'Neill, M. (1997). Prostitute Women Now. In G. Scambler and A. Scambler (eds.), *Rethinking Prostitution: Purchasing Sex in the 1990s.* London: Routledge.

Overall, C. (1992). What's Wrong with Prostitution? Evaluating Sex Work. *Signs, 17*:705–724.

Potterat, J. J., L. Phillips, R. B. Rothenberg, and W. W. Darrow. (1985). On Becoming a Prostitute: An Exploratory Case-Comparison Study. *The Journal of Sex Research, 20*:329–336.

Potterat, J. J., R. B. Rothenberg, S. Q. Muth, W. W. Darrow, and L. Phillips-Plummer. (1998). Pathways to Prostitution: The Chronology of Sexual and Drug Abuse Milestones. *The Journal of Sex Research, 27*:233–243.

Russell, D. E. H. (1988). The Incidence and Prevalence of Intra Familial and Extra Familial Sexual Abuse on Female Children. In L. E. A. Walker (ed.), *Handbook on Sexual Abuse of Children.* New York: Springer.

Scambler, G. (1997). Conspicuous and Inconspicuous Sex Work: The Neglect of the Ordinary and Mundane. In G. Scambler and A. Scambler (eds.), *Rethinking Prostitution: Purchasing Sex in the 1990s.* London: Routledge.

Seng, M. J. (1989). Child Sexual Abuse and Adolescent Prostitution: A Comparative Analysis. *Adolescence, 24*:665–675.

Silbert, M. H. and A. M. Pines. (1983). Early Sexual Exploitation as an Influence in Prostitution. *Social Work, 28*:285–289.

Simons, R. L. and L. B. Whitbeck. (1991). Sexual Abuse as a Precursor to Prostitution and Victimization Among Adolescent and Adult Homeless Women. *Journal of Family Issues, 12*:361–379.

12

Male Street Hustling: Introduction Processes and Stigma Containment

Thomas C. Calhoun

Individuals engaged in discrediting behavior (i.e., male street prostitution), but who are not yet discredited, employ strategies to prevent others from learning about their involvement. Since their behavior makes them vulnerable to severe legal consequences and can damage their self-concept, they strongly avoid discreditation. This research, using the negotiations that transpire between the hustler and customer as they seek to arrange a sexual transaction, highlights the strategies used by male street hustlers to cover their involvement in street prostitution.

The male street hustler is the most visible of prostitutes because he often operates on street corners, out of bus terminals, or in hotel lobbies (Butts, 1947; Reiss, 1961; Weisburg, 1984). Unlike the call boy, who either operates alone by advertising in an underground newspaper or works with a pimp, the street hustler neither advertises (excluding the signs conveyed by dress or physical demeanor) nor works for anyone else (Caukins and Coombs, 1976). It is difficult to gather data on kept boys because they generally have relationships with only one other individual who meets most of their needs. Since street hustlers operate in the open, they are most accessible to the researcher.

Given society's negative view toward those who engage in homosexual activity, a hustler usually prevents others from learning of his participation. Should his homosexual activities become known, the hustler risks others important to him redefining him negatively. He may face social and familial ostracism.

Reprinted from *Sociological Spectrum,* Vol. 12, No. 1 (1992), pp. 35–52. © 1992 Taylor & Francis, Inc. Edited and reprinted by permission of the publisher.

This article discusses the process used by male street hustlers as they attempt to negotiate a sexual transaction with their customers. The focus is on the nuances and subtleties in the interaction between hustler and would-be customer, which are designed to prevent others from learning about their discrediting behavior. (This article does not address "covering" and "passing" strategies with significant others such as family members or peers.)

The research literature provides limited reference to the process whereby street hustlers and their tricks arrive at a decision to engage in sex. Six pickup methods commonly identified in the literature for initiating contact are: got a light (Butts, 1947; Jersild, 1956; Raven, 1963); got a cigarette or time (Butts, 1947; Jersild, 1956; Reiss, 1961); eye contact (Butts, 1947; Reiss, 1961); cruise (Bell and Weinberg, 1978; Coombs, 1974; Humphreys, 1970; Lenoff and Wesley, 1956; Rechy, 1977; Reiss, 1961); smile or nod of head (Coombs, 1974; Reiss, 1961); and hitchhiking (Reiss, 1961). These methods relate to initial contact; they do not explain systematically what happens after initial contact is made. Prus and Irini (1980) discuss other steps in the process; however, their research is directed toward female prostitutes. Although much has been written recently about male prostitution (Bour, Young, and Henningsen, 1984; Boyer, 1989; Coleman, 1989; Earls and David, 1989; Humphreys, 1970; Lowman, 1987; Mathews, 1988; Sullivan, 1987), only one scholarly article provides a detailed discussion of the entire interaction that transpires between male customer and the male street hustler (Luckenbill, 1984). Luckenbill identifies seven stages: making contact; assessing suitability; agreeing to a sale; coming to terms; moving to a suitable setting; making the exchange; and terminating the sale. The stages identified here parallel those identified by Luckenbill (1984).

Methods and Sample

The data were obtained from interviews with 18 young male prostitutes over the course of 3 months in 1984; all subjects were from a southern community with a population of just more than 200,000. In addition to the formal interviews, information was also obtained from other hustlers through informal conversations and by systematic observations.

The subjects were between the ages of 13 and 22 years. The average age is 17.6 years and the model age is also 17. Of the 18 subjects, 15 are white and the remaining three are black. The overall education level of the street hustlers in this sample is low. Half of the 18 subjects were currently not attending school, 7 of these dropped out before obtaining a high school diploma, and the other 2 subjects completed high school. Sixteen of the 18 subjects were single and living at home with a parent or adult guardian. The remaining 2 subjects were married and had established independent households.

In this community, only one part of town was used by male prostitutes to arrange for sexual encounters with other males—the downtown area behind a gay bar. Female street walkers operated in another section of town, approximately five blocks away.

Entrance into the "subculture" of male prostitution is difficult because many young male prostitutes are mistrustful and suspicious of outsiders, especially those seeking information about street prostitution and their involvement in it. Meeting the principal informant occurred quite by accident. While observing informally one evening, Tony approached me as I sat in the parking lot directly across from a popular pickup spot. Because Tony was interested in "turning a trick," I could only identify myself as a researcher and state my purpose.

Each time following our first encounter, when Tony would come on "the block," he would come over and talk with me. As time passed, a mutual trust developed between us. After we became friends, he helped introduce me to other hustlers. The recorded interviews took place at locations convenient to both the hustler and myself; some lasted only 30 minutes, whereas others lasted more than two hours.

Entry

Before we can appreciate the intricacies of hustlers' defense processes, we need to focus first on (1) how they learn about street hustling; (2) what instructions, if any, they are provided; and (3) then move to the process used by hustlers to negotiate a sexual transaction.

The data indicate two major pathways leading young males to street prostitution: peer introduction, including friends, siblings, and/or relatives; and situational discovery, including those situations in which a young person learns about male prostitution without conscious effort.

The data indicate that the majority of these hustlers learn about street hustling from their friends who are participants. From these interactions the new recruit is given (in varying degrees) instructions, motives, and techniques for carrying out this deviant activity (Sutherland and Cressey, 1978). In rare instances some hustlers stumble on this activity and subsequently become participants, lending credence to Matza's (1964) notion of "drift."

Peer Introduction

Research on teenage male prostitution has demonstrated that the majority of juveniles are introduced to street prostitution through their associations and interactions with significant others (Allen, 1980; Butts, 1947; Ginsburg, 1967; James, 1982; Jersild, 1956; Raven, 1963; Reiss, 1961; Ross, 1959; Weisberg, 1984). Most of the subjects in this study confirm this finding. Fourteen of the 18 respondents indicated that they were introduced to street hustling by a friend. In discussing how he became involved in male prostitution, Mike "C" said:

> This dude told me about it. I went with him behind "The Bar" and he kept talking about it. It seemed like he didn't want to tell me. He just wanted me to be there and watch or something. I was standing there just freaking out on all of it. He went across the street and talked to somebody. He said "Mike, this dude will give you 50 dollars to do so and so . . ." I said, "no," cause I was freaking out.

Perhaps Mike "C"'s friend was intentionally vague because he did not know how Mike "C" would react to the knowledge that he was a street hustler. Yet another plausible explanation for his friend's vagueness is that it would make it easier for Mike "C' to reject the chance to participate in this kind of sexual activity.

In some situations a friend takes an active part in exposing the minor to street hustling. James related the following story about how he learned about hustling from his friend:

> One night we was sitting down there on "The Wall"—we was just sitting there. Cause I didn't know nothing about it. This guy comes up and says, "Let's go up to my apartment for awhile." He says "I ain't into it tonight. I'm trying to break my friend into it. He ain't never been out."

The presence of an experienced hustler can serve two functions: It may reduce the anxiety the new recruit feels about participating in homosexual encounters; and, secondly, having an experienced street hustler with the novice can help him learn the necessary skills.

Some juveniles who have friends that are prostitutes will indicate a need for money, and the friends may then offer a way to eliminate the financial hardship (Allen, 1980; Butts, 1947; Caukins and Coombs, 1976; Raven, 1963; Reiss, 1961). Bill said:

> I know this friend. I said "Damn, I need some money." He said, "I know how to git it." He showed me the tricks so that I would know what to do. So I tried and the guy gave me money.

Although friends constitute the largest group of people who introduce others to prostitution, siblings and/or other relatives are also influential (Reiss, 1961). Of the 14 subjects who were introduced to hustling by another person, two were introduced by a sibling or other relative. Boo said:

> I followed my brothers down there. I said, "What are y'all doing there?" They said "hustling." I said, "What do you do?" They said "Just go up to one of these cars and just make sure it ain't no cop— ask if they're a cop first. Then you can name your price."

In this case the young person was introduced and given instructions about hustling by his older brothers. Other juveniles learn about street prostitution from a relative, other than a sibling, who recognizes the financial benefits. Henry, a black teenager, related the following:

> I first found out about hustling from my cousin. He said "do you want to make some money?" I said, "What are you talking about?" He said, "down to the gay bar." I'd never really thought about it. So one night he asked me about it again and I said, "Yeah, I'll go down there with you." I had made up my mind to hustle myself because I wanted to see what it was all about.

An offer to earn money was extended; however, it was not initially accepted. Money may be the primary inducing factor, but Henry's response suggests that other factors may also be important.

Situational Discovery

Although 14 teenagers were introduced to street hustling by a significant other (i.e., family member or friend), the remaining 4 subjects learned about street prostitution by chance in the literature about street male prostitutes there is limited reference to this method of introduction (Allen, 1980; Butts, 1947; Caukins and Coombs, 1976; Ginsburg, 1967; MacNamara, 1965). Kenny stated:

> I was out riding around on my bike, and I seen a man sitting. I stopped
> and talked to him for a while and I said, "What are you doing down
> here?" He says, "I'm making money." I said, "How?" He said
> "Letting these queers suck my dick." I said, "What do you mean?" He
> says, "Fags, you know what fags are, don't you?" I said "Yeah, I've
> heard of them." "Well, I'm letting them suck my dick." I said "Is that
> how you're making money?" He said, "Yeah you should try it." So
> that night, that same night that he told me about it, I took my bike and
> I hid it. I came back down here. I was scared 'cause it was the first
> time I had ever done something like that. And I went out with this
> dude. He gave me 30 dollars to go out with him. Me and him went
> out, and he sucked my dick. Ever since then I've been down there.

The male prostitute Kenny spoke with provided him incentives for
participating in this activity—money and sex—and by implication, conveyed a dislike for homosexuals. During their conversation, participation in prostitution was portrayed as "no big deal." Also the tone of the
conversation implies that one can participate in hustling and maintain a
sense of masculinity. The usage of terms such as "fags" and "queers"
suggest that men who buy sexual services from other males are not
"normal." In this sense, the prostitute is able to separate his sense of
self from his perception of homosexuals (Goffman, 1963; Warren,
1972).

Peer Socialization

The literature on male prostitution does not give specific information
concerning what young males are told by their introducer as they begin
hustling. In his now classic study, Reiss (1961) identifies norms that
govern the interactions between hustlers and their tricks, such as: the
interaction must be for monetary gains and sexual encounter must be
restricted to mouth–genital fellation; the participants must remain effectively neutral during the sexual encounter; and violence can only be used
when the shared expectations between the participants is violated.

    Each subject was asked what instructions, if any, were provided by
the person who introduced them to street prostitution. The most common instruction given the soon-to-be hustlers by their mentors were: the
location of the prostitution area; which acts a hustler should perform
and an idea of the cost for performing these acts; assessment of the
potential customer as a law enforcement agent; and something about
customer behavior. Ron reported the greatest number of instructions
during the interview. He said he was told:

Let them give me head, $20 and nothing else. Be careful about some
of the motherfuckers . . . not to let 'em fuck you in the ass, not to give
them no head . . . Be careful about the police, they'll stop and ask you
a bunch of shit.

The hustling instructions given to Ron contain at least three themes:
(1) he was told what sex acts were acceptable; (2) he was given some
idea about how much to charge for the specific type of sex; and (3) he
was warned about law enforcement.

Although some hustlers reported receiving extensive instructions,
others were given few. They had to learn on their own. David said:

He didn't know how it was going on or anything but he did tell me
one thing, "Make sure that you'd ask if they was a cop." Other than
that he really didn't tell me a whole lot about it.

Some young people were given no instructions whatsoever and
they, too, had to learn for themselves. Mink stated, "I learnt it on my
own. Really, I learnt it the hard way."

The Negotiation Process

During informal conversations, interviews and observations with street
hustlers, the following sequence appears as the typical order in which
sexual interaction occurs; however, not all interactions pass through
each stage as presented. Some stages may be skipped. The stages to be
discussed are: initial contact; confirmation; negotiation of the sexual act
and fees; and negotiation of location. For analytical purposes, the initial
contact stage, the confirmation stage, and the negotiation of location
stage are used to illustrate how these hustlers manage the threat of stigma (i.e., arrest and subsequent labeling as homosexual prostitute). The
negotiation of acts/fees stage of the process is used primarily in managing an identity as nonhomosexual.

Initial Contact

For the trick and hustler to reach a mutually acceptable agreement about
the buying and/or selling of sexual favors they must be able to talk with
each other. Although the hustler and potential customer may occupy the
same physical space, there is no guarantee their copresence indicates
desire or availability for sex. Hustlers must develop strategies for iden-

tifying potential tricks and strategies for making the initial contact once a potential trick has been identified.

One method of identifying a potential trick is *cruising*. Mink, a 20-year-old hustler, with typical views about the subtleties and intricacies of this process, stated:

> They circle around the block, and they'd look at you, and they'd circle the block again. They'd pull over and stop. And so you are thinking to yourself, in you mind, "This guy is wanting me. I'm gonna go up and see what he wants.'

In this case, the hustler is aware of the fact that perhaps the individual who is cruising the block might be a potential customer; however, he does not commit himself initially to being recognizable as a male prostitute.

Once a potential customer has been identified, the hustler may "nod his head or wave" at the trick. This gesture can signal a willingness by the hustler to enter into conversation with the potential trick, which may result in a sexual transaction. As the customer is cruising the block trying to determine if the young male is a hustler, he generally uses gestures to communicate his interest. One respondent told me:

> When somebody's trying to pick you up, they're staring at you. They wave at you, they nod their head for you to walk on down the street so they can talk to you.

Although an initial gesture has been offered, neither the sender of the message nor the hustler is sure that the other is the kind of person he seeks. The hustler may not respond to the gestures for a number of reasons, such as prior knowledge about the trick; the hustler may be waiting for a specific individual; he may have to be home early; or he may be just "hanging out" and is not interested in pursuing a sexual encounter. Assuming the hustler has identified a potential trick, additional efforts may be made to further verify the assessment.

The hustler initially does not commit himself, and his message may be vague and structured so as to force the potential trick to state his purpose. One respondent said after he makes contact with the potential customer: "I'm gonna ask him for a cigarette or I'm going to ask him for a light, and then you tell him, "Hey man, look you doing anything tonight.'" In other situations, the hustler disguises his purpose from the customer by making reference to a need for employment. One hustler said:

> I go up and say, "Hey man do you know where I can get a job?" He'll say, "I might." Then I say, "Where? Do you care if I get in and sit down a minute." He says, "O.K." And I get in there and sit down, and they drive, and then we start talking about it.

Structuring the interaction in his manner, the hustler is using disidentifiers by not linking himself initially to prostitution. He only tries to verify if the individual is a potential trick. Before the interaction proceeds any further, the hustler needs to know that the person to whom he is talking is not someone (i.e., the police) who could officially sanction his behavior by arresting him and attaching the label "deviant" to him.

Confirmation

If the hustler is satisfied with his assessment of the potential trick, then he will generally ask if the potential trick is a policeman before discussing negotiating sexual favors. Bill said:

> I talk to him, I say, "Hi, my name is Bill, how are you doing." Then I ask them if they are the police or anything to do with the police. And sometimes, if they got an antenna or two on the car, I don't get in. Then I ask them what they looking for tonight.

Hustlers believe that if a potential trick is a police officer he must say so, for failure to do so constitutes entrapment. According to Mitch, "It's a law that requires that he cannot say he is not a policeman if he is." James, in discussing an encounter he had with a potential trick and how he deals with them if he thinks they are the police, said:

> "Are you a cop?" That's the first question I ask and if they say yes–you run like hell. If they are a cop, they have to tell you; if they don't they can't arrest you.

Asking the potential trick if he is a cop then serves two functions. First, hustlers believe if the potential customer does not answer the question truthfully the court case will be dismissed should he be arrested for prostitution. Second, if a policeman informs the hustler of his identity, the hustler can terminate the conversation without telling the policeman he is a prostitute.

The hustlers" understanding of this law is incorrect; however, whether or not hustlers are correct in their interpretation, they make a concerted effort to avoid arrest in an attempt to prevent significant others from learning about their involvement in this type of deviant behavior.

Negotiation of Sexual Act

If the hustler finds the potential trick acceptable, the conversation moves to a more intimate level—sexual negotiation. These negotiations first center around a specific act to be performed followed by a negotiation of the fee.

Negotiating the Act. The potential trick may tell the hustler the sexual activity he desires. At this point the hustler and trick attempt to reach an agreement. If an agreement cannot be reached, the interaction ceases. As one hustler stated: "If I don't like it, I don't go. If he asks me to suck his dick, I say no I don't do that." If the initial offer is rejected, the hustler may make a counteroffer. Bill, when discussing the negotiation process stated: "There is a couple of things that I don't do. I tell them, and if they still want to do something then they tell me. If it's alrights with me then we do it." In some situations the hustler can be rather adamant about which sexual acts he will perform. Mink illustrated this when he said:

> I always told them that all I wanted was to get sucked off, and that was it. If they'd ask me, do you do more than that, I'd tell them, "No that's all I do." You give me head, that's it.

A trick may want the hustler to provide other sexual services, but the hustler generally holds his ground about what he is willing to do. If the trick accepts the counter offer, the conversation continues; if it is rejected, the trick or hustler may make another offer or terminate the conversation.

The negotiations between the trick and hustler are complex. The hustler generally enjoys a dominant position in these encounters because he has the option of deciding whether or not he will engage in the requested sexual activity. Male prostitutes, as a category, will not perform any and all sexual acts.

Negotiating the Fee. When the hustler and trick have agreed on the act or acts to be performed, the hustler must decide how much to charge and the trick must decide if he will pay the price. Many factors influence the cost: the nature of the act being requested; the perception of the trick; and other situational factors, such as a need to be home early or an inability to get picked up.

Nature of Act

The number of acts requested are diverse, but the acts hustlers say they are willing to provide is limited. David best reflects the importance of the act when he stated:

> If they just want to suck my dick that's fine. He'll suck you off. Suck each other off for a reasonable price. But after that I'd ask for more. If somebody's going to fuck me they have to look decently—really appealing to me. I don't let anybody that don't look appealing fuck me or vice versa. But even if he was appealing there's going to be a jacked up price, about $60.

At least three themes are evident in this quote: (1) David is aware that tricks may request a number of sex acts; (2) the sexual act requested influences the cost (e.g., anal sex more than oral sex); and (3) participation in some acts (i.e., anal sex) is influenced by his perception of the customer. Generally, the more atypical the act requested the more the hustler will charge.

Perception of Trick

If the hustler suspects the trick is under the influence of alcohol or drugs, he will try to extract more money. Asking Mitch why he charged one customer $15 and the other $75 to perform the same act, he said: "Well, the one that I would be charging $75, he would be tore up on drugs, and I would be taking advantage of the situation." Aside from attempting to take advantage of the trick's condition, one respondent said that "if I think he is rich I charge him high." Believing a trick is rich is based on dress, the presence of jewelry, or the automobile driven.

Other Constraints

Most hustlers in this study live at home, and their parents expect them home by a certain time. If the hustler is pressed for time, the price he normally would charge may be lowered. Reflecting on time restrictions, Glenn stated he lowered his price "lots of times on nights when I had to be home early and couldn't make a trick." Two conditions are operating in Glenn's case: (1) time and (2) the difficulty in getting picked up. This young male, like other hustlers, may have difficulty in being picked up for several reasons: the number of available tricks may be limited; tricks may be available but they may not want this hustler for a variety of reasons; and the number of hustlers on the street may exceed the number of available tricks. These conditions may force the hustler to lower his price.

Negotiation of Location

If the hustler and trick have agreed to the act(s) to be performed and the price, one final decision must be made: where to consummate the deal. The 18 hustlers in this study reported having sex with tricks in three locations: 16 in apartment/houses; 11 in cars in parking lots; and 8 in motels or hotels.

The trick is given some latitude in choosing where the sexual transaction is to take place; however, a major concern of the hustler is how best to protect his privacy. Although information was obtained only from hustlers, it is also reasonable to assume that privacy is also a concern of the customer, since arrest could lead to loss of family, friends, and perhaps his job. One hustler said:

> Sometimes you might go to a hotel that they have already rented or you might go to their houses, you might even stay in the car, but you would go away from society. You would go where you wouldn't have any attention.

Despite the variety of locations, it is not clear from the data if hustlers have a preference as to where the sexual encounter should take place. Again, privacy is a common concern. Performing these acts in public increases the probability of detection by law enforcement, and to be caught in the act is the easiest way for one's cover to be blown (Goffman, 1963).

The sexual act can influence the location, since some activities cannot easily be accomplished in a car (i.e., anal intercourse). Some activities require the trick to either take the hustler to his house, with an attendant risk of discovery should a family member come home unexpectedly, or to rent a room in a motel where the risk of discovery is minimal. The latter, however, would require additional expenditures, therefore, the sexual desires of the trick must also be balanced with practical considerations.

Once the act is complete, the trick will return the hustler to the downtown area or take him to another location. Most hustlers in this study did not return to the prostitution site but were dropped off at other locations—a strategy used to avoid detection. If the hustler has been successful in negotiating and completing the sexual transaction, he can continue to engage in this discrediting behavior without being publicly labeled and identified as a discredited person.

Discussion

The majority of these hustlers became involved in male prostitution as a result of peer introduction. Their friends provided them with the necessary instructions, motives, and techniques for carrying out this deviant activity. As presented here, one of the key instructions given these hustlers by their introducers was the type of sexual acts they should engage in with their tricks. Other instructions included the location of the prostitution area, how to minimize police detection, and ideas about customer behavior.

In the negotiation process between hustlers and customers, several techniques were highlighted that help these hustlers avoid arrest and the subsequent label of homosexual prostitute. Particular emphasis is placed on three stages of the negotiation process: initial contact, confirmation, and location of the sexual act. In each of these stages, hustlers made every attempt to prevent others, particularly those with official sanctioning powers, from learning about their involvement in street prostitution. Of those strategies identified, making sure the individual who is cruising is a would-be customer; ascertaining if the customer is connected with law enforcement; and carrying out the sexual transaction out of the public's view are all designed to avoid arrest.

This research suggests that the interactions between a street hustler and a trick are a complex process requiring each party to "read" the other. The hustler must be skilled in these negotiations, for failure to do so could result in arrest and subsequent stigmatization.

References

Allen, D. M. (1980). Young Male Prostitutes: Psychosocial Study. *Archives of Sexual Behavior*, 9:399–425.

Bell, A. P. and M. S. Weinberg. (1978). *Homosexualities: A Study of Diversity Among Men and Women*. New York: Simon and Schuster.

Bour, D., J. Young, and R. Henningsen. (1984). A Comparison of Delinquent Prostitutes and Non-Prostitutes on Self Concept. In S. Chaneles (ed.), *Gender Issues, Sex Offenses, and Criminal Justice.* New York: The Haworth Press.

Boyer, D. (1989). Male Prostitution and Homosexual Identity. *Journal of Homosexuality, 17*(1–2):51–84.

Butts, W. M. (1947). Boy Prostitutes of the Metropolis. *Journal of Clinical Psychopathy, 8*:673–681.

Caukins, S. E. and N. R. Coombs. (1976). The Psychodynamics of Male Prostitution. *American Journal of Psychotherapy, 30*:441–451.

Coleman, E. (1989). The Development of Male Prostitution Activity Among Gay and Bisexual Adolescents. *Journal of Homosexuality, 17*(1–2):131–149.

Coombs, N. K. (1974). Male Prostitution: A Psychosocial View of Behavior. *American Journal of Orthopsychiatry, 44*:782–789.

Earls, C. M. and H. David. (1989). A Psychosocial Study of Male Prostitution. *Archives of Sexual Behavior, 18*(5):401–419.

Ginsburg, K. N. (1967). "The Meat Rack": A Study of the Male Homosexual Prostitute. *American Journal of Psychotherapy, 21*:170–184.

Goffman, E. (1963). *Stigma.* Englewood Cliffs, NJ: Prentice-Hall.

Humphreys, L. (1970). *Tearoom Trade: Impersonal Sex in Public Places.* Chicago: Aldine Press.

James, J. (1982). Entrance into Juvenile Male Prostitution. *Final Report.* Washington, DC: Department of Health and Human Services.

Jersild, J. (1956). *Boy Prostitution.* Copenhagen: G. E. C. Gad.

Lenoff, M. and W. A. Wesley. (1956). The Homosexual Community. *Social Problems, 3*:256–263.

Lowman, J. (1987). Taking Young Prostitutes Seriously. *The Canadian Review of Sociology and Anthropology, 24*:99–116.

Luckenbill, D. F. (1984). The Dynamics of Deviant Sale. *Deviant Behavior, 5*:337–353.

MacNamara, D. E. J. (1965). Male Prostitution in American Cities: A Socioeconomic or Pathological Phenomenon? *American Journal of Orthopsychiatry, 35*:204.

Mathews, P. W. (1988). On Being a Prostitute. *Journal of Homosexuality, 15*(3–4):119–135.

Matza, D. (1964). *Delinquency and Drift.* New York: John Wiley.

Prus, R. and S. Irini. (1980). *Hookers, Rounders, and Desk Clerks: The Social Organization of the Hotel Community.* Salem, WI: Sheffield.

Raven, S. (1963). Boys Will be Boys: The Male Prostitute in London. In H. Ruitenbeck (ed.), *Problem of Homosexuality in Modern Society.* New York: E. P. Dutton and Company.

Rechy, J. (1977). *The Sexual Outlaw: A Documentary.* New York: Grove Press.

Reiss, A. J., Jr. (1961). The Social Integration of Queers and Peers. *Social Problems, 9*:102–120

Ross, H. L. (1959). The "Hustler" in Chicago. *Journal of Student Research, 1*:13–19.

Sullivan, T. (1987). Juvenile Prostitution: A Critical Perspective. *Journal of Marriage and Family Review, 12*:113–134.

Sutherland, E. H. and D. R. Cressey. (1978). *Criminology.* 10th ed. Philadelphia: Lippincott.

Warren, C. A. B. (1972). *Identity and Community in the Gay World.* New York: Wiley.

Weisberg, D. K. (1984). *Children of the Night: A Study of Adolescent Prostitution.* Lexington, MA: Lexington Books.

13

Bathhouse Intercourse: Structural and Behavioral Aspects of an Erotic Oasis

Richard Tewksbury

Gay bathhouses, also sometimes referred to as gay saunas, sex clubs, or "the tubs" (Hogan and Hudson, 1998) have been a part of urban gay communities for several decades and have served as centers of sexual and social interactions. As a social institution bathhouses provide a setting in which men can gather, meet other men (often anonymously), and engage in sexual activity. Bathhouses provide men seeking male sexual partners an environment where they can have a high degree of confidence of finding willing and interested sexual partners. Bathhouses have stood as a central, although infrequently discussed, aspect of urban gay culture for nearly five decades (Hogan and Hudson, 1998).

On the threshold of the 21st century bathhouses remain one of the "dirty secrets" of many gay communities. As commercial establishments bathhouses continue to flourish, and attract large numbers of men seeking men for sexual purposes. However, community perceptions of bathhouses have ranged from benign tolerance to intense distain. In the 1980s bathhouses were vehemently attacked as scourges of the gay community, institutions contributing to the downfall of communities and relationships and to the deaths of many men (see Bailey, 1998; Brigham, 1994; Miller, 1995; Rabin, 1986).

Reprinted from *Deviant Behavior,* Vol. 23, No. 1 (2002), pp. 75–112. © 1996 Taylor & Francis, Inc. Edited and reprinted by permission of the publisher.

The Present Study

The purpose of the present research is to revisit gay bathhouses and examine the social and sexual dynamics of the setting. In essence, this work seeks to explore the way that men use the bathhouse, and how interactions are structured and conducted. Focus is centered on understanding how, where, and when sexual opportunities are encountered/constructed, how they physical features of the setting both bound the experience and provide a safe environment and how both physical and social features of bathhouses promote congeniality among patrons, comfort, and hence sexual interactions. In short, the present study seeks to enhance, complete, and update understandings of bathhouses as provided by others, with a focus on physical and social structures, interactions, and setting-specific norms.

The sociological study of bathhouses—assessing the culture, organized facilitation of sexual activities and patrons—has been essentially neglected, especially in the past two decades. In fact, Bolton, Vincke, and Mak (1994:257) have gone so far as to say that "no serious ethnographic work on saunas has ever been published" (see Weinberg and Williams, 1975). To be accurate, Bolton and his colleagues may have overstated the issue. It would be more accurate to note that while overall relatively few researchers have ventured into bathhouses (as is the case with many, if not most, erotic oases), there has been some research, but it was produced either during the "sexual revolution" of the 1970s (Styles, 1979; Weinberg and Williams, 1975) or during the initial years of the HIV epidemic. The present study seeks to fill this significant gap in our understanding of the culture, activities, and patrons within this largely understudied social context.

The Bathhouse as an Erotic Oasis

The bathhouse is a prime example of what Delph (1978) defined as an "erotic oasis" (see also Tewksbury, 1995). By definition, an erotic oasis is a location considered as physically and socially safe (according to subculturally defined standards) from threats to exposure. Erotic oases provide individuals with opportunities to gather and pursue mutually desired sexual interactions. Erotic oases include both private and public settings. Some such settings are commercially operated businesses (such as bathhouses or adult bookstores) while others are natural environments co-opted by men for sexual purposes (public restrooms, public parks, etc.). Generally speaking, then, there are two basic varieties of erotic oases. First, some erotic oases are public settings usurped for erotic activities. The best-known work in such locales is Humphreys's (1970) *Tearoom Trade*. Alternatively, some erotic oases (as in the case of a bathhouse) are subcultural sites expressly designed for sex and "that specifically encourage erotic posturing if not outright sex. Privately owned, they are not nearly as accessible to the public as natural settings" (Delph, 1978: 36). However, regardless of the specific nature of the setting, the defining characteristic of an erotic oasis is that sexual expressions are not only permitted, but openly encouraged.

To facilitate sexual expressions and activity, erotic oases are physically bounded and guarded settings that employ screening devices to separate the sexual world from the conventional world (Delph, 1978). Bathhouses clearly fulfill such a definition. Although they typically advertise and present themselves as "social clubs" or "health clubs" catering to gay men, in reality, there is little confusion about the real purpose of such commercial establishments. Bathhouses are social venues, but environments that "provide a highly charged erotic environment where the possibilities for sexual gratification are always just around the corner. It is small wonder, then, that baths became extremely popular institutions for gay men, especially in view of the ethos of sexual freedom that was part of the process of gay liberation" (Bolton et al., 1994: 258).

Because of both the normative structure of the setting and the fact that most patrons strive to hide the fact that they patronize such settings (Bolton et al., 1994; Tattleman, 1999; Weinberg and Williams, 1975), relatively little is known about the men who go to the baths. Bolton et al. (1994), studying Belgian men and Richwald, Morisky, Kyle, Kristal, Gerber, and Friedland (1988) studying men in Los Angeles show that while bathhouse clients are diverse in age, more than three-quarters are under the age of 40, most are white, they are typically college educated, most frequently are involved in a steady, long-term relationship, and are diverse in terms of their religious affiliation (see also McKusick, Horstman, and Coates, 1985). Furthermore, the majority self-identify as "exclusively homosexual" or report only male sex partners; however, between 4% (Richwald et al., 1988) and 14.9% (Bolton et al., 1994) report either being currently or previously in a heterosexual marriage. Similarly, Earl (1990) reports that 15% of men engaged in same-sex sexual interactions in bathhouses and pornographic bookstores are married, and essentially none of the men who also reported female sexual partners informed their female partners of their sexual activities with men.

As discussed above, the primary reason for patronizing a bathhouse is for sexual purposes, but this is not universal. Although Richwald et al. (1988) report that 72% of their sample attend a bathhouse "to have sex," other nonsexual purposes are also cited as alternative or complementary reasons for bathhouse patronage. For instance, nearly one-half (48%) report going to the baths to use the health club facilities/equipment, more than one-third (37%) go to meet friends, and 6% go to have a safe place to sleep. In terms of the sexual nature of the settings, baths also provide an outlet for men who have voyeuristic tendencies (Bolton et al., 1994; Tattleman, 1999; Weinberg and Williams, 1975). Due to the pervasiveness of sexuality, opportunities for observing the sexual activities of others are common. However, a few men in bathhouses do not engage in sexual activities; fully 18% of men in one study reported engaging in no sexual contact during bathhouse visits (Richwald et al., 1988; see also Tattleman, 1999).

As a sexualized setting, bathhouses are especially attractive to men with a wide range of sexual tastes and desires (Bolton et al., 1994). When comparing the sexual activities of a predominantly gay male sample, Bolton et al. (1994) found that men who went to bathhouses were more likely to engage in group sex, rimming (oral-anal contact), water sports (inclusion of urine in sexual interactions), anal intercourse (but only when condoms are involved), and actively cruise a variety of public settings for sexual partners. However, drawing on data from the mid-1980s Richwald et al. (1988) report that "only" 29% of men in Los Angeles bathhouses reported engaging in anal intercourse during their most recent bathhouse visit, and only 10% of all men in bathhouses engaged in anal sex without condoms. As the political and public outcry against bathhouses in the mid 1980s shows, common belief is that bathhouse sex is high-risk. However, at least one set of researchers (Bolton et al., 1994) claim that gay men who do go to bathhouses have high rates of condom use. Therefore, they conclude that bathhouses, "may be safer sexual venues than the alternatives" (see also Richwald et al., 1988: 269).

Structural and Cultural Aspects of Bathhouses

As an institution designed to facilitate and host sexual activities between men, bathhouses possess unique sexually facilitating features.

This structure has been best and most comprehensively discussed in Weinberg and Williams's (1975) work on the organization and activities of gay bathhouses. Specifically, they identify six critical factors for the facilitation of impersonal sex: protection; a good opportunity structure; a known, shared, and organized opportunity structure; bounding of the experience; congeniality; and comfortable physical settings. All six factors—critical for the attraction and "success" of any erotic oasis—are maintained by the organization and structure of bathhouses.

The anonymity of any erotic oasis, and the (near) exclusive focus on sex are perhaps the most important aspects for attracting patrons. In the case of the bathhouse, patrons enter a world centered on depersonalization and objectification, and can interact with a set of other men seeking similar experiences and interactions (Weinberg and Williams, 1975). However, attendance at an erotic oasis (including bathhouses) has always been believed to be confined to a minority of gay-identified men (see Bolton et al., 1994; Miller, 1995; Communication Technologies, 1986, cited in Richwald et al., 1988). Men have almost always hidden their participation, or shown some degree of embarrassment when "caught" in an erotic oasis by others they know (Bolton et al., 1994; Styles, 1979; Tattleman, 1999; Tewksbury, 1990, 1995, 1996; Weinberg and Williams, 1975).

As with any subcultural setting, participants in erotic oases are regulated by a set of situationally defined norms. In baths, these norms include restrictions on modes of communication, style of comportment (i.e., "no campy behavior"), and regulations about the appropriate use of physical space (some areas are unofficially deemed "non-sexual zones"). The importance of these norms is that they are central to the structuring of interactions and sexual opportunities (Tattleman, 1999; Weinberg and Williams, 1975). However, despite the best of intentions of some (Tattleman, 1999), a full explication of the norms and structure of activities, and how the setting functions to structure sexual communications, negotiations, and encounters remains absent in the literature.

In terms of situational norms, bathhouses show important divergence from the structure and organization of other erotic oases in terms of the communication modes the men use. In most instances, erotic oases are largely silent environments (see Delph, 1978; Desroches, 1990; Donnelly, 1981; Humphreys, 1970; Tattleman, 1999; Tewksbury, 1990, 1993, 1996). Silence is important in most erotic oases, as a way of both maintaining anonymity and protecting oneself from committing to a course of action before deducing whether others are seeking similar lines of action. However, bathhouses are generally not silent places where patrons actively avoid verbal communication; the reason for this difference is that silence is only necessary in "spaces susceptible to direct coercion and control" (Delph, 1978: 25). However, when verbal exchanges occur, anonymity is eroded. Therefore, while not necessarily silent locations, conversation has traditionally been discouraged, by bathhouse management (see Hogan and Hudson, 1998: 74). A lack of verbalization is intended to provide opportunities for *anonymous* sex (Weinberg and Williams, 1975).

The fact that conversation is typically held to a minimum does not mean that communication between men in bathhouses does not transpire (see Tattleman, 1999). Rather, intentions, desires, and propositions are not communicated verbally, but rather through nonverbal communication. Messages and intentions are communicated through eye contact, posturing, body language, and movement (Tattleman, 1999). However, the ways in which these means of communication are used remains unexplored.

Erotic oases host such pervasive sexuality that Delph (1978) claims that posturing and performances designed to attract sexual partners begin as soon as an individual enters the setting (also see Humphreys, 1970). The posturing and performing is most commonly based on initial communications exchanged via eye contact. Meaningful eye contact is "not merely an empty glance but a holding or penetrating look shot directly into the other's eyes" (Delph, 1978: 49). If a line of communication is opened in this way, the exchange of signs and cues between potential sexual partners will usually escalate in intensity and directness. It is in this exchange of ever increasingly direct and focused signaling that individuals determine if they will have sex with one another. As with all sexual oasis interactions, conversation is held to a minimum, although some researchers have indicated that any conversation between patrons can be interpreted as an indication of sexual interest (Styles, 1979; however, see also Tattleman, 1999; Weinberg and Williams, 1975).

The anonymity of the bathhouse, and the pervasive sexuality, "generate a high level of sexual excitement—so much so that the physical characteristics of participants seem to recede in importance" (Weinberg and Williams, 1975: 130). This is not to say that those who rank lower in patrons' eyes in terms of cultural definitions of attractiveness are not at a disadvantage in finding sexual partners. For "the standards of the wider homosexual culture, in which youth and physical attractiveness are highly valued, pervade the baths. Thus, older or very overweight patrons may spend much of their time cruising with little success"

(Weinberg and Williams, 1975: 129). Delph (1978) suggests that there is a competition between the attractive/desirable and unattractive/undesirable in erotic oases for sexual partners, and perhaps roles. In some instances the presence of physically less attractive men may discourage others from engaging in sexual communications and transactions. Similar arguments have been made regarding other erotic oases (Tewksbury, 1990, 1996) as well.

Methods

The present analysis is based on 45.5 hours of participant observation in two bathhouses located in a major Midwestern city. The use of data gathered by way of participant observation allows the research to assess the actual activities and culture of the settings, while avoiding obstacles of response bias and respondent selection. The reliance on participant observation data allows the research to assess the actual events and cultural patterning of both social and sexual activities "as they really are."

The author entered and spent several hours in the bathhouse, circulated with and among patrons, carefully observing others, their activities, movements, interactions, and use of the physical features of the environment. Field notes were written during periodic retreats (usually every ten to fifteen minutes) to one of the private rooms available for rent to patrons.

After leaving the setting, field notes were elaborated and expanded, with methodological and analytical notes added to the documentation of witnessed events (see Berg, 1998). Field notes comprised the primary data for analysis. An analytic-inductive process was used in organizing and interpreting the data (Miles and Huberman, 1984). Data analysis included three activities: data reduction (identifying emergent themes in the data), data display (organizing and clustering of information for deriving conclusions), and conclusion drawing and verification (interpreting the meaning and patterning of experiences).

Research Settings

Facility A

Facility A is located in the downtown, business area of the city, on a street with little pedestrian traffic. The building is close to the street,

with glass double doors providing entry off of the sidewalk; an inconspicuous sign on the front of the building identifies the establishment. A
parking lot for about 30 cars is immediately adjacent to one side of the
building.

Immediately upon entering the front doors there is a glass window
through which a clerk greets, checks, or sells memberships, and rents
patrons either a locker or private room (with or without closed-circuit
porn videos). Rates vary by day of the week and number of hours a
patron wishes to stay. The facility is open 24 hours a day.

There are a total of approximately 100 lockers located in a room
immediately adjacent to the front entrance. Just inside the front door is
a television lounge with seating on either benches or couches for
approximately a dozen men. The large-screen television shows network
programming. Also immediately inside the door is a gym area, enclosed
by glass walls, with treadmills, weight machines, and stationary bicy-
cles; the gym area is used rather frequently, always by men dressed in
shorts and (usually) t-shirts. As one progresses down the hall, going
deeper into the facility, there is a small area with vending machines and
three small tables with two chairs. Beyond the snack area is a large rest-
room, and then the private rooms. All areas between the entrance and
the private rooms are brightly lit, carpeted, and very clean.

There are also 50 private rooms on two floors, with rooms on the
second floor having 19" televisions suspended from the ceiling showing
pornographic videos on closed-circuit. Each private room is approximately 8' x 8' with dark wood paneling, a light on a dimmer switch, and
a 1' x 1' window in the door. On the inside of the door, above the window is a clothes hook, allowing a room occupant to cover the window
with their clothing. Each room has a small shelf and a bed parallel to
the door. Mattresses are approximately 4" thick and accompanied by a
worn, very thin pillow. Rooms with televisions have the television suspended from the ceiling behind the door, allowing a room occupant to
lie on the bed and simultaneously watch the video and other patrons
walking past the open room door. In the hallways where private rooms
are located lights are dim, carpet has well-worn traffic patterns, and
speakers play pop and dance music at a fairly high volume.

On one end of the second floor is a 19" televison hanging from the
ceiling in the hallway showing porn videos; this hallway also has one
small bench about 10 feet from the television, and a larger bench at the
far end of the hallway for patrons watching videos. On the opposite side
of the second floor is a railed balcony overlooking a two-story glass
wall separating the "wet area." As one enters the wet area on the first

floor there is a 5-head open shower area on the left, and on the immediate right is an 8-person sauna with a large glass window in the door. Next to the sauna is a large steam room. The glass-doored steam room has three primary areas. As one enters the steamroom there is a narrow, approximately 25'-long passageway leading to a 6'-high wall. Around the wall is a two-tier, tiled set of benches, and standing room for approximately 10 men. The third area of the steam room is a sitting area with a bench for four men immediately inside the door, separated from the passageway by a 6'-high wall. Beyond the steamroom and showers is a whirlpool that can accommodate 8 men, and beyond the whirlpool is a door to an outdoor, in-ground pool, surrounded by tables and lounge chairs.

Facility B

Facility B is located in a commercial area of town, along a major, 4-lane road. The building is all-brick, with an inconspicuous sign on the front of the building. Surrounding the front and one side of the building is a 8'-high wooden fence; a driveway along one side leads to a well-lit parking lot behind the building. As in Facility A, immediately inside the building entrance is a glass window through which a clerk greets, checks or sells memberships, and rents patrons either a locker or private room (with or without closed-circuit porn videos). Rates vary by the day of week and number of hours a patron wishes to stay. The facility is open 24 hours a day.

There are a total of 50 private rooms on three floors and 40 lockers. All lockers are located in a hallway at the bottom of a stairwell on the first floor. Private rooms are on all three floors; one-half of all rooms are on the top floor, with one quarter on the first and second floor each. Additionally, there are two televisions showing pornographic videos in public lounges (one 52" television is located in a third-floor lounge with bench seating along three walls for about ten patrons, and one 19" television is located at one end of the workout area on the first floor. The gym equipment is located in the middle of a large first-floor room lined on three sides by private rooms. The second floor contains a large, projection screen television lounge, a small snack area with 4 small tables and 19" television (showing network programming, and a room with a tanning bed. Restrooms are located on each floor. Each private room is approximately 6' x 8' with dark wood paneling and painted metal doors. Each room is equipped with a mattress (about 5" thick) and one thin pillow (with dark maroon sheets) on a bench positioned either parallel or perpendicular to the door. All rooms are carpeted and have a wall hook for hanging one's clothing, a small shelf, and a dimmer switch. The carpeting throughout the facility is indoor-outdoor with a dark blue and gray pattern; little wear shows on the carpet. Lighting is by recessed ceiling lights throughout; most areas are kept fairly dim.

The wet area is located on the first floor and consists of an open four-head shower area, steam room, sauna, two sinks, and a wall of benches facing the showers, sauna, and steam room. This facility also has a large outdoor patio with approximately 30 lounge chairs and 4 tables and chairs which is shielded from outside view by the surrounding wood fence.

Findings

Pervasiveness of Sex

As a physical and cultural institution devoted to providing men with a safe, clean, and open environment for sexual activities the bathhouses studied are highly successful. In the simplest of terms, sex in the bathhouses is common and pervasive. Men can be found engaging in sex in a variety of locations throughout the setting, participating in a variety of sexual acts, partaking in sexual endeavors with a number and range of partners, and centering their time in the setting around the pursuit and consummation of sexual activities.

It is rare to see a man who leaves without having been seen engaging in at least some form of sexual activity. Throughout all observation periods, nearly every man in the setting was witnessed negotiating, engaging, or leaving a sexual encounter at least once. Many men were witnessed sexually involved with more than one individual, and on more than one occasion during their time in the setting.

Each bathhouse provides a maximum length of time that an individual may stay in the setting (without paying an additional fee). When first entering the bathhouse an individual rents either a locker or a private room for a specified period of time. Depending on which bathhouse an individual patronizes, lockers and rooms can be rented for either 3, 6, or 12 hours. Most men remain in the setting for all (or nearly all) of the time they purchase. When an individual's allotted time has expired they will be paged through the public address speaker system (using their locker or room number, not their name), and informed that their "time is up." Such announcements are common, especially during the hours between 11 p.m. and 8 a.m.. After midnight it is common for 10 or more room/locker numbers per hour to be announced and informed their time has expired. Clearly then, men do often remain on site for the duration of the time they purchase.

Sexual activity is common in numerous areas of the bathhouse at a variety of hours. The number of men on-site is highest in the late evening (after 10:00 p.m.), but the greatest amount of sexual activity appears to occur during the early evening hours (from approximately 8:00 p.m. until 10:00 p.m.). It is interesting to note that patron turnover occurs every few hours. This is especially noticeable during midafternoon, early evening, and late evening hours. The majority of men present during the early evening leave, and a new influx of men arrive between 10:00 p.m. and midnight. Also, lights are often dimmed yet further sometime after 10:00 p.m. When this occurs there is a corresponding increase in the frequency of public nudity and public/semi-public masturbation to be witnessed. This suggests that the dimming of lights not only facilitates a sexual environment, but is also perceived as an enhancement of the setting's protective features. However, regardless of the hour, men can be found engaging in oral and anal sex in private rooms (with doors sometimes widely, or more often slightly, open), in the sauna and steam rooms, in the pool or whirlpool, or less frequently in the television lounges and hallways.

Sexual activity is most common when the bathhouse is only moderately busy. During the late evening, or during weekend days when the facility is very crowded, sexual activity (both in publicly visible areas, and presumably in private rooms) is less pervasive. On a "typical" day during the late afternoon and early evening hours the bathhouse may have between one-quarter and one-third of the rooms occupied and lockers in use. During these hours there is a less intense attitude among patrons (evidence by more relaxed facial expressions and body posture), and cruising involves more overt and obvious sexual posturing and propositions. It is during these hours that any physical touching between men in public areas is most likely to occur, especially when passing in the hallways. Additionally, these hours are when men are more likely to simply approach a man in a public area and commence massaging his chest, legs, ass, or genitals, or simply to say hello and verbally invite another to engage in sexual activity. However, as the facility becomes more crowded (which generally correlates with late night hours) the patrons become younger on average, less aggressive in approaching others and cruising takes on a more subtle (or, perhaps more selective) nature. (See below for a discussion of the means by which men communicate sexual interests and negotiate sexual contacts.) This suggests that either a greater density of patrons reduce the setting's protected features or that as men age they become more sexually forward ("free"?) and less concerned about the consequences of a rejected sexual proposition/approach.

During late mornings, afternoons, and early evenings, most men in the setting are in their 30s and 40s; relatively few (perhaps 10–15%) bathhouse patrons appear younger than 30, and only somewhat more common are men in their 50s or older. However, during late-night/early-morning hours (after 11:00 p.m.) almost all older men leave and the mean age of patrons becomes significantly younger (late 20s or early 30s). Additionally, bathhouse patrons are primarily white. African Americans, Hispanic Americans, and Asian Americans are present, but only in small numbers (this is likely due to the demographic homogeneity of the community in which the bathhouses studied are located.) Hispanic and Asian men appear well-integrated to the setting, interacting and engaging in sex with men of all races; however, this is not the case for African-American men. First of all, African-American men are far more likely to be present during later hours, when younger patrons are also more common. Those African-American men observed on-site were primarily either very young and effeminate men or extremely overweight. When present, African-American men are only rarely seen interacting or sexually engaged with white men.

Where Sex Occurs

Sex primarily occurs in three areas of bathhouses: inside private rooms, in communal, semiprivate facilities (saunas, steam rooms, whirlpools, and dormitories), and in communal, open facilities (pools, Jacuzzis, porno lounges, etc.). Also, on rare occasions men will engage in some sexual activities in public areas intended for nonsexual uses (hallways, restrooms, and gyms).

There is a clear set of norms structuring the seeking, negotiating, and consummating of sexual activities. As others (Tattleman, 1999; Weinberg and Williams, 1975) have shown, there are physical areas inside the baths that are designated "sex free zones." These include the "regular television" lounge (as opposed to lounges showing pornography), the areas containing vending machines, and the areas immediately surrounding the main entry to the facility. While some sexual activity does occur in these areas, it is rare and most often consists only of manual stimulation of self or a partner. The fact that sex and sexual approaches are clearly "deviant" in these areas is communicated to patrons by the fact that these are the areas with the brightest lights, the most open space, and areas in which some men can be found fully clothed as they enter or exit the facility. In this way, these sex-free zones of the bathhouse serve as transitional areas, mediating between the norms and culture of the "regular world" and the sexual oasis of the bathhouse.

The most common locations for sexual activities are private rooms. There are two basic varieties of private rooms in bathhouses: those with and those without closed-circuit sexually explicit videos. Most sex in private rooms is performed behind closed doors. This means that most sex that occurs in private rooms is not directly witnessed; however, when seeing men enter a room together, or one man entering a room already occupied by another man, it is assumed that sexual activity does follow. Men that are witnessed entering or exiting private rooms are of all demographic categories. However, two patterns can be discerned about men's ages and the use of private rooms. First, the youngest men only rarely rent a private room, instead opting for a locker. Second, among men who cruise hallways seeking possible sexual partners there are relatively few men under the age of 30; those who cruise rooms are typically older men. When younger men do cruise the halls, they tend to walk more quickly than older men, and to gaze into rooms less frequently and for shorter durations.

Whereas the very young men tend to not cruise other men in private rooms, those who do rent a room frequently present themselves as sexually available from inside the room. Men who remain in their private rooms with open doors (i.e., presenting themselves as sexually available to others) represent the full range of ages of patrons, but are almost exclusively white men. When presenting themselves as sexually available in a private room it is typical for the lights in the room to be dimmed, although not so much as to inhibit passersby from adequately assessing the desirability of the room's occupant. Only in instances where the man in the room is elderly, excessively overweight, or extremely unattractive will the lights in the room be completely off while the door is open. In most instances men in their rooms will sit or lay on the bed in a way that exposes either their genitals or asses. When exposing one's genitals, it is normative to slowly masturbate, or in some way maintain either a partial or full erection. The presentation of men inside private rooms is focused, if not exclusively centered, on sexualized body parts: genitalia, asses, chests/abdomens, hands, and on occasion mouths. This focus on sexualized body parts is most clearly seen in instances when men shield their faces, while positioning their genitals/asses to be directed toward the open room door, maximizing exposure to passersby. Rooms containing men with the lights off, or men shielding their faces but presenting their genitals or asses to the door, are more commonly seen during very late-night/early-morning hours.

If a passerby is interested in a man in a room he will pause outside the open door (sometimes after making one pass without pausing) and attempt to make eye contact with the man in the room. Alternatively, some men will enter the threshold of an open room and offer brief comments about how crowded (or not) the bathhouse is, or will comment on the porn playing on the video screen (if a room has video). At this point the responsibility for determining the outcome of the possible interaction shifts to the man in the private room; he can either indicate a lack of interest (breaking eye contact, shaking his head no, or covering himself) or invite the other into his room (with a nod of the head, a gesture to enter, or much less frequently a verbal invitation). Only on very rare occasions do men inside rooms initiate contact with passersby.

In Facility A room doors contained a small (approximately 8" x 8") window that could be covered from the inside by hanging one's clothing on a hook just above the window. Many times this will leave a small portion of the window uncovered, allowing passersby to easily see inside the room. Also, some private rooms in bathhouses have doors that close but leave small cracks between the frame and the door. It is common to see men stop in front of these doors when they are closed and peer through the cracks.

On occasion men will engage in sex in a private room leaving the door open or ajar. In these instances, the men in the room are inviting others to watch, or even join in. It is common for men to stop in the hallway outside an open/ajar door and watch those inside engage in sexual activity. The men watching are usually older men who are among the least attractive patrons. Some men outside rooms with open doors will initiate sexual contacts with other men watching, not infrequently leading to two or more men moving to another private room, presumably to continue with a sexual encounter. This is a pattern seen throughout bathhouses; when one set/group of men initiate sexual activity others witnessing the encounter frequently and quickly initiate a sexual contact of their own. The occurrence of sexual activity appears to clearly communicate to others a "permission" to be sexual, in what is then constructed as a safe location within the bathhouse. Once one man (or couple/group) crosses the boundary from cruising to engaging in sexual contact, others witnessing the movement often quickly follow suit.

The second common type of area in which sex occurs in a bathhouse is communal, semiprivate areas. Communal, semiprivate areas of the facility include all areas that are open to any patron, but are secluded from general observation, unless an individual passes through or beyond a visual barrier (such as a wall or door).

Communal, semiprivate areas are primary areas of sexual activity for three reasons. First, these are areas in which most, if not all, men will spend at least some time. Second, some men do not rent a private room, and therefore will spend all of their time in public or semipublic areas of the facility; this means their sexual activity must occur either in the room of another man, or in a public/semipublic area. Third, communal areas offer gathering places that are semiprivate (as well as semipublic), thereby facilitating exhibitionism, multiple-partner sexual encounters, and opportunities to receive visual "permission" to engage sexually.

The most common communal, semiprivate area for sex between men is the steam room. In both facilities a steam room is located immediately adjacent to a dry sauna, but the sauna is rarely the site of sexual activity (with the exception that some men will openly masturbate in the sauna, usually in an attempt to gain the attention/interest of another). The primary reason for the steam rooms to serve as central locations for sexual activity is that although their doors are entirely made of glass, they provide a visual barrier that is not provided by the saunas. In both facilities the sauna door is more than 75% glass, and located so that all men passing through the area can easily see inside. In Facility B the sauna also has a small, shoulder-high window (approximately 18" high and 3' feet wide) that allows continuous surveillance by passersby. In fact, as most men pass the sauna, if anyone is inside they will significantly slow their pace or stop and peer in the window. However, the steam rooms' doors are continually fogged over, preventing seeing anything more than the outline of a body immediately inside the door. Additionally, once inside the steam rooms, there are areas that cannot be seen from immediately inside the door. Rather, one must enter and walk at least ten paces and proceed around a wall to a darker area. It is in these areas, behind two visual barriers that most steam room sex takes place. However, especially when the steam room is crowded, initial contacts and manual, oral, and anal sex will occur in the "more public" areas (i.e., closer to the doors) of the steam rooms.

In most instances, men who engage in sex in communal, semipublic areas enter the areas completely naked, either carrying or leaving their towel outside. Nudity in the steam room facilitates efficient assessments of one another as sexually desirable objects; this is in line with Delph's (1978) claim that assessments of the size of others' penises is perhaps the most important way men in sexual oases assess potential sexual partners. Sexual contacts typically begin by one man stroking his genitals or slowly masturbating, which will lead to an observer mirroring this behavior. Touching of another rarely happens without at least a brief period of mirroring self-manipulation of one's genitals. In most (although not all) instances, the first touching of another is initiated by the man who first touched his own genitals. Once contact between two men begins, it is not uncommon for other individuals to either insert themselves into the dyad or to replace one of the participants when he exits the interaction/location.

There are no apparent patterns or sets of traits to distinguish men who do and do not engage in sexual activities in communal, semipublic areas of the bathhouse. However, younger men are somewhat more likely to be found in communal, semipublic areas. Older men are slightly more likely to seek sexual partners in private rooms.

The mere presence of a man in a steam room, and to a lesser extent a sauna or whirlpool, is taken by others as an indication of one's sexual availability; this is further enhanced by one's self-presentation in the nude. Availability as a function of presence can be seen in the apparent acceptance of touching in these locations. Whereas touching another is only rarely, or "accidentally" done in other areas of the bathhouse, inside these areas to touch and be touched is situationally normative.

Men of all races, all ages (although younger men are somewhat more common), and all degrees of physical fitness are found engaged in manual and oral sex in communal, semipublic areas; however, anal sex is relatively rare in communal, semipublic areas, and typically involves younger men. However, anal sex is the only form of sexuality for which there appears to be a pattern (in terms of age) regarding who is and is not involved in sex in communal, semipublic areas of a bathhouse.

Communal, semiprivate areas are attractive locations for sexual activity because they bring many men together in close physical proximity, and while open to observation, they also provide some degree of seclusion. Also, due to either temperature, humidity, or immersion in water, most men will (either prior to entering or immediately after entering) remove their towels and present themselves completely naked. This, clearly, facilitates the continued and constant assessment of one another as potential sexual partners (especially as the penis is revealed), as well as creates a yet more sexually charged air for the area.

However, the fact that these locations are not entirely private is also an important facilitating factor for their frequent sexual activity. In a communal location men can truly "perform" sexually for others, both those with whom they are engaged and others in search of sexual contacts. In this way a man can demonstrate his desirability, sexual skills, and the fact that he is able to attract sexual partners while others have not and/or cannot; in essence, sexual activity in a communal location allows a man to display his virility and his "evolutionary superiority." The communal, semiprivate areas of the bathhouse, then, are the truly sexualized—and most sexually active—regions; although the bathhouse as a whole serves as a host and facilitator of sexual activity, it is in these communal, semiprivate areas that sexual activities are most strongly facilitated and (apparently) most commonly performed.

Communal, public areas of bathhouses are relatively sex-free zones. In hallways, restrooms, snack areas, and gyms men may initiate sexual negotiations—going so far as briefly groping another or exposing their genitals—but sexual activities are rarely performed in these locations. On the rare occasions when sex does occur in these areas it almost always involves men who appear to be younger than age 25. It is the youngest men in the setting that engage in truly public (i.e., performing) sex, but even they do so very rarely.

What is most common in communal, public areas is solicitations for sex. When an individual passes another man in whom he is sexually interested in a hallway he may make and hold eye contact, "inadvertently" allow his hand to touch or stroke a hand, arm, or leg, or may initiate a short verbal exchange. However, communal, public areas are restricted to these types of interactions. Patrons as a whole enforce the general norm of "no sex" in public areas through their rejection of advances that are too strong, or displays of frustration or disdain for those observed crossing the line.

Sexual Acts Performed

There is a restricted range of sexual acts that occur between men in bathhouses. What distinguishes bathhouse sex, however, is the anonymous nature of many sexual interactions, and the inclusion of multiple partners, both sequentially and concurrently. Although a variety of sexual acts can be witnessed in a bathhouse, the vast majority of sexual interactions involve either one man masturbating another (sometimes reciprocated, sometimes not) or oral sex. Anal intercourse does occur, but with significantly less frequency. Contrary to the expectations of some, both "more exotic" forms of male-male sexual interaction (fisting, watersports, bondage, sadomasochistic scenes) and displays of intimacy (kissing, caressing, holding hands) are relatively rare, if present at all.

Manual stimulation of another is the most commonly observed and most frequently engaged in form of sexual interaction for men in bathhouses. There are several structural reasons that facilitate this fact. First, in communal, semiprivate areas stroking, grasping, and fondling another man's genitals is a typical "first step" in any sexual encounter. This means that regardless of what an individual desires for his sexual interaction with another, he will almost always initiate "actual sex" with manual stimulation. Touching another man's genitals is also a way of assessing his willingness to engage in sex. If, when an individual touches another man's genitals, the second man either allows the contact to continue or reciprocates, there is an enhanced likelihood of contact progressing to oral or anal sexual contact.

A second structural factor facilitating manual stimulation as the most common sexual activity in the bathhouse is that in communal, semiprivate areas of the facility touching of genitals will often occur in a group setting, and men may move from partner to partner relatively quickly. Most sexual contacts and interactions in a communal, semipublic area do not result in ejaculation. Rather, many men will engage in sexual contact with numerous men sequentially, seemingly seeking a range of diverse and varying sexual contacts rather than one (or several) longer interactions. In this respect, then, manual stimulation of another is an easy, quick, and exploratory form of sexual interaction. For most men in a bathhouse they will have manual-genital contact with a large number of others, and oral or anal sex with only one or a very few others. (This is not a universal, however, as some men will engage in oral or anal sex with multiple men during a single visit to a bathhouse.)

Oral sex is the second most commonly observed form of sexual interaction in a bathhouse. When men engage in oral sex it is usually a nonreciprocal interaction; one partner performs oral sex on another without the second man performing oral sex on the first. This appears to be a desirable arrangement for most men in the bathhouse.

When soliciting another man for a sexual encounter a man seeking only to perform or receive oral sex will communicate his desired role in several ways. For one, if a solicitation is verbal it will almost always be clearly articulated. When verbalizations are clear, direct, and unambiguous, statements are short and usually preceded by little if any additional conversation. As such, men who verbally solicit will simply approach another and inquire in words such as "Can I suck your cock?" or "Do you suck?" However, verbal solicitations are not the norm; even when soliciting another for a sexual encounter using nonverbal communications, roles are clearly delineated. When a man is seeking someone to perform oral sex on him, he will approach a desired sexual partner and either expose or present for manual stimulation his own genitals, avoiding contact with the desired partner's genitals. In most instances the man soliciting another for oral sex will avoid touching the desired partner, unless it is to guide a hand to his genitals, or to grasp, stroke, or massage the back of the other's head and neck (as an indication to move one's head, so as to be in a position to perform oral sex).

When seeking to perform, rather than receive, oral sex a man may solicit another by first touching a targeted sexual partner; this may be a caress of the buttocks, chest, leg, or groin. Or, an approaching man may reach under or open another man's towel to gain access to his genitals; in these cases the approaching man will keep his own towel securely knotted. If the approached man attempts to touch the body—and in most cases especially the genitals—of the approaching man, he will have his hands redirected or simply pushed away. If he attempts again to gain access to the first man in a sexual manner he can expect to be told in a succinct, direct, yet polite way that such is not expected nor desired. Such messages are communicated with language such as "It's okay, just let me do this" or "I'm fine, . . . sit back" or "Just enjoy."

In a somewhat more subtle, yet just as clear approach, desired sexual activities are communicated by how and where a man positions himself in the environment. Men who rent private rooms will typically spend at least some of their time in their room with the door open. During this time they will position themselves in the room in such a way as to inform passersby about the type of sexual activity they are seeking. A man who wishes to receive anal intercourse will lie naked on his stomach with his buttocks facing the door, perhaps with his legs spread or his ass slightly elevated. A man seeking to perform anal intercourse will sit naked on his bunk, often with an erection, with lubricant (and perhaps condoms) visible and within arms' reach.

Those seeking oral sex also use body posture and positioning to communicate sexual desires. A man wishing to perform oral sex will sit on his bunk wearing his towel and when a desirable other looks into his room he will lick or slowly move his lips, usually while shifting his gaze to the passing man's groin. A much more direct approach would

be a man inside his room squatting in the doorway or otherwise positioning himself so as to have his head approximately at waist level for
those passing by. Similar approaches are used in communal, semiprivate areas where a man squatting in the sauna, steam room, or porn
lounges can be assumed to be seeking others upon whom he can perform oral sex. The least clearly communicated sexual role—and the
role that is populated by the most men—is that of someone seeking
another to perform oral sex. To communicate this desire a man might
sit on his bunk and display his genitals (perhaps masturbating slowly),
or he might sit or lie on the bunk (with or without his towel covering
his genitals) and when another man looks in he will shift his gaze or
nod his head toward his own groin. However, men seeking others to
perform oral sex are the least successful at soliciting those passing a
private room. However, these men are not without opportunities to find
others interested and willing to perform oral sex on them; men seeking
to perform oral sex can easily and quickly be found in their own private
rooms or (sooner or later) in any of the communal, semipublic areas of
the bathhouse.

Anal sex also occurs in bathhouses, in both communal, semipublic
areas and in private rooms. It is assumed that anal sex most often occurs
in private rooms, and therefore the typical dynamics and frequency of
this sexual interaction are more difficult to assess. However, on all
observation visits men were observed engaged in anal intercourse in
communal, semipublic areas, and numerous men were seeking anal sex
partners in open-door private rooms. In communal, semiprivate areas of
the facility anal sex is often an activity in which the receptive partner
either has sequential partners and/or is simultaneously involved performing oral sex on other men.

The other common form of sexual activity found in bathhouses is
manual self-manipulation (i.e., masturbation). At least 75% of all men
in a bathhouse will engage in some form of masturbation during their
visit in a location visible to other men. For some this means sitting,
standing, or lying in a private room and masturbating with the door
open; this is typically a slow and unfocused activity that is not necessarily intended to achieve sexual stimulation or release, but rather is a
means for either attracting a sexual partner or maintaining an erection.
The other common places to observe men masturbating are in communal, semipublic areas and in porn lounges. When men gather in a sauna,
steam room, or other communal area that hosts significant amounts of
sexual activity men will masturbate both as a way to attract a sexual
partner, and as a way of sexually stimulating themselves while watching

others engage in partnered sex. Similarly, men watching videos in communal lounges will often masturbate.

An interesting aspect about masturbation, however, is that men never appear to masturbate to the point of ejaculation. Masturbation, then, is clearly not for sexual release as much as it is for maintaining an erection and for signaling one's sexual readiness and availability to others.

Across all sexual activities and all men in the bathhouses, there are virtually no condoms used. Condoms are readily available, however, they are not used. This finding is in direct contrast to those of Bolton et al. (1994) and Richwald et al. (1988). The reasons for this difference in findings is unclear. It may be a difference based on geographic location of the study sites, it may be that condom use has decreased since these earlier studies were completed, or it may be that what men actually do in bathhouses differs from what they report on surveys. When a man first checks in he is provided with a key to his rented private room or locker, a towel, and (usually) at least one condom. Condoms are available in at least two locations in both facilities studied (and on occasion are in private rooms), and safer sex posters and messages are located throughout both facilities. In fact, on the inside of all rooms at Bathhouse B is a list of "Safe, Possibly Risky, and Risky" sexual activities, and instructions that using condoms can reduce the risk of contracting a sexually transmitted disease. Despite their availability and pervasive messages about safer sexual practices, at no time were any condoms seen being used and no used, discarded condoms or open condom wrappers were ever seen in either facility. This does not mean that condoms are never used; it is likely that condoms are most likely to be used for anal sex (Tewksbury and Moore, 1997) which presumably is most likely to occur in private rooms. Therefore, if condoms are used for anal intercourse it would not be readily known to an observer. However, based on verbal solicitations of the research team it is clear that condoms are not consistently used even for sex in private rooms. Comments such as "want to fuck? You don't have to use a condom" were heard on multiple occasions.

Interactions and Communications Among Men

Although advertised as "social clubs" for gay men, bathhouses are places where conversation is minimal, and interactions are focused, and based on the pursuit of individual not social goals. Bathhouses are not silent locations, such as adult bookstores and video peep shows

(Tewksbury, 1990, 1993) but rather more similar to cruising (i.e., seeking of sexual partners) that occurs in usurped public areas that serve as erotic oases (Delph, 1978; Tewksbury, 1995, 1996). Communication takes place, often frequently and for protracted periods of time, but it is primarily nonverbal in nature. Men communicate with their gaze, gestures and body language, and touch, in addition to occasional brief verbal statements.

Verbal statements, when they are uttered, come in three forms. Men who speak do not possess any distinguishing set of characteristics compared to men who do not speak; however, almost all conversation is brief and in volume lower than that of normal daily conversation. As indicated above, when negotiating a sexual encounter some men will verbally state what they are seeking or offering to a potential partner. However, these are almost always short, succinct, and direct statements that are made in a hushed voice, and usually spoken when the speaker is less than an arm's length away from the man to whom he is speaking. A second general form of verbal interaction is the short conversation which occurs in communal, public areas. Men will interact in "regular" ways in the sex-free areas of the facility. On numerous occasions men have been observed sitting, standing, or otherwise lounging in front of televisions and having exchanges about news, sports, or movies. Some men will make comments about other men present; such comments are usually about the very high or low level of attractiveness of particular others, or inquiries about whether a particular man (or type of man) has been seen. Information that is shared in these conversations is almost always of the "public information" variety; conversation very rarely reveals personal information. Some men do ask "personal" questions (name, where one is from, occupation, age, etc.); such questions almost always elicit nervous responses, and conversations tend to end rather quickly. There are exceptions to this, however. The third general form of conversation that is observed is between men who are friends or acquaintances. Among men who come to the bathhouse together, conversations do have a "normal" appearance, although they are usually conducted in hushed tones, and are not lengthy exchanges. For other men, those who encounter others they know, but did not expect to see, verbal exchanges are short, and often include either an acknowledgment of embarrassment at being "caught" in the setting or individuals will attempt to explain their presence as a "first time" thing, or something that they have done "on a lark/dare."

The primary modes of communication among bathhouse patrons are nonverbal forms of communication. This includes gaze/looks, touch and gestures, and body language. Each of these communication modes is used to indicate interests, sexual preferences, and an individual's commitment to both current activities (or lack thereof) and desire for making sexual contact with particular others.

The most subtle, yet perhaps most constant, means by which men present messages and seek to establish "conversations" with other men in bathhouses is through directing, holding, and shifting of gazes. Where a man directs his gaze is an important means of communicating interest (or lack of interest) in another man, or sexual activity in general. When an individual is interested in another man he will look at him. On the initial level it does not matter how one looks at another, or where on another's body one looks; to direct a gaze at another individual communicates an interest in communicating, and possibly sexually connecting.

While it may be sufficient for communicating a general interest in another (and possibly a sexual exchange) to simply gaze at or toward another man, the direction and placement of one's gaze communicates more specific messages. Gazes directed toward and held on another man's eyes or crotch are especially informative communications. When a man directs a held gaze at another man it conveys a message of either general or specific sexual interest. A gaze into another's eyes expresses a desire to make a connection, without specific sexual activities intended. However, when a man holds a gaze on another's eyes, and strokes, gropes or otherwise draws the gazed-upon object's attention to a location on the gazer's body this is an indication of the type of sexual activity that one is seeking. Men can also communicate specific sexual desires by where they direct their own gaze. A look directed and held at a specific location on another man's body indicates a desire to have sexual contact with that area of the gazed-upon individual's body.

Commonly accompanying communicative gazes are gestures and body language. Sexual interests communicated via gestures typically involve movements of a hand or the head. Meaningful gestures include hand waving for a man to come closer (or enter a private room into which he is gazing), rubbing or caressing of one's own body, and nods of the head indicating a direction for another to move.

Gestures are most commonly employed when an individual seeks to communicate with a specific man, but attempts to do so when in the presence of multiple others, or when he wishes to conceal his message from others. Gestures are silent and can be employed without the knowledge or notice of others nearby. A simple wave, while keeping one's hand hidden from view of others, or a nod of the head from inside one's room will communicate a message to an intended recipient, but be immune from observation by others. Or, as is fairly common in communal, semipublic areas (especially steam rooms and saunas), men will look towards (but avoid eye contact with) a desired other and slowly stroke or manipulate their genitals. Simultaneously gazing at another while manipulating one's genitals rather clearly communicates a sexual interest and availability.

Body language is also a powerful mode of communication inside a bathhouse. Body language—as discussed above as a means for presenting oneself in open-door private rooms or communal semipublic areas—can be used in both subtle and obvious ways. The way a man presents himself, and how he emphasizes his body (and the parts of his body he emphasizes in presentation), are ways to suggest one's sexual interests and availability.

One of the primary ways that men communicate sexual interests and availability via self presentation is through the wearing (or not wearing) of a towel. Nudity is generally seen only in wet areas (pool, showers, sauna, or steamroom) or when a man is displaying himself in a private room. However, even in these locations some men will be attired, whether in a bathing suit, designer underwear, or a towel. When presenting himself nude in a private room, a man will usually be lying or sitting on the bed, or less commonly, simply standing (and idly occupying himself with a menial task such as arranging clothes or adjusting a video monitor) in a private room.

Some men do present themselves naked in communal areas of the bathhouse, however they are the rare exceptions. There are two varieties of men who present themselves in the nude. First, there are older, white men who, although having a towel, will openly display their genitals (and often masturbate) while viewing pornographic videos in a communal, public area. The second variety of men who present themselves in the nude are more physically fit, smooth-chested, white men in their 30s. Most often these men will walk through the hallways or loiter near showers, steam rooms, or saunas, while either holding or draping a towel over their shoulder. In almost all instances men who present in the nude avoid eye contact with other men, projecting an indifferent attitude about their nudity. In essence, it appears that these men use nudity to present themselves as available for sexual solicitations, although they do not actively solicit others.

Clearly, the way a man presents himself in a communal, semipublic area (including his attire), is an important means for communicating interests and desires. Although there are variations, the vast majority of bathhouse patrons wear a towel, and in similar fashion: unfolded, somewhat loosely wrapped around the waist and knotted at one side, with the entire upper half of the legs covered. Variations on this mode of attire are seen in only about 10% of all bathhouse patrons, and are primarily seen either during late night/early morning hours or when the bathhouse is less crowded.

Variations on how men wear towels are present (also see Tattleman, 1999). Each variety of attiring oneself emphasizes different body parts (through what is and is not revealed). The way a towel is worn can be varied by both folding/rolling it to make it shorter, or by knotting it in varying ways and at differing places around the hips (so as to have an opening at the side, front, or back of the body). For men who modify their attire by knotting their towel so that the ends do not overlap and an opening remains, the location of the opening is important for understanding their pursuit of sexual partners. Additionally, the part(s) of the body that is revealed via the opening is an important indicator of a man's sexual desires. A towel that is knotted in the front of a man's body, so as to reveal his inner thighs and genitals indicates a man who is seeking a partner to stimulate his genitals. Men wearing their towels in such a way are always among the youngest men (early 20s) and white men. Similarly, men who wear their towels in ways that facilitate views of the backs of their legs or ass are communicating a desire to receive anal intercourse. A bit more complex are men who knot a towel at the side of their body, revealing essentially all of one leg.

Men who wear their towels in very "revealing" ways (i.e., very short or with wide openings) are of two general varieties; either these are older, overweight, and frequently bald/balding men or they are very young and often rather effeminate-appearing men. For some overweight men the fact that their towel does not cover their legs/hips entirely is a matter of body size, not necessarily a sexual message. Interestingly, in contrast to many of the other behavioral patterns in the bathhouse, race does not seem to be correlated with the ways men wear towels. However, age is important in differentiating men who wear towels in revealing ways. Older men are typically among the most dedicated cruisers, continually circulating throughout the facility and attempting to negotiate sexual contacts. Younger men, however, further distinguish themselves by also folding/rolling their towels, and presenting themselves in the equivalent of a short, tight around the hips, slit skirt. As stereotypes in open society suggest, such individuals are actively seeking sexual contact, and also possess a high degree of confidence in their ability to attract sexual partners. The comportment of these younger men supports this belief; these individuals carry themselves in a very confident manner, and can be seen rebuffing the advances of many "average" or unattractive others.

Presentation of self includes more than simply one's attire, however. Gestures and body language are also powerful (yet complex) means by which men communicate inside the bathhouse. Between the subtle complexities of body language and verbalizations, however, is a means for communicating sexual interest that is more direct than body language while also less direct than verbal solicitations: touch. Men communicate with other men using both "intentional" and "accidental" touches.

Intentional touches are most often done in the context of a verbal exchange. These include one man reaching out to touch or grasp another man's hand, a rubbing of another's shoulder or upper arm or less frequently an intentional touch to a man's chest, leg, or ass while commenting on the attractiveness of that particular part of the individual's body. Intentional touches are most often friendly and may or may not be explicitly sexual in nature. Intentional touches are the same type, duration, and pressure of touching that would occur in conventional interpersonal interactions.

"Accidental" touches, however, are (contrary to their apparent accidental nature) a more direct means for communicating sexual interests. Accidental touches most often occur when one man passes another in a semipublic, communal area and lightly brushes a hand—or on rare occasions, his leg, crotch, or hip—against another man. Men who touch others are usually older men (almost always at least mid-30s) and those who engage in sex in communal, semipublic areas. In this respect, it appears that men who "accidentally" touch others are among the more sexually active and most forthright in seeking out sexual contacts.

Men touched by other men most often receive accidental touches on the hip, leg, or hand. When an accidental touch occurs it is almost always light in pressure, and the touch is held for a second; accidental touching is not a bump or deflected touch, but a light brushing or stroking. When one man accidentally touches another he almost always significantly slows (if he is moving) or holds still, as he awaits a response. It is not uncommon for touching men to combine an accidental touch with a direct gaze into the eyes of the other man.

The importance of nonverbal communications through gaze, gestures, suggestive body language, or "accidental" touches is that such modes allow for efficient communications, yet minimize the possibility of awkward and/or embarrassing propositions. When an individual employs nonverbal means to express a desire to sexually connect with another and his interest is rebuffed, he can quickly, easily, and with relatively little loss of composure withdraw from the interaction. This is not so easily done when an interest or proposition is verbally presented. Therefore, the reliance on nonverbal communication modes are important for their efficiency regarding both communicating and withdrawing from interactions where one's desires are not reciprocated. These means of communication also allow for a man to psychologically cope with rejections more easily. Although bathhouses are very sexual environments (i.e., erotic oases) not all men are sexually interested or willing to sexually engage all other men present. By signaling or propositioning another nonverbally it may be easier to define a rejected advance as a failed communication, not a personal rejection.

Discussion

Gay bathhouses clearly meet the definition of an erotic oasis: they are open, yet secluded, settings that facilitate and promote the pursuit of sexual gratification. Additionally, these are locations that are known (and ostensibly accessible) only to those who are knowledgeable about male-male sexual subcultures. However, due to the greater seclusion that bathhouses offer as compared to other erotic oases (public restrooms, public parks, etc.) there are some important normative differences found. Most notably, bathhouses (although containing only a minimal degree of conversation) are not silent locations, and they offer men a greater degree of security and comfort as well as greater assurances that copresent others are also present for sexual purposes.

Common assumptions are that bathhouses are simply about sex, despite the fact that they are advertised as "social clubs" catering to gay men. Sexual activity is the central focus of the bathhouse, but not to the degree that many critics may believe. Frequent, and multiple partner sexual encounters that occur do, however, introduce cause for concern in numerous arenas. Most notably, since the mid-1980s these concerns have centered on issues of public health and control of the spread of HIV.

Bathhouses host an abundance of high-risk sexual activity; oral and anal sex are common, and condoms are rarely used. In response to this concern, the mid-1980s saw the closure (both voluntary and forced) of numerous bathhouses. However, in the 1990s, many bathhouses reopened, and began to appear in some cities that previously did not have such facilities. Consequently, as the HIV epidemic has continued, bath-houses need to be considered as important foci for HIV prevention/intervention efforts. At present, the likelihood of HIV transmission among bathhouse patrons appears to be quite high.

Sex is present, is common, and is consummated between partners who know little if any information about one another. Those who are present in a bathhouse are considered sexually available by copresent others. Sexual relations, are however, guided by locally specific social structures, situational social norms, and imported values and expectations about potential sexual partners. As previously argued by Delph (1978), as soon as an individual enters a sexual oasis, he begins posturing and performing as a sexually available actor. This is largely true of the bathhouse, although bathhouses provide patrons with a brief transitional period not seen in other sexual oases. Specifically, once entering a bathhouse an individual is not engaged in sexual posturing and is not defined as a potential sexual partner until he moves through communal public areas, secures his room/locker and disrobes. Similarly, in transitioning out of the facility, once an individual begins the process of disengaging from sexual availability (via dressing or presenting himself in street attire) he is freed from the expectations and norms of sexual posturing.

One area in which sexual oases, such as bathhouses, both borrow from and modify larger society's norms and structures regarding sexual competition and negotiations is in regard to competition between more and less attractive men for sexual partners. Whereas stereotypical assumptions about which men do and do not pair off for sexual liaisons in open society suggest that only the attractive engage the attractive, and the unattractive (i.e., older, overweight, deformed, etc.) are relegated to few if any sexual contacts, these assumptions (and the reality) are much less valid inside the bathhouse. Although it is not common for men of different "tiers" or "classes" of desirability to sexually interact, it does occur, and the presence of the less attractive does not present a wholly deleterious effect on others' sexual negotiations and activities. This is especially true in the most highly sexualized areas of the bathhouse (i.e., communal, semipublic areas). What transpires in the bathhouse is simply a much softened form of sexual and desirability competition and classification. Although the less physically attractive are at a disadvantage compared to (generally younger) more attractive patrons, they are not relegated to a marginal status, and denied sexual opportunities. In this respect, bathhouses can be seen as providing somewhat of a balancing effect on social stratification. While not reaching the point of being a truly equal-opportunity environment, bathhouses do begin to blur the lines of differentiating variables. And, perhaps most important for many patrons, bathhouses provide opportunities for men who have sex with men to interact in a safe, sex-positive, generally nonstigmatizing environment. This clearly can account for at least a significant degree of bathhouses' popularity and continued existence.

The findings of this research provide strong support, as well as an updating, of previous work in bathhouses. What is significant here, however, is identifying how bathhouses and the men who patronize them have perpetuated the basic social structure and primacy of sexual activities that characterized bathhouses of the pre-AIDS era. Bathhouses continue to function as erotic oases, with men presenting and approaching one another in manners consistent with previous assumptions and research findings regarding interactions. However, where the present work goes beyond the existing literature is in analyzing the microaspects of the structure, organization, and interactions between and among patrons.

References

Bailey, R. W. (1998). Bathhouse Closure. In R. A. Smith (ed.), *Encyclopedia of AIDS*. Chicago: Fitzroy Dearborn.

Berg, B. L. (1998). *Qualitative Research Methods for the Social Sciences.* 3rd ed. Boston: Allyn and Bacon.

Bolton, R., J. Vincke, and R. Mak. (1994). Gay Baths Revisited: An Empirical Analysis. *GLQ, 1*: 255–273.

Brigham, J. (1994). Sexual Entitlement: Rights and AIDS, the Early Years. *Law and Policy, 16*(3):249–265.

Delph, E. (1978). *The Silent Community.* Beverly Hills: Sage.

Desroches, F. J. (1990). Tearoom Trade: A Research Update. *Qualitative Sociology, 13*(1):39–61.

Donnelly, P. (1981). Running the Gauntlet: The Moral Order of Pornographic Movie Theaters. *Urban Life, 10*(3):239–264.

Earl, W. L. (1990). Married Men and Same Sex Activity: A Field Study on HIV Risk Among Men Who Do Not Identify as Gay or Bisexual. *Journal of Sex and Marital Therapy, 16*(4):251–257.

Hogan, S. and L. Hudson. (1998). Baths/Bathhouses. In Hogan and Hudson (eds.), *Completely Queer: The Gay and Lesbian Encyclopedia.* New York: Henry Holt and Company.

Humphreys, L. (1970). *Tearoom Trade: Impersonal Sex in Public Places.* Chicago: Aldine.

McKusick, L., W. Horstman, and T. J. Coates. (1985). Reported Changes in the Sexual Behavior of Men at Risk for AIDS, San Francisco, 1982–84—The AIDS Behavior Research Project. *Public Health Reports, 100*:622–628.

Miles, M. B. and A. M. Huberman. (1984). *Qualitative Data Analysis: A Sourcebook of New Methods.* Beverly Hills: Sage.

Miller, N. (1995). *Out of the Past: Gay and Lesbian History from 1869 to the Present.* New York: Vintage Books.

Rabin, J. A. (1986). The AIDS Epidemic and Gay Bathhouses: A Constitutional Analysis. *Journal of Health Politics, Policy and Law, 10*(4):729–747.

Richwald, G. A., D. E. Morisky, G. R. Kyle, A. R. Kristal, M. M. Gerber, and J. M. Friedland. (1988). Sexual Activities in Bathhouses in Los Angeles County: Implications for AIDS Prevention Education. *The Journal of Sex Research, 25*(2):169–180.

Styles, J. (1979). Outsider/Insider: Research Gay Baths. *Urban Life, 8*(2):135–152.

Tattleman, I. (1999). Speaking to the Gay Bathhouse: Communicating in Sexually Charged Spaces. In W. L. Leap (ed.), *Public Sex / Gay Space.* New York: Columbia University Press.

Tewksbury, R. (1996). Cruising for Sex in Public Places: The Structure and Language of Men's Hidden, Erotic Worlds. *Deviant Behavior, 17*(1):1–19.

Tewksbury, R. (1995). Adventures in the Erotic Oasis: Sex and Danger in Men's Same-Sex, Public Sexual Encounters. *Journal of Men's Studies, 4*(1):9–24.

Tewksbury, R. (1993). Peepshows and "Perverts": Men and Masculinity in an Adult Bookstore. *Journal of Men's Studies, 2*(1):53–67.

Tewksbury, R. (1990). Patrons of Porn: Research Notes on the Clientele of Adult Bookstores. *Deviant Behavior, 11*(3):259–271.

Tewksbury, R. and D. K. Moore. (1997). Men's Sexual Risk Factors for HIV Infection: Racial Differences in Behavior, Knowledge, and Self-Perceptions. *Journal of Men's Studies, 6*(1):91–102.

Weinberg, M. S. and C. J. Williams. (1975). Gay Baths and the Social Organization of Impersonal Sex. *Social Problems, 23*:124–136.

14

S/M Interactions in Semipublic Settings

Charles Moser

The present paper is a description of the social construct called a "party" among S/M (sadomasochistic) practitioners. These social events allow S/M practitioners to display their personal style of S/M behavior in a semipublic setting. S/M parties also serve a social function, facilitating individuals with similar interests to meet for both S/M and non-S/M interactions. S/M parties are similar to other parties, in that they are a place for socializing, refreshments are usually available, and they are an enjoyable way to spend social time.

The present paper is a retrospective analysis of the author's experiences while involved in other S/M research projects; no prospective design was used. Collection of the data and observations on which the present paper is based, occurred over the last 25 years. Over 200 parties have been observed in five metropolitan areas (Los Angeles, New York City, Portland [Oregon], San Francisco, and Seattle). These parties present a perfect environment for observational research, since voyeurism is common and even encouraged.

Size, Invitations, Etiquette, and Other Considerations

Parties can be as small as a few people to over 500 participants. Some parties are limited only by the size of the space available, while others aim for a more intimate atmosphere. A fee is usually charged to cover

Reprinted from *Journal of Homosexuality,* Vol. 36, No. 2 (1998), pp. 19–30. © 1998 The Haworth Press, Inc. Edited and reprinted by permission of the publisher.

the cost of food, drinks, and safer-sex supplies. Parties may be potluck, catered, or a mix of the two. There are individuals who run parties as a source of income; others do so simply to entertain their friends.

Parties may be openly advertised in alternative periodicals, via the Internet, open only to members of a specific group, or by invitation only. Some parties are restricted by role (female dominant/male submissive), gender (women only), or require participation in a specific fantasy theme (Story of O). Membership on selected party lists is coveted within the S/M community, several of which are very exclusive. Acceptance by a segment of the S/M community can be judged by invitations to the appropriate parties. Social crises have been precipitated by failure to receive the appropriate invitation.

Parties are held either at an individual's home or at a commercial space rented for the purpose. In several cities there are dedicated S/M party spaces for rent. The rental and maintenance of these spaces often constitutes a successful business enterprise in the S/M community. Commercial spaces (lofts, warehouses, bathhouses) may also be rented and converted into an S/M party space for an evening. It is not unusual for competing parties to be held on the same night at different locations. Conversely, various party groups may combine to host a joint event.

Some individuals provide S/M interactions for a fee outside these parties. These interactions are devoid of overt sexual interaction, thus avoiding violation of the prostitution laws. These individuals often work in a "house" specifically and elaborately furnished for S/M interactions. "Houses" also may be rented by individuals or groups for private S/M interactions or parties. It is important to note that no one is paid for an S/M interaction at the party itself.

The rules of behavior at a party are quite serious and explicitly stated. Some parties require the guest to sign a written set of rules to signify understanding. Many parties use monitors, also known as dungeon masters/mistresses, to enforce the rules. Arguments over the rules have caused major rifts in groups, which can result in a new group being formed.

The rules relate to an etiquette that is actually quite varied throughout the S/M community, though the issues are constant. Who may talk to whom, who may play (engage in S/M interactions) with whom, who may have sex with whom, how to interact respectfully with other party participants, issues of confidentiality, prohibited S/M or sexual behaviors, and specific interpretation of what constitutes safer sex are the major points of contention. Rules about smoking, cleanup, confidentiality, etc., can also be included. Certain other courtesies, keeping a respectful distance, not distracting from the activity by talking or other disruption, not blocking use of equipment by sitting on it, etc., are also usual.

It would be inappropriate for an individual (either dominant or submissive) to speak to a person who has assumed a submissive role, without permission (formal or informal). Sometimes, this rule is suspended in certain areas (the kitchen) or at certain times during the party, but it is a major concern. Dress and behavior may indicate that someone is in a submissive role and may not be addressed without permission. A common sign is a leash and collar, especially with another person holding the leash. Other signs include lack of eye contact, clear statements that the individual is "in role," and deferring to the dominant partner for any statement directed to the submissive. Some parties become very stilted, because the roles do not allow any personal interaction. Other parties have no limitations, with the norm being some restrictions as part of the etiquette.

Parties have various mixes of singles, couples, or groups attending. The couples that attend a party vary from committed long-standing relationships to a first date. Some couples are comprised of friends, without any romantic or S/M interest. Individuals attend as couples or groups for camaraderie, as a mechanism to meet others, and to share transportation.

Individuals do go to parties alone, occasionally with hopes of meeting a new partner. The usual way singles connect with each other is via a third party making a clear introduction. Even then, it is not uncommon for the dominant to ask if the submissive needs permission to proceed further. It would be a serious violation of protocol, if one assumed that someone would "fall into role" just by requesting/commanding it. It is acceptable and not uncommon for a submissive to approach a dominant and respectfully request the initiation of S/M play.

Rules about alcohol and other drugs are also very specific. Inebriation is never acceptable. Many parties allow wine or beer, but parties that ban all intoxicating substances are also common. Marijuana is common at private parties; hard liquor occasionally shows up at private parties that have a BYOB policy. On rare occasions harder drugs are seen, mostly the snorting of cocaine or "speed." At least at one time "poppers" were common, but are rarely seen now.

Other issues of etiquette may be party specific, for example, dress requirements or appropriate ways to address other party participants. Some parties attempt to promote a dominance and submission theme. For example, by dictating that submissives may not sit on the furniture, they either stand or sit on the floor. One party group allows any dominant to fondle any submissive without requesting permission. Another party group requires submissives to stay in a certain area unless escorted by a dominant.

The Generic Party

Guests are told when to arrive, and a cutoff or door closing time is usually stated, though special arrangements can be made in advance for late arrivals. Parties that occur in someone's home usually require that the participants change into costumes there. Drawing attention to the host with a stream of uniquely dressed people converging on a nondescript home in a residential neighborhood would be seen as a problem.

The beginning segment of the party is usually similar to non-S/M parties, people milling about talking and being introduced to one another. Flirting occurs and promises are made for later in the evening. It is not uncommon to arrange to play with a "date" before the party. These individuals would arrive separately, but then quickly reconfirm the "date." It is also common to meet a previous play partner at the beginning of the party and make arrangements to play later in the evening, without any involved courtship. Some individuals plan first dates for a party, where others are around to assure safely.

Newcomers may or may not find it easy to play at first. Attractive people that exude a sense that they have done this before have no problem. Either less attractive or tentative newcomers tend not to play immediately. After a few parties, people become familiar with the newcomer, and most people become active. Obviously, if someone was not "clicking"with a particular group, they would not be asked back or they might decline the invitation if offered.

The most common situation is the established couple who arrive at the party together. They are not interested in S/M interactions with others, but do want to exhibit their own S/M style. While the involvement of others in their S/M interactions is minimal to nonexistent, these couples are open to friendships and socializing with others. While some people may play with multiple partners at a party, it is unusual. This is distinct from individuals who are involved in multipartnered relationships, in which some or all partners may engage in S/M interactions.

In the beginning segment of the party, individuals might comment on an aspect of another's costume or ask specific questions about the person's S/M preferences. A participant may see something (a bondage technique, toy, or body adornment) and ask about it, but more commonly the references are to other people each might know. Participants may also ask about one's job or variations of the generic "How's the wife and kids?" There are also parties where the roles are in effect from arrival, without any exchange of pleasantries.

People do make business connections, and professional relationships develop, in part due to the knowing that the businessperson or professional understands and is sympathetic to the S/M lifestyle. Friendships flourish, in part because this aspect of their life does not need to be hidden.

If individuals know each other and have engaged in S/M interactions before, they may be no preliminary communication other than "Wanna play?" With individuals that have just met, a period of discussion is usual. This usually focuses upon limits ("Don't hit me in the face"), the style or fantasy to be the focus of the interaction (pain vs. humiliation), and specific requests. The party rules are also reviewed, as well as safewords (code words that signal that the play must slow or end).

As the party ends, people exchange telephone numbers, make dates, and thank people for their interactions ("That was an incredibly hot whipping"). Many individuals say they are returning home to continue the behavior. It is often clear that in privacy the behavior will be more overtly sexual.

Costumes

Common costumes include corsets and lingerie for the women and anything black for the men, regardless of the role. Black is so common that different-colored costumes can lead to comments for being unusual. Submissive women are more likely to wear other colors, especially red or white. In general, the submissive is more likely to wear a revealing outfit, but exceptions abound. Leather is common, PVC (polyvinyl chloride) and latex are also popular. At some parties formal attire (tuxedo) is permissible, but frowned upon at others. Some parties specify "fetish attire, no street clothes," but without further elaboration. Other parties have very specific and elaborate dress codes. Several groups dictate that a "slave" must wear a collar at all times. One group has established a code for colored ribbons attached to the collar, to signify specific liberties that may be taken or restrictions to be observed. Cross-dressing occurs at some parties, but is considered inappropriate at others.

Indications of dominance and submission can vary from being obvious to nonexistent. Sometimes the roles are very changeable and the costumes do not indicate the role or are in conflict with the role. Depending on the party, switching roles is common or discouraged. Some individuals will switch roles to play with a particular partner or even just to play at all.

Costumes are often quite revealing, but total nudity is rare. Even when the genitals and/or breasts are devoid of covering, other aspects of the costume are obvious. One woman commonly seen at parties wears only a collar with ankle and wrist cuffs. Parties may have costume themes, though not always a clearly S/M motif (science fiction, Middle Ages). Costumes may be changed at various times during a party, indicating new roles or just a fashion statement. A participant may arrive in a demure outfit, become involved in S/M play that involves significant nudity and not bother dressing when the interaction is concluded. It is not uncommon to see someone nude next to a fully clothed person engaging in essentially the same behavior. The dominant partner usually does not undress. Not all party participants wear costumes and casual dress in not uncommon.

Reasons for Attendance

There is something counterintuitive about people voluntarily attending a party to see others or to personally engage in what appears to be painful and humiliating behavior. Nevertheless, individuals often look forward to these parties and complaints can be heard if the play is insufficient in either quantity or quality.

As mentioned earlier, voyeurism is encouraged at these parties. Individuals will often remark that they look forward to watching a specific interaction or that a specific interaction was particularly interesting. Some individuals will admit that watching an S/M interaction was sexually exciting or made them desirous of engaging in their own S/M interaction.

Similarly, there is an obvious exhibitionistic motive to many of the S/M interactions. Participants often receive recognition and complaints for their interactions. Many individuals report that having their interaction watched adds to the excitement. Many people gain status within the S/M community for the apparent success of their S/M interactions and relationships.

Clearly individuals are attracted by an atmosphere that encourages them to be themselves and validates their behavior. An acceptance of S/M identity role is clearly part of the reason that individuals attend. It is also an atmosphere where individuals can garner support for their behavior. It can be difficult to be involved in S/M, in a culture that holds subjugation as politically reprehensible for both parties; the dominant for invoking it and the submissive for allowing it to happen.

Education is also a reason some people attend. Some parties have a demonstration or lecture as part of the activity. Safety concerns and correct techniques for other behaviors are commonly discussed informally. Activities may vary from the accepted "safe" technique can lead to interruption by the dungeon master/mistress.

Among the party regulars, people become known for various interests. It is not uncommon to hear someone say "I hope Mary is here tonight, I could really use one of her whippings." Couples may incorporate a new partner into a scene to instruct him/her on how to engage safely in a new behavior. Individuals watching may gain new ideas to incorporate in their own S/M play.

Gender and Sexual Orientation

Some parties are segregated by gender. It is common for a woman's only party to be composed of heterosexual, bisexual, and lesbian-identified women; though parties exist that are clearly only for lesbian-identified women. Attendance at a women's only party would imply that the woman is open to S/M interactions with other women, even if not interested in female-female sexual interactions. Men's parties are usually more orientation specific, meaning that heterosexual men rarely go to all-male parties.

Parties that specify role according to gender (male dominant/female submissive or female dominant/male submissive parties) are common. It would not be surprising for the same couple to attend both styles of parties, adopting the appropriate roles for each party. Parties that specify female dominants may have both male and female submissives present. Parties that specify male dominants rarely include male submissives; if male submissives are included, they are usually cross-dressed. Of note, this follows the pattern among swingers, where female-female interactions are common, but male-male interactions are rare.

Mixed play was once unheard of, but now occurs with some regularity. This involves individuals engaging in S/M interactions, but whose stated sexual orientation would preclude any interaction (a lesbian playing with a gay man). There is usually no suggestion of overt coitus or other orgasm-seeking behavior among these individuals. Parties that mix male-male, female-female, and female-male interactions are common.

There are parties that are nominally open to everyone, all genders or orientations, but do discriminate against heterosexual males. There are various stated reasons for this, but it appears to be an attempt to make female party participants more comfortable, meaning not being approached by heterosexual men. This phenomenon is seen at a minority of parties and is clearly not supported by the larger S/M community, but may be a new trend.

Sexual Activity

Most parties have no rule against sexual activity, but overt coitus or genitally focused orgasm-seeking behavior is rare. Most party spaces do not have mattresses or beds conducive to sexual activities, though slings are often used for this purpose. Clearly parties that are not structured for comfortable sexual activity are less likely to display the behavior.

A few parties promote sexual activities, and on rare occasions the sexual activity takes precedence over the S/M activity. Some S/M participants reported that traditional swing parties (group sex) led to S/M encounters during those parties, but that discussion is beyond the scope of the present paper.

Much of the overt sexual activity at S/M parties is between established couples. It is rare for people who just met to engage in coitus. While this at first seems reasonable, it is contrary to the atmosphere of these parties. Participants see themselves as sexually adventurous and open, many have experience in group sex settings. Several participants were asked what stops them from engaging in coitus. They suggested that it is too personal an activity for such a public setting. When it is pointed out that being stripped naked and whipped in public seems a more personal activity, the response is usually a variation of "That's different." Many do indicate that coitus with a partner is private in the culmination of the evening. Overt sexual activities were more common before the AIDS epidemic, but even then were not usually the focus of the party. Several respondents did suggest that the "messiness" of sex and safer sex restrictions were considerations in not pursuing coitus at S/M parties.

To be clear, fondling of genitals is relatively common. Oral sex may happen, but usually not to orgasm. Genital to genital contact is rare. Reciprocity is also rare, one person gives and one receives with rare reversals. The active person is usually the dominant partner. The submissive partner is more likely to orgasm than the dominant partner. Safer sex is not an ever-present part of the experience.

Some individuals clearly state that coitus or genitally focused stimulation leading to orgasm is not a regular part of their sex or S/M life. It appears to be especially common between female dominant/male submissive couples, that penile-vaginal coitus never takes place. Nevertheless, orgasm-seeking behavior is still present in those relationships. A common aspect of many scenes is controlling the orgasm of the submissive partner. This involves either forbidding orgasm, requiring the dominant's permission to orgasm, or "training" the submissive to orgasm on command.

S/M Play

S/M play is quite varied and different parties often have different foci of activity. In general, people engage in a variety of bondage and whipping exhibitions. Usually music is playing in the background, and it is common that the dominants are whipping the submissives in unison to the beat of the music.

The general style is to start in a soft, caressing manner, slowly increasing the frequency and strength of the strokes. There are short breaks to massage and caress, as well as to add unpredictability to the routine. Sometimes there is more caressing than painful-appearing stimulation. Occasionally, welts or other marks are left. Usually, the only objective sign that the submissive has engaged in an S/M scene is some generalized redness, which typically disappears in a few hours.

These sessions can go on literally for hours. They end due to fatigue or a desire to move on. Orgasm is not necessarily an endpoint. Occasionally they end because the participants are not happy with the scene, too hard or too soft for particular tastes. Some interactions are devoid of physical interactions and only exhibit psychological aspects of S/M (kneeling, bowing, following orders, doing menial tasks).

Sometimes the S/M play appears to culminate in a crescendo. The submissive's body stiffens, then relaxes or actually goes limp; pleasurable screams or moans often accompany the event. The partners then hold each other for a few minutes in an intimate and gentle manner. When asked about this event, respondents deny orgasm; the men do not ejaculate. The submissive partner often states that it was a great experience, but often does not have words to explain the phenomenon. Some individuals in the submissive role do orgasm as a result of direct stimulation from the S/M play (usually genitally directed); that is clearly a different phenomenon.

Most parties have a "play space," which is a large area usually filled with a variety of S/M bondage devices. These include a variety of sturdy structures with appropriate places to tie or otherwise attach someone to the device. Some are tables that allow the person to be restrained horizontally. Individuals may also be tied to crosses (T- or X-shaped) or to hooks set in walls while standing. Leather slings suspended from the ceiling and posts are also used. Some parties have unique objects (motorcycle, gynecological table) which can also be used. People usually bring their own "toys" (handcuffs, whips, etc.). Once the negotiation is concluded, the participants go to the play space and find an unused bondage device or just an area to engage in S/M play.

Discussion

The present paper is limited by the observation of only one investigator. Due to the author being male, observation at women's-only events was severely limited. The author's reputation and personality may have facilitated entry to some parties and hindered entry to others. It should also be noted that the present paper is the result of observations while the author was involved in other research projects. No observation protocol was created nor was any attempt made to document the findings at the time of the observation.

Discussions with women who regularly attend women's-only parties, report no differences in those parties and the mixed or all-male parties discussed here. One female respondent felt that women's-only parties were much more sexual than other parties, but not all women's-parties respondents agreed.

The lack of coitus is both interesting and curious. Naerssen, Dijk,

Hoogeveen, Visser, and Zessen (1987) report a similar phenomenon among male homosexual S/M practitioners. They note that "the satisfaction was derived from the non-orgasmic aspects of the interaction" (117), but that was contrary to how the pornography depicted the interaction.

There clearly have been parties where most participants engage in coitus with multiple partners, but these are the exceptions. The lack of coitus has been touted by some as a virtue, since a stated goal is adherence to the safer-sex guidelines. A common fantasy among S/M participants is being sexually used or being given away by their partner to be sexually used. There are indications that this happens, but outside these S/M parties.

The individuals who attend these parties often have experience as swingers or participate in other alternative sexual lifestyles or behaviors. When discussed outside the party atmosphere, most individuals have no explanation for the lack of orgasm-seeking behavior. These participants agree that it violates neither the mores nor the sensibilities of the participants. They do not deny that the behavior is clearly sexual for most of the participants. They confirm that dates are made at these parties for a later time to include both S/M and overt sexual activity.

It is much more common to be invited to engage in S/M behavior with a relative stranger (though supervised) than to be asked to join someone for a sexual encounter. One can conclude, participants at these parties find sexual fidelity a more pervasive value than S/M fidelity.

It should also be noted that several groups have formed for those that wish to engage in more overt sexual behavior, but most of these eventually evolve into holding the less sexually active party. The author was present at one party, where several couples left en masse to return to one couple's apartment where the S/M was mixed with more overt sexual behavior. It seems reasonable to conclude that the atmosphere of the party is conducive to the exhibition of overt S/M behavior, but not sexual behavior.

In general, hosts of S/M parties do not make the party space conducive to overt sexual activities. The party participants do not request a change in the space to make it more conducive to sexual activities. The individuals that host S/M parties are not the same individuals that host swing (group sex) parties and vice versa. These observations explain the lack of sexual activity, but the underlying reasons are still not clear.

In summary, why there is a lack of overt genital sex play at S/M parties is another unanswered sexological question. These parties serve to allow participants to display their behavior in a non-stigmatized setting. Rules at these parties work to make the setting safe, avoid harassment, and allow participants to show off their particular S/M style. Friendships and a sense of community generally flow out of the party.

References

van Naerssen, A. X., M. van Dijk, G. Hoogeveen, D. Visser, and G. van Zessen. (1987). Gay SM in Pornography and Reality. *Journal of Homosexuality, 13(2–3)*:111–119.

15

Swinging Revisited

Alan S. Bruce and Theresa A. Severance

Recent absence of scholarly interest in swinging may be attributed to belief that it "has died a natural death" (Fang, 1976: 236). In the introduction to his popular deviance text, Thio (1998) reflects this belief when describing topics omitted from the text: "Moreover, subjects that are no longer important or relevant to today's society, such as bar girls, massage parlors, and swinging, have been deleted" (xiii). Although swinging has failed to gain the popularity once anticipated (Ramey, 1972), it is still widely practiced. For example, recent media attention (Chen, 1998; *The Hartford Courant,* 1999; *Los Angeles Times*, 1998; *USA Today,*1999:) demonstrates the ongoing popularity of swinger clubs. Furthermore, the number of swinger-related internet sites shows the enduring status of swinging.

In addition to signifying the continued existence of swinging, internet sites also indicate many swinger groups are highly organized, with swinger conferences and vacations being offered. Swingers are clearly utilizing this technological revolution to promote their behavior, communicate with other swingers, and recruit people to this activity. This chapter presents a summary of swinging research, an examination of internet use by swingers and classification of swinger internet sites, identification of characteristics making the internet an important tool for the promotion of swinging, and a suggestion for future research.

Written exclusively for this reader.

Literature Review

A variety of terms are used to describe the activity commonly known as "swinging." Thio (1995) provides the following list: "wife-swapping," "mate-swapping," "co-marital sex," "consensual adultery," and "faithful adultery." These terms all identify the distinctive characteristic of swinging: both partners agreeing to, and engaging concurrently in, sexual activity with others. Bartell (1971) defines swinging as "having sexual relations (as a couple) with at least one other individual" (713) and recognizes that crucial to swinging is the shared willingness and acceptance of both partners to participate in such activity. Swinging does not involve an alternative lifestyle and most research finds swingers are "remarkably uninteresting" in all aspects of their lives except sexual behavior (Bartell, 1970, 1971; Denfeld, 1974; Fang, 1976; O'Neill and O'Neill, 1970; Varni, 1972; Walshok, 1971).

Existing research describes types of swinging, swinger characteristics, the process of becoming involved in and continuing with swinging, and the consequences of swinging. Each of these topics is discussed below.

Types of Swinging

Swinging consists of different forms and types of swingers. In most instances couples are involved, and married couples are preferred. Bartell (1971) observed great fear of discovery among his research subjects and believed married couples are preferred because they are trusted to be more discreet than singles or non-married couples. Swinging may involve just one other couple or multiple couples. In some instances only one other individual will be involved and the third person is almost always female. Homosexual relations among males are very uncommon in swinging and much more common among females. Very few instances of homosexuality among men are reported in existing swinger research (Denfeld and Gordon, 1970; Fang, 1976; Palson and Palson, 1972; Ramey, 1972, 1975). Swinging can be either "closed" or "open" depending on participant preference. With closed swinging, couples exchange partners and enter separate rooms for sexual activity. Neither partner witnesses the behavior of the other during closed swinging. In open swinging, couples exchange partners and engage in sexual activity within sight of each other (Fang, 1976).

The different types of swingers reflect the range of benefits sought from swinging. Symonds (1971) distinguishes between "utopian" and "recreational" swingers. Utopian swingers want more than sexual activity from a swinging relationship and are interested in creating a new lifestyle. Utopian swingers are very open about their behavior and more likely to favor living in a communal group. Recreational swingers engage in swinging only for the sexual activity and are not interested in establishing a new lifestyle.

Gilmartin (1975) identifies three types of swingers. Purely sexual swingers are only interested in the sexual activity and are most likely to swing with different couples every time. Emotional swingers are interested in sexual activity but also wish to form close emotional bonds with other couples. Finally, recreational swingers regularly attend swing parties and clubs and are interested in swinging as much for the social life, which comes through mixing with like-minded individuals, as the sexual activity.

Varni (1972) sees swingers as occupying places along a continuum ranging from hard core to communal. Hard-core swingers want no emotional involvement and swing with a different couple every time. Hard-core swingers are very sexually active and swing as often as possible. Egotistical swingers also place an emphasis on sexual activity but are more discriminating in their choice of swinger companions. Recreational swingers value both the social and sexual aspects of swinging, and thus belong to a relatively stable group of couples who regularly swing together and know each other well. Interpersonal swingers wish to form emotional bonds with other couples, and this bond is just as important to them as the sexual activity. Ramey (1975) describes this type of relationship as "intimate friendship." Those involved in intimate friendship may not regard themselves as swingers and reject the term, although they still engage in consensual sexual activity with other couples. The final group of swingers Varni (1972) identifies is communal swingers, who are similar to interpersonal swingers except that group living is preferred.

Bartell (1970) did not find an emotional connection among the swingers he studied, and his research subjects rarely reported swinging with the same couple more than once. His subjects were interested in swinging only for the sexual activity. In contrast, Palson and Palson (1972) "had no difficulty finding couples who either wanted to or had succeeded in having some degree of emotional involvement and long-term friendship within a swinging context" (29).

Clearly no single type of swinging exists and motivations for involvement vary among individual participants. While some swing purely for the sexual activity, others display a desire for emotional attachment. The perceived benefits of swinging are often those traditionally associated with marriage; the activity may therefore be motivated in part by an effort to satisfy needs not being met within the marital relationship.

Swinger Characteristics

According to the existing research, swingers share a number of common characteristics. They are predominantly white, with few documented instances of nonwhite swingers. While early research on swingers found interracial swinging to be virtually nonexistent (Bartell, 1970, 1971; Fang, 1976; Gilmartin, 1975; Jenks, 1985; Palson and Palson, 1972; Schupp, 1970; Varni, 1972), new research is clearly needed to determine whether such racial distinctions still exist.

Swingers tend to have routine jobs, and swinging thus appears in part to be an effort to generate excitement in an otherwise routine existence. A number of researchers (Bartell 1970, 1971; Bell, 1971; Gross, 1975; Palson and Palson, 1972; Smith and Smith, 1970) report that other than in their sexual behavior, swingers are remarkably uninteresting in most areas of their lives. For many, swinging is a way to escape from their everyday routine: "By affirming one's freedom from sexual restraint one obtains a feeling of personal freedom; this in turn, sustains one in the routine activities of day-to-day living" (Walshok 1971: 492).

Independence is a common characteristic of swingers. Researchers find swingers less likely to be members of conventional institutions such as churches (Bartell, 1970, 1971; Fang, 1976), less likely to report having had strong childhood attachments to parents or other relatives, to have had more and earlier premarital sex, and to have married much younger than non-swingers (Gilmartin, 1975, 1977). These characteristics are interpreted as evidence of independence, and swingers typically claim freedom from the constraints of society in at least one area of their lives (Cole and Spaniard, 1974; Gilmartin, 1975).

The age range of swingers varies by study but there is general agreement that the majority are aged 25–40 years. Great variation exists in the length of time swingers have been married, and Palson and Palson (1972) report the length of marriage from 6 months to 30 years. Finally, most swingers tend to be conservative in their general outlook and political beliefs. They are intolerant of deviant activities other than swinging and regard their behavior as acceptably different from the norm rather than deviant (Miller, 1984).

Getting Involved and Staying Involved

The literature on swinging (Bartell, 1970, 1971; Fang, 1976; Gross, 1975; Palson and Palson, 1972; Thio, 1995) indicates five general methods swingers use to contact potential partners: advertisement, swingers' clubs/bars, personal reference, seduction, and swinger parties.

Advertisement.   Advertising is the most common way for couples to meet. Contact or "trade" magazines enable swingers to advertise, and such ads usually list a description of their couple, a description of the desired "ideal couple," and some preferred sexual activities. In some magazine ads couples provide photographs of themselves. In addition to magazines catering exclusively to swingers, ads are placed in general interest magazines and newspapers, so the print media is a common method swingers use to contact each other. The role of advertising has changed dramatically with the emergence of personal computers and the internet, however, and this will likely have a great impact on the number of swingers.

While technological revolutions bring about positive change, they are often accompanied by the emergence of unintended effects. As noted by Durkin and Bryant (1995), just as the automobile and the telephone were adapted for sexual activities, so too have personal computers been used for unanticipated sexual purposes. According to Wysocki (2001) "the increased availability of technological products such as computers, modems, computer bulletin boards (BBS), and the internet, along with their declining prices, have had a dramatic effect on social life as we know it" (293). Given the rapid spread of access to the internet and the quantity of swinger-related material on the World Wide Web, this latest technological revolution will likely contribute to sustained interest in swinging, further justifying renewed academic interest in the activity.

The World Wide Web is unique in the opportunities it provides "individuals interested in identifying like-minded partners for sexual experimentation" (Gauthier and Forsyth, 2001: 203) and the unprecedented access it provides to controversial matter. Exposure to material extolling the virtues of swinging may once have been restricted to adult bookstores, but internet sites are not limited in this way, and many swinger-related sites do not even require internet users to acknowledge meeting legal criteria to access sexually related material. The internet is further unique in the ease of access it affords. "Web rings" enable easy access to multiple sites dealing with specific topics. Recent examination of one such Web ring revealed 224 swinger-related, associated sites.

The growing popularity of personal computers and the internet makes it easier and less costly for swingers to advertise. The potential "audience" is much greater with internet advertising than is the case with newspapers and magazines. Internet ads also can contain more information and photographs, and with e-mail access swingers can contact each other quickly and easily. While considerable overlap among swinger internet sites exists, examination of content from different sites reveals the following classification of swinger websites.

Promotional sites provide general information about swinging. The emphasis is on "education" about swinging, and the subjects presented illustrate some of the underlying swinger concerns. Common topics include jealousy and how to deal with it, benefits of swinging, swinging etiquette, and sexually transmitted diseases. These sites typically provide information on contacting swingers and may publish a list of on-premises and off-premises swing clubs throughout the country. Swinger activities such as vacation packages and conferences are also promoted. While potential negative effects are often mentioned, these sites clearly emphasize the purported benefits of swinging. Promotional sites often provide links to additional information on relevant topics although, as discussed below, information links often lead to biased or inaccurate information.

Advertisement sites have also been created for swingers. Couples can typically advertise free of charge. Ads reflect the range of swinger types discussed above. Some ads emphasize sexual activity and are pornographic in nature, while others emphasize the social aspect of swinging. Photographs are frequently included and many are sexually explicit. Advertisement sites often include ads for swinger clubs and publications, and provide further evidence of the range, extent, and popularity of swinging. Such ad sites differ from promotional sites as they typically do not provide general information about swinging and are primarily targeted at participating couples.

Commercial sites are classified as such because while they may include ads and information on swinging, they charge fees for both membership and the placing of ads, they sell videos and magazines, and they advertise products. These sites promote the sale of pornographic material and appear more concerned with sales than promoting swinging.

Pornographic sites are those claiming to be concerned with swinging, but are actually sites promoting pornography. Rather than containing information about swinging, or contact ads, these sites provide sexually explicit images. They are easily accessed when searching for swinger-related sites. While pornographic sites are typically unrelated to swinging, they are included here because they are often found when using popular search engines to search for swinger sites, and they may be linked to genuine swinger sites. Pornographic sites differ from commercial sites as they typically do not attempt to sell merchandise.

Swingers' Clubs/Bars. Swingers' bars and clubs provide another popular way for couples to contact each other. Thio (1995) states swingers' bars and clubs may be viewed as a "sexual marketplace" where people gather for the purpose of locating partners for sexual activity. While similar types of clubs for singles and gays exist, Thio describes the behavior of couples at swingers' bars as more explicit because couples tend to approach each other and immediately ask whether the other wishes to engage in sexual activity. When couples express an interest in swinging they may leave the premises and have sexual relations that day or make future arrangements. In some instances a club may provide the opportunity for "on-site" sexual relations.

Personal Reference. Couples may also become involved with each other as a result of personal reference. This occurs only among couples who have already engaged in swinging and in some instances swingers keep books with names, phone numbers, physical descriptions, and ratings of sexual performance, for the purpose of passing this information on to other swingers (Thio, 1995). While this is another common way for couples to meet, information is not passed along without permission.

Seduction. Seduction only occurs among couples who are close friends. A couple who already engages in swinging may attempt to seduce another into swinging with them. This method is believed to be least common because it poses a threat to existing friendship and the secrecy of practicing swingers (Fang, 1976).

Swinger Parties. Swinger parties take place in the home of established swingers. They begin like any other party although it is understood that couples remaining after a certain time are expected to engage in sexual activity. In some instances couples curious about swinging may be invited to attend so they can meet swingers and ask questions without commitment to swinging. It is quite common for curious couples to be introduced to swinging in this way, and there is no forced participation (Fang, 1976).

Staying Involved

Because swinging involves departure from traditional norms concerning marriage and sexual behavior, it is expected that swingers will utilize strategies enabling them to reconcile their behavior with traditional beliefs. Without such strategies it seems inevitable that swinging will have a negative effect upon marriage as one or both partners become concerned over their actions. An important swinger strategy involves characterization of swinging as a distinct form of extramarital behavior. Extramarital behavior typically occurs without the knowledge or consent of one partner, and discovery can have very negative consequences. Swingers claim, however, that because there is no deceit involved in swinging it does not have this negative impact (Cole and Spaniard, 1974). Gilmartin's (1975) findings support this claim as he found swingers were significantly more satisfied in their marriages than traditional adulterers. In addition, swingers do not believe their behavior is deviant because of the consensus between partners and so "swingers do not think of themselves as adulterers" (Varni, 1972: 510). Varni (1972) suggests swingers use this strategy to not only avoid viewing themselves as deviant but to view adulterers as much more deviant than themselves.

While the consensual nature of swinging makes it easier for swingers to rationalize and justify their behavior, it is still necessary for them to develop other strategies to deal with this activity (Bartell, 1971). The most important swinger strategy appears to be separation of love and sexual activity. Swingers maintain that they can engage in sexual activity without harming their marriage because sexual activity does not involve emotional investment, and emotional investment is the prominent feature of marriage. Swingers also assert that the decision to swing is a joint one emphasizing the degree of equality in marriage, and so swinging is interpreted as evidence of marital health (Palson and Palson, 1972).

Another common swinger strategy involves viewing themselves as part of an elite movement or group of people. In his research, Bartell (1970) found swingers viewed themselves as more liberated, as "jet setters," and as part of an exciting new movement. This is also apparent from ads in which swingers refer to "the lifestyle" rather than to swinging.

Finally, swingers place great emphasis on swinging etiquette, and participants are required to adhere to an unwritten code of behavior (Fang, 1976; Society for Human Sexuality, 1998). The emphasis on mutual respect stemming from this etiquette may further enable swingers to regard themselves as part of an elite group.

Consequences of Swinging

Most early studies on swingers suggested involvement has a positive impact upon marriage. Swingers typically claim their behavior is motivated by boredom with their day-to-day existence or the need to improve an unhappy marriage. Because swinging is used as a strategy for improving marriage, however, it is unlikely subjects will report swinging has been detrimental as this would thus acknowledge failure to improve the relationship.

Bartell's (1970) subjects reported better relationships with their spouses and improvements in their social lives as consequences of swinging. Couples claimed a general increase in sexual activity after swinging because of their new experiences and shared interest. Female subjects often reported swinging made them feel good about themselves as different males desired them. Some swingers, moreover, believed their participation. Served to solidify their marriages, to expand their circle of friends, and to contribute to a more general sense of well-being. In this sense, participation in the sexual subculture may give a sense of competence and fulfillment which for many is lacking in their day-to-day work and living (Walshok, 1971).

In their study, O'Neill and O'Neill (1970) also reported that swinging had positive consequences. Their respondents conveyed that "the openness and communication about their group sexual activity extends into other areas of their marriage and frequently forms a bond between them which was previously lacking in their relationship" (110).

Gilmartin (1975) reports about 85 percent of couples studied felt swinging posed no threat to their relationship, and no couple reported swinging had any negative effects upon their marriage. Such findings do suggest swinging can be beneficial to marital relations and are consistent with the claim that "the family that swings together clings together" (Denfeld and Gordon, 1970).

There is evidence, however, that swinging can have a negative impact, and Denfeld (1974) surveyed marriage counselors to determine the types of problems ex-swingers reported. While negative consequences were not reported by all couples, Denfeld discovered a number of problems related to swinging including jealousy, guilt, disappointment, and resulting in divorce or separation. The frequency with which these problems occurred, however, was not described.

The potential for jealousy to develop from swinging is obvious, and jealousy, consequently, is the most common reason for dropping out of swinging. In "closed swinging" spouses may become jealous because they do not know whether their partners experience emotional involvement. "Open swinging" may contribute to jealousy as one partner may perceive the other as benefiting more from their sexual encounter. Jealousy may also occur if one partner views themself as less desirable than the other. At swingers clubs and parties, one partner may be jealous because the other appears to be more popular and to receive more attention. For husbands, jealousy may occur as a result of less sexual activity. Finally, both spouses may experience feelings of inferiority as a result of comparing themselves to other couples. Some couples may come to believe they are less desirable than others and that they do not perform as well sexually (Bartell, 1970; Fang, 1976; Smith and Smith, 1974).

Masters and Johnson (1974) also found jealousy to be a common negative effect of swinging. They noted that while swingers are quick to acknowledge their behavior creates great potential for jealousy, they are also quick to deny any jealousy because they have managed to separate love from sexual activity. They argued that this claim is merely a facade, however, used to hide deep-seated jealousy swingers experience but are unable to express. In this situation jealousy is likely to persist within each partner, and Masters and Johnson (1974) reported "under these circumstances the dissolution of the marriage would not be unexpected" (167). Further evidence of the problem of jealousy comes from the promotional swinger internet sites discussed previously, where advice on dealing with jealousy is commonly provided. The level of concern over jealousy suggests this may in fact be a significant problem for swingers.

Masters and Johnson (1974) also reported swinging can lead to anxiety concerning sexual performance and subsequent performance difficulties. They cited cases in which both partners have sexual performance difficulties arising from fear of failure to perform adequately. Such fear is especially likely to occur in swinging as the public nature of the activity exposes participants to greater risk of humiliation as a result of sexual performance difficulties.

Masters and Johnson (1974) also were skeptical of claims that swinging has positive effects upon marriage, believing that the necessary conditions for any benefit are unlikely to exist. They concluded that swinging can only have a positive effect if the sexual activity is equally stimulating for both partners and increases the desire of each for the other, if swinging is an activity that each enjoys to the same extent, and if in the long term the behavior improves communication between husband and wife. They believed that it is extremely unlikely such conditions will exist, especially for couples experimenting with swinging for the first time. In the absence of these conditions swinging is only likely to have a negative effect upon marital relations.

A final disadvantage of swinging, which has encouraged some to drop out, is the fear of sexually transmitted diseases (STDs) including AIDS. While the AIDS scare of the early 1980s may have led to a reduction in swinging and an increase in precautions against the spread of STDs (Buunk and Van Driel, 1989; Jenks, 1998), a common feature of swinging is that couples are supposed to keep themselves "clean" and refrain from swinging if they believe they might have an STD. Because of this norm, protection—such as the use of condoms—is often not used during sexual activity, exposing couples to the risk of contracting STDs. More research concerning the impact of AIDS on swinging and swingers' attitudes toward AIDS is strongly warranted.

Many promotional internet sites offer information about swinging with the goal of reducing the anxiety of potential swingers, and this information may be a key factor for those considering involvement in swinging. Information provided on promotional internet sites is often misleading, however, creating the impression that swinging is an exciting activity with many benefits and few risks. Swinger sites present the activity in a positive light, but those seeking information about swinging will be gravely misinformed. For example, while there is often information on STDs on promotional sites, discussion typically claims there is virtually no chance of contracting STDs through swinging. Some web sites go so far as to discourage condom use during sexual activity and refer visitors to alleged "expert" opinions critical of condom use. Many internet sites provide reference to articles by Peter W. Plumley (1997, 1998), who argues that condom use is not only undesirable and unnecessary, but is also dangerous. Such information helps create the impression that swinging is an activity with exclusively positive consequences.

While there is evidence of concern (Jenks, 1998), skepticism remains among swingers concerning that AIDS, and some deny AIDS is a serious problem. Indications of such doubt come from promotional sites where swingers claim they have never heard of swingers with any STDs even though they have been swinging for many years. Also, promotional sites provide references denying the seriousness of AIDS, referring to the "AIDS myth," and arguing that healthy middle class heterosexuals (such as swingers) are not at risk of contracting HIV. Finally, promotional sites direct internet users to publications where they can improve their understanding of AIDS, and these are generally publications denying the risk of contracting HIV (Fumento, 1988). Further evidence that swingers refute the threat of STDs and AIDS comes from Newman (1993), who attended sessions dealing with STDs at a swinger convention. Newman found these sessions dealt with STDs only briefly, and that they mainly focused on advertising surgery for penis enlargement and breast implants. As a result of denying the serious risk of healthy heterosexuals contracting STDs or the HIV virus, and in light of recent evidence on the continuing prevalence of HIV, swingers are likely to contribute to the spread of these conditions.

Limitations and Suggestions for Future Study

The above findings summarize available information on swinging, and while early research revealed positive effects for married couples there is also evidence that swinging can have very negative consequences. Complete understanding of the effect of swinging is not possible from existing research because of methodological limitations.

Sampling techniques may contribute most significantly to evidence that swinging improves marriage (Biblarz and Biblarz, 1980; Denfeld, 1974). Most prior research used snowball samples in which swingers referred each other to researchers who then gathered information through surveys, interviews, or observation. Such findings must be interpreted with caution, however, because of the risk of sampling bias. Subjects are typically a self-selected group of couples identifying themselves as swingers willing to discuss their sexual experiences. Thus, such research findings should not be generalized to the population of swingers.

Also, the use of convenience samples is likely to result in findings of positive effects of swinging. Subjects are volunteers and unlikely to classify their behavior as wrong or to emphasize its negative effects. Administering surveys in swinger bars and clubs is another common approach with limitations that may result in misleading evidence. Club and bar attendees do not represent all swingers, preventing generalization from such data. Those attending such clubs are also likely to be committed swingers who identify themselves as such, and committed swingers are unlikely to regard themselves or other swingers negatively. Again this approach to sampling will result in an overrepresentation of those who feel most positively about swinging.

Existing research provides only limited information on the effects of swinging. In many instances research questions concern the act of swinging or the rules involved, and while this may produce a good supply of descriptive data, such inquiry does not allow assessment of the impact of swinging upon participants. Efforts must be made to gather data independent of the perceptions and beliefs of the swingers themselves. Denfeld (1974) made a move in this direction with his survey of marriage counselors, which provided information from sources other than the swingers themselves. The development and implementation of scales measuring different dimensions of marital happiness and quality of marriage would also be useful for understanding causes and effects of swinging.

A final limitation of existing research is the failure to conduct longitudinal studies. While cross-sectional studies have provided a good deal of information, participants' attitudes toward swinging and its effects may change over time. A longitudinal approach might lead to more complete understanding of the changes swingers go through and of the long-term impact of swinging upon marriage. Finally, longitudinal data would provide a more accurate image of dropout rates and allow examination of such dropouts.

The potentially harmful effects of swinging for both marital relations and individual health make it a topic worthy of more attention. The availability of swinger magazines and the number of clubs, ads, and discussion groups found on the internet indicate swinging remains popular and may even be increasing. The internet provides a valuable research tool with great potential for studying swinging. Many swinger ads placed on the internet provide immediate access to advertisers through e-mail, and this too might be a useful data source. While a sample of swingers advertising through the internet does not represent the general population of swingers, the internet presents an opportunity for prolonged contact with swingers, which could be useful for a longer-term study.

Caution must be used for data collection via the internet. The potential for e-mail users to adopt false identities is clearly a major problem of this approach. Swingers ads frequently present detailed personal information, however, including e-mail addresses and photographs, and this reduces the likelihood that subjects will be able to present a convincing false identity. Continued correspondence will further provide researchers the opportunity to determine whether subjects are providing valid data.

The internet also offers greater access to subjects as they can be contacted regularly by e-mail. The researcher is also less limited by time constraints in gathering information. Typically when meetings are arranged or subjects are approached in clubs, the contact period is limited, and the researcher spends little time communicating with subjects. Internet surveys can be widely distributed and subjects are able to complete them at their leisure, giving researchers the opportunity to ask more questions than they could in other research settings. Finally, the internet offers researchers a less costly and more efficient alternative to traditional research approaches.

Conclusion

Since the 1970s surprisingly little research examining swingers and the consequences of swinging has developed. The existing research provides mainly descriptive data, and little is known about the impact of swinging upon health or marital relations. Lack of research is understandable if evidence revealed swinging was either rare or dying out. The availability of swinger magazines and the number of swinger internet sites and ads, however, suggest this remains a popular activity and may even be on the increase. The study of swinging, therefore, may be increasingly important as the potential for negative effects increases. More research on swinging must be conducted, and internet access presents a good opportunity to improve our understanding of swinging and its consequences.

References

Bartell, G. D. (1971). *Group Sex*. New York: Wyden.
Bartell, G. D. (1970). Group Sex Among the Mid-Americans. *The Journal of Sex Research, 6*(2):113–130.
Bell, R. R. (1971). Swinging—the Sexual Exchange of Married Persons. *Sexual Behavior, 1*:70.
Biblarz, A. and D. N. Biblarz. (1980). Alternative Sociology for Alternative

Lifestyles: A Methodological Critique of Studies of Swinging. *Social Behavior and Personality,* 8(2):137–144.

Buunk, B. and B. Van Driel. (1989). *Variant Lifestyles and Relationships.* Newbury Park, CA: Sage.

Chen, D. (1998). What Goes on at a Swingers Club? *Mademoiselle,* (November):167–192.

Cole, C. L. and G. B. Spaniard. (1974). Co-Marital Mate Sharing and Family Stability. *The Journal of Sex Research,* 10(1):21–31.

Denfeld, D. (1974). Dropouts from Swinging. *The Family Coordinator,* 23(1):45–49.

Denfeld, D. and M. Gordon. (1970). The Sociology of Mate Swapping: Or the Family That Swings Together Clings Together. *The Journal of Sex Research,* 6(2):85–100.

Durkin, K. F. and C. D. Bryant. (1995). Log On to Sex: Some Notes on the Carnal Computer and Erotic Cyberspace as an Emerging Research Frontier. *Deviant Behavior,* 16:179–200.

Fang, B. (1976). Swinging in Retrospect. *The Journal of Sex Research,* 12(3):220–237.

Fumento, M. (1988). *The Myth of Heterosexual AIDS.* New York: Basic Books, Inc.

Gauthier, D. K. and C. J. Forsyth. (2001). Bareback Sex, Bug Chasers, and the Gift of Death. In A. Thio and T. C. Calhoun (eds.), *Readings in Deviant Behavior.* Needham Heights: Allyn and Bacon.

Gilmartin, B. G. (1977). Swinging: Who Gets Involved and How? In R. W. Libby and R. N. Whitehurst (eds.), *Marriage and Alternatives: Exploring Intimate Relationships.* Glenview, IL: Scott, Foresman and Company.

Gilmartin, B. G. (1975). Suburban Mate-Swinging: That Swinging Couple Down the Block. *Psychology Today,* 8:54–57.

Gross, L.(1975). *Sexual Issues in Marriage: A Contemporary Perspective.* New York: Spectrum Publications, Inc. *The Hartford Courant.* (1999). States' Swing Clubs Keep Low Profile. 18.

Jenks, R. J. (1998). Swinging: A Review of the Literature. *Archives of Sexual Behavior,* 27(5):507–521.

Jenks, R. J. (1985). Swinging: A Test of Two Theories and a Proposed New Model. *Archives of Sexual Behavior,* 14:517–527.

The Los Angeles Times. (1998). '90's Swingers Give Monogamy the Kiss-Off. 1.

Masters, W. H. and V. E. Johnson. (1974). *The Pleasure Bond: A New Look at Sexuality and Commitment.* Boston: Little, Brown, and Company.

Miller, P. (1984). The Miller Report: A Survey of Swingers in America Today. *Gallery*:11, 59–75.

Murstein, B J. (1978). *Exploring Intimate Lifestyles.* New York: Springer Publishing Company.

Newman, J. (1993). Strange Bedfellows: At the Swingers' Convention, You Can't Help but Make Good Friends. *GQ,* (October):161–173.

O'Neill, G. C. and N. O'Neill. (1970). Patterns in Group Sexual Activity. *The Journal of Sex Research,* 6(2):101–112.

Palson, C. and R. Palson. (1972). Swinging in Wedlock. *Society.* 28–37.

Plumley, P. W. (1998). Latest Proof of Low Heterosexual AIDS Risk: CDC HIV/AIDS Surveillance Report 1997 Year-End. Online. Available at: http://www.libchrist.com/std/cdc/html

Plumley, P. W. (1997). Condomania-Common Sense or Nonsense? Online. Available at: http://www.libchrist.com/std/condomania.html.

Ramey, J. W. (1975). Intimate Groups and Networks: Frequent Consequences of Sexually Open Marriage. *The Family Coordinator* (October):515–530.

Ramey, J. W. (1972). Emerging Patterns of Behavior in Marriage: Deviations of Innovations. *The Journal of Sex Research, 8*(1):6–30.

Schupp, C. E. (1970). An Analysis of Some Social Psychological Factors Which Operate in the Functioning Relationship of Married Couples Who Exchange Mates for the Purpose of Sexual Experience. Ph.D. dissertation, United States International University, San Diego, California.

Smith, L. G. and J. R. Smith. (1974). Co-Marital Sex: The Incorporation of Extra-Marital Sex into the Marriage Relationship. In L. G. Smith and J. R. Smith (eds.), *Beyond Monogamy: Recent Studies of Sexual Alternatives to Marriage.* Maryland: The John Hopkins University Press.

Smith, J. R. and L. G. Smith. (1970). Co-Marital Sex and the Sexual Freedom Movement. *Journal of Sex Research, 6*(2):131–142.

Society for Human Sexuality. (1998). A Modern Guide to Swinging. Online. Available at: http://www.sexuality.org/mgswing.html.

Symonds, C. (1971). Sexual Mate Swapping and the Swingers. *Marriage Counseling Quarterly, 6*:1–12.

Thio, A. (1998). *Deviant Behavior.* 5th ed. New York: Addison Wesley Longman, Inc.

Thio, A. (1995). *Deviant Behavior.* 4th ed. New York: Harper-Collins College Publishers.

USA Today. (1999). Schools See Lesson in Arrest of Two Teachers at Sex Club. 6A.

Varni, C. A. (1972). An Exploratory Study of Wife Swapping. *Pacific Sociological Review, 15*(4):507–522.

Walshok, M. L. (1971). The Emergence of Middle-Class Deviant Subcultures: The Case of Swingers. *Social Problems, 18*:488–495.

Wysocki, D. K. (2001). Let Your Fingers Do the Talking: Sex on an Adult Chat Line. In A. Thio and T. C. Calhoun (eds.), *Readings in Deviant Behavior.* Needham Heights: Allyn and Bacon.

Afterword:
Understanding Deviance

Christopher Hensley and Richard Tewksbury

Deviant acts and deviant actors are central aspects of social organization and culture. Being able to identify what members of a society define as wrong, unacceptable, or intolerable is perhaps the clearest way to establish what a society values and what behaviors fall within the parameters of "acceptable" activities. But, deviant actions are not necessarily rare or extreme behaviors with which non-deviant persons are completely unfamiliar. In simple terms, deviance is pretty common.

All aspects of our lives contain both deviant and non-deviant acts. This includes everything from the most mundane aspects of our lives—how we dress, the language we use to communicate, how we decorate our homes—to our most private activities, such as our sexual behavior. Social definitions and the collective values of our society greatly influence people's behaviors. For some of us, knowing that a particular action is socially defined as deviant is enough of an influence to dissuade us from performing that action. For others, knowing that something is defined as deviant makes a particular behavior more attractive; to engage in a deviant act shows our rebelliousness and defiance of authority. Our sexual behavior is not immune to such responses. As we have seen, although most persons believe that their sexual activities are their own business and not something open to societal critique, sexual behavior is subject to societal critique, regulation, and sometimes—such as when defined as so deviant as to be criminal—subject to sanction.

Although an important aspect of our personal and social lives, sexual behavior (especially deviant forms of sexual activity) is not widely assessed scientifically or systematically. Certainly sexual images and messages pervade our society. However, these messages and subsequent discussions of sexuality tend to be anecdotal in nature. Attention devoted to "deviant" aspects of sexuality most commonly focus on extreme cases that garner media attention, either due to their criminal nature or the attempts of participants to publicize their actions (such as via television talk shows and social activism). Again, it is helpful to keep in mind that there are four basic ways to assess the normalcy or deviance of sexual behaviors.

Cultural standards are those guidelines developed and imposed by a society to facilitate smooth social interactions. These includes legal definitions and are based on (supposed) majority views of acceptable and unacceptable behavior. Religious standards are the second way to determine normalcy/deviance. This approach relies on the teachings and values of individuals' spiritual/faith perspectives. While some aspects of sexual behavior (rape, pedophilia) are viewed rather consistently across religious groups, other aspects of sexuality (premarital sex, masturbation, homosexuality) are viewed differently by different religions.

The third way of assessing normalcy/deviance of sexual behavior is to use the subjective approach, wherein individuals apply personal values and beliefs to their actions in order to determine whether particular actions fit with their world views, or whether such actions violate the expectations that they hold for how the world should be.

Finally, perhaps the easiest way to determine whether some action is deviant is to use a statistical approach. This method simply determines how many persons engage in a particular action; those actions found among only a certain small proportion of society are defined as "deviant." Numbers, however, are rarely the final arbiter of social approval; for example, there is no set standard for what percentage of society must engage in an action for it to rise above a deviant label. This is, rather, a subjective and cultural determination.

What should be clear at this point is that the four methods of assessing the normalcy/deviance of sexual behaviors are deeply intertwined. Our cultural and subjective perspectives are influenced by our religious beliefs, for example. Our religious beliefs, in turn, are a product of historical and cultural development. Statistical determinations are subject to interpretations of how many participants deem something as "normal." Deviance is always a social not a strictly statistical construct, even in the realm of sexuality.

Differences across cultures make universally categorizing any type of behavior as deviant difficult. Polygamy, for example, is rarely practiced and is illegal in the United States. However, in some cultures, polygamy is an expected and revered behavior.

The continual changes within cultural structures also affect the definitional boundaries of deviance. One such internal societal change has been the increased acceptance of out-of-wedlock pregnancy. In the past, this social phenomenon was stereotyped as one reserved for the underclass and poor, and wealthier families quietly sent their pregnant single daughters away. Today, however, shifting definitions of deviance have allowed many middle- and upper-class women to openly pursue single-parenthood.

Another example of a behavior that has been redefined with regard to class and gender is tobacco use. Until recently, all patrons of restaurants and passengers on airlines were allowed to freely engage in their smoking behaviors; today, increasing numbers of public facilities restrict smoking.

As one can see from these examples, paradigm shifts can occur which make a pathological, deviant act normal—or vice versa. New behaviors are continuously being defined as deviant based on the dynamics of societal norms. Hopefully, the study of deviance illuminates how norms are created—and offers important clues as to who shapes society through definitions of deviance.

Index

About the Book

This comprehensive reader is the first to cover sexual deviance in its many forms, including topics as diverse as abstinence, public sex, and sex work. Illustrating pathological, sociological, and "normal" sexual deviance, the editors identify key strands of research within the contemporary literature. Brief introductions to each selection underscore the importance of the essays, chosen for their thematic emphasis and broad classroom appeal.

Christopher Hensley is director of the Institute for Correctional Research and Training and assistant professor of sociology at Morehead State University. He is author of *Prison Sex: Practice and Policy.* **Richard Tewksbury** is professor of justice administration at the University of Louisville. He is coeditor (with Patricia Gagne) of *Deviance and Deviants: An Anthology.*